Using Technology in Teaching

Using Technology in Teaching

William Clyde and Andrew Delohery

Yale University Press   New Haven and London

Designed by Sonia Shannon.
Set in Bulmer type by Integrated Publishing Solutions.
Printed in the United States of America by Sheridan Books.

Library of Congress Cataloging-in-Publication Data
Clyde, William.
    Using technology in teaching / William Clyde
and Andrew Delohery.
        p.   cm.
    Includes bibliographical references and index.
    ISBN 0-300-10394-8 (pbk. : alk. paper)
        1. Education, Higher—Computer-assisted instruction. 2. College
teaching—Aids and devices. 3. Educational technology.   I. Delohery,
Andrew. II. Title.
    LB2395.7.C59 2004
    378.1′7344678—dc22   2004023495

A catalogue record for this book is available from the British Library.

The paper in this book meets the guidelines for permanence and durability of the Committee on
Production Guidelines for Book Longevity of the Council on Library Resources.

10 9 8 7 6 5 4 3 2 1

To my dear wife
—W. C.

To Jodie, whose sensibilities make all things possible
—A. D.

Contents

Acknowledgments

We begin by thanking all of our colleagues at Quinnipiac University, from whom we learn new things about teaching, learning, and technology every day. In particular, we are indebted to Rich Ferguson, Frank Villa, Judy Villa, Maureen Schorr, Frances Rowe, Gary Pandolfi, Richard Beck, Joe Jasinski, David Vance, Vin Buccino, Sally Nagy, Lynn Dorsey, Stephanie Caruso, Phil Devit, Cindy Gallatin, and Josh Kim for their endless ideas, experience, and enthusiasm—and for providing many valuable suggestions for the book.

At Yale University Press, we would like to thank Jean Thomson Black, Molly Egland, Heidi Downey, and Laura Davulis, whose thorough and careful work made this book a reality. We also thank the reviewers, whose many constructive comments and observations made the book more accurate and useful.

We would like to thank J. Alex Schwartz, who helped get this project started.

We are very grateful to Frank Villa, Judy Villa, Frances Rowe, David Clyde, Paul Clyde, and Bill Keep, each of whom spent many hours reviewing the manuscript and offering important changes, corrections, and improvements.

The manuscript would never have come together without the expertise and careful work of Radhika Ippatoori, Alyson Heffernan, and Jonathan Potokin, who transformed the text and images into the formats needed for publication.

Finally, we thank our families for their patience and support—and the joy they give us each day.

Introduction

Can you recall . . .

- Standing at the copy machine five minutes before your class begins, having just discovered a reading you'd like to get to your students today. There are three people ahead of you in line to use the copier—which just ran out of paper.
- Watching television on a Friday night when a preview comes on for a program, airing on Sunday, that relates to topics you will discuss in class Monday morning. You would like your students to know about it so they may watch it.
- Reading student papers with a strong suspicion that some of them contain large amounts of plagiarized materials.
- Assigning readings to be covered next class. Before students come to class you want to make sure they have read the material, and to find out which concepts from the readings most confused them so you can use class time to clarify.

Our lives as faculty are full of everyday frustrations, challenges, and unrealized potential. While we have worked out solutions and strategies for dealing with many of these, it is clear that, given the right tools, we could be more efficient and effective.

Technology now offers an increasing number of intuitive, reliable, "ready for prime time" tools to help faculty do the things they do every day. The strategies described here do not depend on the software or hardware you are using to access these tools. Whether you are using a Mac or a PC, Blackboard or WebCT, WordPerfect or Word, Outlook or an AOL email account, what matters is that you have access to Email, the Internet, threaded discussions, online assessments, and the other basic tools used in this book.

This book is not for the technology innovators, nor is it for the skeptics. It is for the 75 to 80 percent in the middle: the mainstream faculty who are using some technology but have not had the time to explore the variety of technologies now readily available, or to contemplate how these technologies might help them meet challenges they face daily.

You can read this book cover to cover or piece by piece. It might be thought of as a guide for doing what you already do in ways that may save time and make you more productive and effective. We expect that you will often use it to look up what you're trying to do—preparing class materials, giving students feedback, or helping students become researchers—and to explore the options technology offers.

This book is not about pushing a paradigm shift. Faculty resistance to such pushing was made clear in an overheard lunch-table conversation. One faculty member, complaining about the pushiness of another faculty member, was heard to say, "Paradigm, paradigm, paradigm. All he ever talks about is changing my paradigm. If I hear him say paradigm one more time, I'm going to . . . " Faculty naturally don't like to be pushed, and they anticipate that learning everything they need to in order to "shift paradigms" (should they want to) will take more time than they have.

This book will help you use technology as you need it, to do better and more easily what you are already doing. Rather than attempting to use a whole package of course-altering technology, you will see how specific instructional activities and tasks might be more easily and more effectively accomplished by using pieces of technology. Little by little, you will be able to decide which tools fit your needs and how to use them—and even be better prepared to consider shifting paradigms, should you decide to.

The Problem

Increasingly, faculty wrestle with the idea of incorporating technology into the classroom. We'd like to think, indeed, we are increasingly told, that technology will help all parties concerned:

- ourselves, by expediting traditionally cumbersome tasks;
- our students, by taking advantage of more and better learning opportunities; and
- our academic community as a whole, by simply facilitating the exchange of information.

Faculty are responding to the attention being paid to instructional technology by experimenting more and more. However, with the glut of technologies on the market and the recognition of early innovators, it is easy to forget that technology is only a tool. The focus often seems to be on technology rather than our teaching objectives. We often feel that we are asked to change our teaching styles and methods to accommodate technology rather than to use technology as a tool to accomplish our goals. Yet, despite the acclaimed ease propounded by so many software developers, we remain frustrated, feeling that the successful use of technology requires time and energy beyond our resources.

Still, we listen to what others are doing. We notice our peers on the cutting edge of this technology—some more vocal than others—and are aware of the increasing attention their use of technology receives during department meetings and in newsletters. We also notice the level of technology proficiency that our students bring to the classroom, where they fully expect us to offer opportunities supported through technology. Administrators love to promote the use of technology to prospective students and to accrediting organizations, and they appreciate the wealth of data that can be gathered through institutional use. Faced with so much optimism, we think, "This makes sense. I really could use some of this technology." So we begin to ask questions, or we begin to push buttons and open icons on our computer that we have never used before.

And so the avalanche begins. Just a little at first, of course, because we really do think that technology can offer something for us; after all, so many have told us how easy it can be to use and how worthwhile will be the investment of a little time. Tempered by our sincerely progressive attitudes, we hold at bay the growing stress produced by our learning curves. We notice that one question leads to another, that one answer leads to three more questions. We find ourselves the subjects of information overload—**Hypertext**, **Browsers**, **Chat Rooms**, **Threaded Discussions**, **Simulators**, **Formative Assessment**, **Summative Assessment**, **Video Clips**, **Course Management Systems**, **Portfolio Assessment** packages, **CD Texts** prepackaged by publishers, and **URLs** to **Web Sites** for support all sound great, but in attempting to sift through these myriad offerings we begin to change our focus. The surfeit of technology available, the many opportunities for its incorporation, and the increasing arc of our learning curve all compel us to focus on the technology and not on our original motivation. What was optimism begins to change into white noise. Increasingly frustrated, we begin to feel that we cannot invest the time needed for this professional development. (Note: underlining and boldfacing a word or phrase in this book imitates the model of hypertext, indicating that the word or phrase appears in the glossary—and the first time it is used in context it will be defined in the margin.)

Technology Is a Tool

Despite the frustration, using technology to help achieve your instructional outcomes can be manageable—and even rewarding—when taken just one piece at a time. Consider, for example, some simple classroom assess-

Hypertext—a word or phase in a document, presentation, spreadsheet, etc., that is linked (via hyperlink) to additional information, often something on the Internet. Hypertext is almost always underlined and in a different color from the rest of the text. When you click on a hypertext word or phrase, you are automatically taken to the additional information on that term or phrase. You can return to the original passage (where you found the hypertext) by clicking the Back button on the browser screen

Browser—a program that lets the user view a list of files and folders and/or their contents, most commonly Web pages

Chat Room—a location on the Internet or on a network that users can visit to Chat; Chat rooms on the Internet are often dedicated to a specific topic

Threaded Discussion—an ongoing collection of electronic submissions or postings on a particular subject, arranged by "threads" of the subject, with each posting being submitted as the creation of a new thread or a reply to ideas expressed in an existing thread; also an application that provides this capability

Simulator—a software package that allows the user to experience some aspect or aspects of a real-world object, environment, situation, etc.

Formative Assessment—assessment given in the midst of a course, the results of which are used by the students and/or the instructor to adjust activities and behavior in what remains of the course

Summative Assessment—assessment done at the end of a project or course, usually for the purpose of assigning a grade

Video Clip—a small segment of video footage that, if in digital format (storable in a file on a computer instead of just on a videotape), can be inserted into Web pages or otherwise accessed through a network or over the Web

Course Management System—a system of software that allows faculty to easily create and manage a range of online classroom tools, including announcements, file posting, threaded discussions, and online assessments; Blackboard and WebCT are two well-known examples

Portfolio Assessment—a strategy that relies on evaluation of student projects (in a student portfolio) for assessment of the student or of a program, instead of, or in addition to, the use of tests

CD Texts—some textbook publishers offer some of their textbooks—complete with all text, illustrations, tables, etc.—in a digital form on compact disk. In this form textbooks are usually cheaper and include such features as video, audio, and simulators

URL (Uniform Resource Locator)—the unique string of characters assigned to, and used to access, material posted on a network or the Web (in the case of material posted to the Web, the URL is the Web address)

Web Site—a location (made up of a Web page or set of Web pages) on the World Wide Web (abbreviated as WWW or Web) that is uniquely identified by, and found by accessing, the Web address(es) or URL(s) assigned to it

ment. You may use various techniques now, such as the one-minute paper or a short objective quiz at the end of the class. From this assessment you will learn what your students heard, how they are processing it, and where you might reinforce your delivery or change it, all very useful bits of feedback.

This feedback, however, is costing you time—in class and out of class. Usually, you ask students to do these tasks in class, which takes away from class time. Also, you would probably use paper copies, requiring time at the copier or printer, time to hand out and time to collect. If you want this experience to be meaningful to—or validated by—your students, you would have to provide feedback to them, the more specific the better, which means more time reading, evaluating, and responding. And still, if you are after higher-order thinking, you have increased the time you need to develop meaningful questions that require application of information rather than soliciting facts. Tempus fugit, as we all know. With some bits of technology, however, we can make this process more efficient and more effective.

Take, for example, electronic mail, or Email. This piece of technology is very easy to acquire, even if your campus does not have a centralized source or Information Technology department. It can allow you to:

- Contact students outside of class, using the advantage of engaging them on nonclassroom time.
- Prompt students to think about a certain issue prior to class, which can facilitate future discussion.
- Prompt students to reflect on recent information, such as asking them to reply with the most important point they heard during the previous class.
- Follow up a discussion cut short in class or redirect students' engagement by asking leading questions.
- Know who read the Email and who deleted it without reading it.

This book will help you pick out bits of technology that will help you now. We assume that the reader is interested in using technology as a tool to support instructional goals important to the person leading the class. You don't have to buy the whole package. You do not need to redevelop your entire course. This book is more about an evolution than a revolution. You can pick and choose from the many ideas offered—ideas on how to insert usable technology into your course. To this end, the book is arranged in the following manner.

Organization of the Book

The chapters of this book are arranged by instructional activities, many of them objectives you already accomplish through more traditional means.

In Chapter 1 we delineate the importance and value of between-class communication. We discuss opportunities to clarify an assignment, alert students to outside opportunities (TV shows, local events, etc.) that are relevant to the course, reviewing and redirecting students' work, or even canceling or changing a class. The traditional mechanisms for addressing this need include office hours, notes on the office or classroom door, and phone trees; these contacts can be enhanced and even replaced with technology solutions that include Email, threaded discussions, Chat, and **Web Postings**.

In Chapter 2 we explore traditional mechanisms for distributing course material. Syllabi, readings, assignments, and quizzes necessitate trips to the campus copy center. More spontaneous offerings usually mean frantically waiting in line to use the local copy machine to make copies just before you run into class. Technology solutions, which include Web postings, Email, and **Online Assessment**, can make a big difference in your time on task, and can also promote **Learner-Centered Learning**.

In Chapter 3 we describe various situations in which technology will assist your efforts to promote collaboration among students. Traditional mechanisms for promoting collaboration include in- and out-of-class group discussions and assignments, all of which can be improved by using different pieces of technology. These include threaded discussions, Chats, Email, **Annotation**, and **Change Tracking** features in **Word Processors**, and other tools.

In Chapter 4 we discuss the value of actually dissecting a frog as opposed to just reading about it, or of trading in a financial market instead of just talking about it. The sciences have traditionally offered the most in terms of helping students experience ideas through labs. But technology is offering **Experiential** activities to a wide range of other disciplines, mostly in the form of simulators that let students participate in currency markets, practice city planning, fight famous battles, or travel the Oregon Trail.

Web Posting—a Web page and or file that has been posted to a Web site

Online Assessment—a quiz, test, or survey that can be taken on a computer through a network or the Web; when online assessments are made up of objective questions, the results can almost always be generated automatically, often along with summary statistics

Learner-Centered Learning—a perspective and strategy for learning in which learning (as opposed to teaching) is emphasized

Annotation—a feature (sometimes called Comments) available on most word processors that allows the reader of a document to insert suggestions or comments as a bubble or margin note that does not disrupt the flow of the original document

Change Tracking—a feature of word processors in which the reader can edit a document in a way that highlights or otherwise marks all changes made by that reader

Word Processor—a software package (such as Word or WordPerfect) that allows users to easily create, edit, format, and otherwise manipulate a document

Experiential Strategy—a strategy for learning built on the idea that students learn best by experience, or that experience is a critical component of learning

Hyperlink—programming associated with an onscreen item (a word, phrase, image, etc.) that creates a link between that item and another, target, resource, usually something on the Internet; the user accesses the resource targeted by clicking on the hyperlink; often the cursor will change into a hand or other shape when moved over an item with a hyperlink

Disguised Identity—when a user represents himself as someone else or uses a fictitious name when working on a computer, network, or the Internet

Video Projector—a light-emitting device that can project the output from a VHS player, DVD player, or computer (showing what is on the screen of the computer) onto a large movie screen so that everyone in the room can see it

Virtual Library—a collection of digital materials (documents, images, videos, audio files, etc.) that is usually accessible to a community of workers and/or learners

In Chapter 5 we investigate the challenge of helping students see the relevance and connectedness of ideas and activities in ways that help them construct their knowledge. Students are often so used to missing the forest for the trees—moving from one activity or concept to another without seeing how they relate to each other or fit into the big picture—that their knee-jerk reaction when confronted with new material is not to ask "Where does this fit into what I already know?" or "What am I learning from this?" but "Will this be on the test?" A variety of technology tools is helpful in clarifying these linkages, none more than hypertext. The ability to allow students to **Hyperlink** to more detail (a definition, a picture, an assignment, a Website, a quiz) but always to revert to the big picture is invaluable in helping students begin asking the right questions.

In Chapter 6 we discuss various opportunities to address the problems associated with student writing quality. The traditional mechanism for helping students develop writing skills involves students handing in papers to be reviewed by instructors with comments for revision and/or a grade. Technology can significantly increase the efficiency of this process though Email submission and the use of annotation or "track changes" features available in word processors. Beyond that, technology offers new processes to help develop student writing, such as the ability to post **Disguised-Identity** drafts to threaded discussions so that work can be critiqued by other students in an online "writers' workshop" and in-class writing/critiquing exercises using laptops and **Video Projectors**. The impact of technology on plagiarism—both its practice and its prevention—is also discussed.

In Chapter 7 we discuss the increasingly critical need for students to be able to find and evaluate information on their own in terms of life-long learning and the thrilling speed at which new knowledge is being created. The traditional library has been transformed over the past fifteen years, and the use of technology in this arena is really no longer an option. Still, many faculty are not comfortable with techniques related to online research and **Virtual Libraries**, nor are they fully aware of new issues arising from the use of these media, such as unreliability of data and copyright complications (see Appendix).

In Chapter 8 we describe situations demonstrating the value of assessment and offer a reference to the growing literature on the importance of formative assessment. Traditional mechanisms for assessments tend to be very labor intensive and generally offer little in terms of systematic evaluation of which concepts the student understands and which she does not. Technology offers a growing variety of assessment tools that can

- reduce the busywork associated with grading,
- provide targeted feedback and follow-up instruction to the student, and
- provide systematic assessment of student learning to the instructor,

all of which will help students and faculty refine activities and increase learning.

In Chapter 9 we catalogue the traditional sources of course materials, both in terms of the processes for finding them and in terms of the value of materials found. These selections are contrasted to technology-based sources of course materials, including the **Course Cartridges** and other **Ancillary Resources** available with most textbooks, as well as the plethora of free information available on the Web. The opportunity for **Student-Centered Learning**—in which students are asked to find their own materials for a given project—that these Web resources represent is also discussed.

> **Course Cartridge**—a set of Web pages and online course materials (assessments, videos, presentations, threaded discussions, etc.) that have been created to accompany a textbook and can be loaded directly into a course management system and used without editing (though editing is possible); course cartridges are often among the free ancillary materials available to an instructor upon adoption of a textbook
>
> **Ancillary Resources**—additional materials available, often for free, from publishers upon adoption of a textbook. These may include PowerPoint presentations, digital video clips, online tests, and a wide range of Web resources
>
> **Student-Centered Learning**—a perspective and strategy for learning in which the activities of the student (as opposed to those of the instructor) are emphasized

Organization of the Chapters

Each of these chapters is organized using specific scenarios for ease of use and includes sections giving a description of several scenarios in which faculty often find themselves— and may find themselves frustrated.

And then for each scenario,

- traditional solutions to that scenario's challenges, including strengths and weaknesses of those traditional solutions in terms of efficiency and effectiveness,
- possible technology-based solutions and how they relate to the traditional solutions,
- potential pitfalls in the technology solutions.

When proposing technology solutions to these scenarios we confine ourselves to tools that are reliable, widely available, and relatively intuitive. At the time of this writing, these technologies are

- Email—sending a letter electronically remains a very easy way to keep in touch with students. With various assumptions explained, faculty can remain in close contact with their students.
- Internet Access—your institution, your cable company, your phone company—at least one of these groups is interested in your using this technology, so they make it as easy as possible.
- Word Processing—if you can type, you can use a word-processing application. The bonus here is the portability and easy sharing of information, both discussed in this book.
- Presentation Software—create your own slideshows using material you have already developed; send them to students to view on their own time; post them to a Web Site.
- Video Projection—a very nice touch for the professor interested in learner-centered learning, video projection is simply taking the image from your computer screen and putting it on your classroom wall. Walk students through an essay revision; guide them through research material.
- Video Cameras—available in most homes and the audiovisual departments in virtually all universities, a video camera on a tripod allows easy recording of student presentations, lectures, and other activities.
- Course Management Systems (such as Blackboard or WebCT)—the ability to easily post pages and files; easy creation and use of threaded discussions; easy creation and use of tests and surveys.

The **Campus Computing Project** and other studies support the notion that these are increasingly widespread technologies: the use of Email has grown exponentially over the past few years, and the use of Internet resources and course Web pages in higher education also continues to increase. Course management systems are available on the vast majority of campuses—even if most faculty have not yet figured out how, when, or why to use them.

An Invitation

And so we offer you the following pages as a guide to help you explore and experiment with technology. There will be no pitch that you should be integrating technology, no guilt that you are not already doing so—just opportunities to become a competent user of technology for the best possible reason: because it helps you do what you want to do.

Campus Computing Project—an ongoing study of the impact of technology on higher education in America, based on annual surveys going back to 1990

Using Technology in Teaching

CHAPTER 1

Communicating with Students

SCENARIO 1: Sending Information to Students Between Classes

You are watching television on a Friday night when a preview comes on for a program, airing on Sunday, that relates to topics you will discuss in class Monday morning. You would like your students to know about it so they may watch it.

SCENARIO 2: Making Last-Minute Changes and Canceling Class Meetings

It's 8 A.M. and you feel a stomach flu coming on (or your car won't start, or something else has come up). You feel certain you will not be able to make your 10 A.M. class and would like to let your students know—particularly those traveling to school just to take your class. You would also like to give them some projects to work on so that the day is not lost entirely.

SCENARIO 3: Leveraging the Value of Good Questions (and Answers)

A student comes to your office for clarification on an assignment, and you realize that the entire class would benefit from that discussion. You would like to make the student's questions and your answers available to everyone in the class.

SCENARIO 4: Students Contacting You Between Classes

You have a big exam coming up in your class. You expect several last-minute questions as your students prepare for the exam. Unfortunately, you must be at a conference the two days before the exam and will miss office hours both days.

SCENARIO 5: Students Submitting Work

One of your assignments is due at 5 P.M. Friday. You will not be in your office until Saturday morning, when you will pick up the assignments to grade over the weekend.

**SCENARIO 1: Sending Information to Students Between Classes and
SCENARIO 2: Making Last-Minute Changes and Canceling Class Meetings**

Because the traditional and the technology solutions to these two scenarios are the same, we deal with them together.

TRADITIONAL SOLUTIONS

Attempting to get information to students between classes can be time-consuming and in-effective. One simple strategy is to post information in a main hallway, on a classroom door, or in a commons area. If students learn to check the board regularly, physical posting can be useful in getting the word out. There are limitations to this strategy:

- students must travel to the posting place (which may be problematic if students live off campus or if the posting place is locked when you are trying to convey the information—like over a weekend);
- someone may remove the message if it is not enclosed behind glass;
- if it is a long message, students may be forced to spend a long time writing it down;
- it is difficult to know who saw the message.

A second strategy for getting information to students between classes is to send the message through campus mail. This should get the information to each student, but it requires that a lot of copies be made and that enough time be allowed for the campus mail system to work. A third strategy is the use of phone trees—the professor calls a few students who each call a few students who each call a few more students. This can be fast and effective, but it is not good for conveying long messages. Its effectiveness also relies on students' willingness to carry it out.

Because of their shortcomings, these strategies are seldom employed, and the time-saving and learning opportunities that might be afforded by timely delivery of between-class information are usually forgone.

TECHNOLOGY ALTERNATIVES

Technology, in the forms of **Announcements** and **Email** in **Course Management Systems** and stand-alone Email (outside of a course management system—your campus almost certainly has a campus Email system such as Outlook), offers a few ways of easily delivering information that is timely and widely accessible to students—and can even indicate which students have seen it. What follows describes the use of announcements and

Announcements—a feature of all course management systems (usually the first thing a student sees when entering the Web pages for a course) that allows faculty to easily post information they want their students to see
Email—broadly speaking, the transmission of messages and associated data over a network or the Internet; this broad definition would include submissions to Chat and threaded discussions, but Email is most commonly treated as a distinct system for sending, receiving, and collecting messages to and from the user's account (mailbox) to the account or accounts of other users

Email within a course management system. The use of a stand-alone Email system such as Outlook is described in Scenarios 1, 2, and 4 of Chapter 2.

All course management systems give the course instructor the ability to **Post** announcements that are available whenever students access the course Web site. The process for creating an announcement need involve nothing more than typing text (though pictures, **Hyperlinks,** and other features can be added as needed) into a **Template**, as in figure 1.1.

This five-minute process results in immediate posting of the announcement, usually to the entry point of the **Course Web Pages**, meaning that every student accessing the course pages after you have posted the announcement will see your message (figure 1.2).

> **Post**—to submit data (text, an image, a file, etc.) to a computer on a network or the Web for display to others
> **Template**—a page in a software program with prompts for information or data (including files holding documents, presentations, video, etc.), and a space accompanying each prompt in which the information or data may be typed or pasted
> **Course Web Pages**—a set of Web pages and online classroom tools created for a specific course

Course management systems also automatically collect statistics regarding students' use of course Web pages. A report such as that in figure 1.3 would assure you that your two students would have seen any announcements posted before January 24, since both visited the course Web pages on that date. You can usually get this information by hour of the day if you need that much detail.

Course management systems also allow you to send Email to

- everyone in your class,
- designated groups of students (when you have students working in teams), or
- select students,

as indicated in figure 1.4.

Clicking on the boxes to the left of Jane Student and John Student in the "To" column in figure 1.4, for instance, adds those students to the "To" box in your Email, as shown in figure 1.5. This feature allows you to easily add the students you want to reach to an Email generated in the course management system.

The advantage of using the course management system's Email as compared to announcements is that the message is sent to students' Email accounts, even off-campus accounts, as shown in figure 1.6. Since most students check their Email several times a day, this can be an effective way to get messages to your students quickly—even on weekends.

The downside of sending Email from the course management system (as compared to posting announcements) is that there is often no way to track who has read your Email—though that capability is present in some stand-alone Email systems (such as Outlook). In other words, the current Email feature is more likely to get the message to your students quickly, whereas the announcements feature allows you to assess which

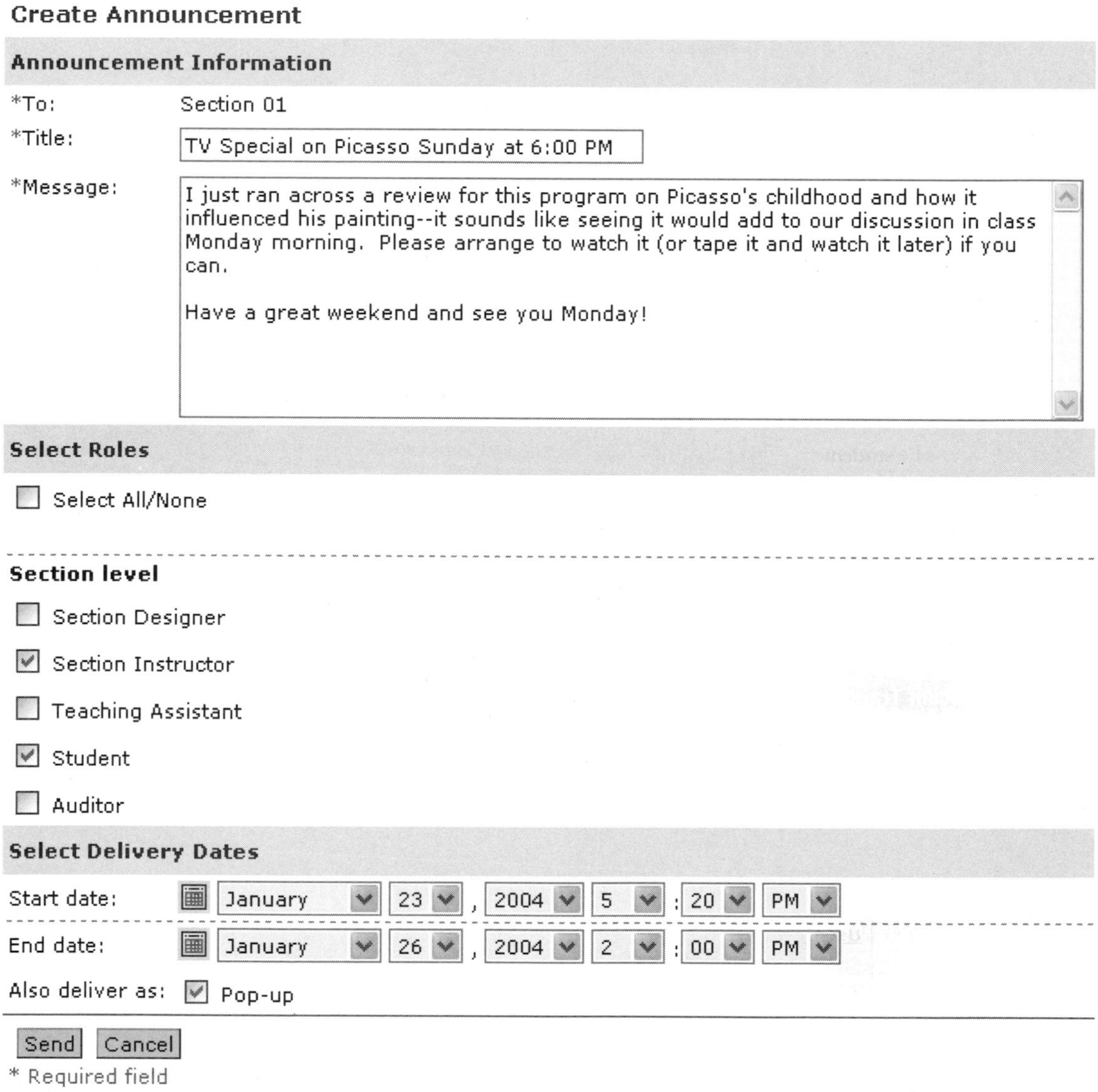

Create Announcement

Announcement Information

*To: Section 01

*Title: ┌───┐
              │ TV Special on Picasso Sunday at 6:00 PM   │
              └───┘

*Message: ┌───┐
              │ I just ran across a review for this program on Picasso's childhood and how it │
              │ influenced his painting--it sounds like seeing it would add to our discussion in class │
              │ Monday morning. Please arrange to watch it (or tape it and watch it later) if you │
              │ can.   │
              │   │
              │ Have a great weekend and see you Monday!   │
              │   │
              │   │
              └───┘

Select Roles

☐ Select All/None

- -

Section level

☐ Section Designer

☑ Section Instructor

☐ Teaching Assistant

☑ Student

☐ Auditor

Select Delivery Dates

Start date: 🗓 January ▾ 23 ▾ , 2004 ▾ 5 ▾ : 20 ▾ PM ▾

End date: 🗓 January ▾ 26 ▾ , 2004 ▾ 2 ▾ : 00 ▾ PM ▾

Also deliver as: ☑ Pop-up

[Send] [Cancel]

* Required field

Fig. 1.1: A template for posting an announcement through a course management system. WebCT Campus Edition
and WebCT Vista are registered trademarks of WebCT, Inc.

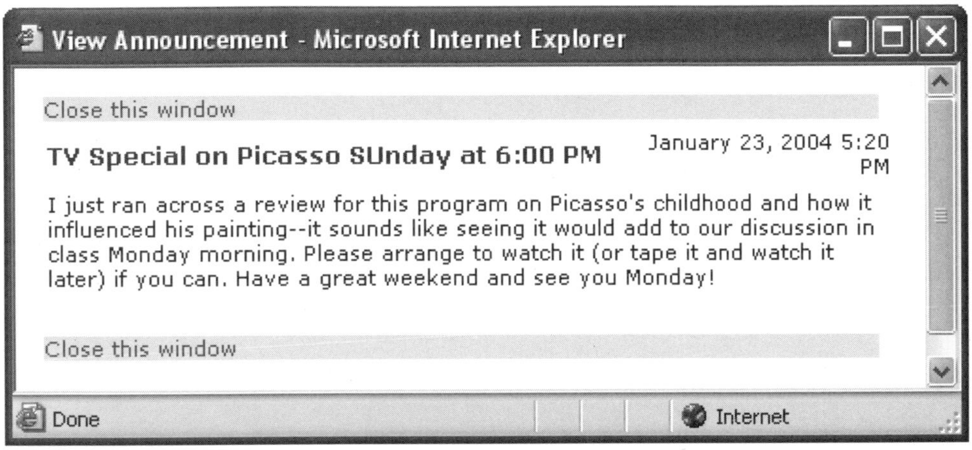

View Announcement - Microsoft Internet Explorer

Close this window

TV Special on Picasso SUnday at 6:00 PM January 23, 2004 5:20 PM

I just ran across a review for this program on Picasso's childhood and how it influenced his painting--it sounds like seeing it would add to our discussion in class Monday morning. Please arrange to watch it (or tape it and watch it later) if you can. Have a great weekend and see you Monday!

Close this window

Done   Internet

Fig. 1.2: The student view upon entering the course Web pages of a pop-up box displaying an online announcement. Microsoft Internet Explorer™ screenshot reprinted by permission from the trademark holder, Microsoft Corporation. WebCT Campus Edition and WebCT Vista are registered trademarks of WebCT.

Student Tracking Report: Survivor's Guide - Section 01 - Microsoft Internet Explo...

Student Tracking Report: Survivor's Guide - Section 01

Report generated January 24, 2004 9:08 AM
Clyde, William
January 17, 2004 9:08 AM to January 26, 2004 6:08 AM

Export Close

Student	User Name	First Access	Last Access	Sess
For an individual report, click the student's name.				
Student, xJohn	jostudent	Jan 23, 2004 2:33:11 PM	Jan 24, 2004 6:25:39 AM	
Student, xJane	jastudent	Jan 23, 2004 2:22:10 PM	Jan 24, 2004 6:05:30 AM	

Internet

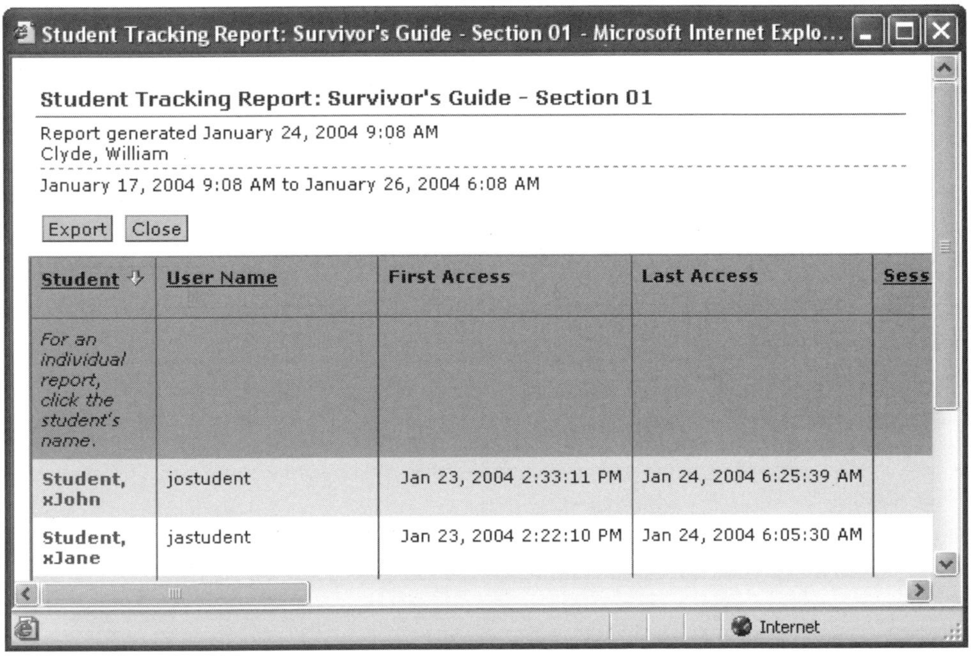

Fig. 1.3: Report of student visits to the course Web pages in a course management system. Microsoft Internet Explorer™ screenshot reprinted by permission from the trademark holder, Microsoft Corporation. WebCT Campus Edition and WebCT Vista are registered trademarks of WebCT.

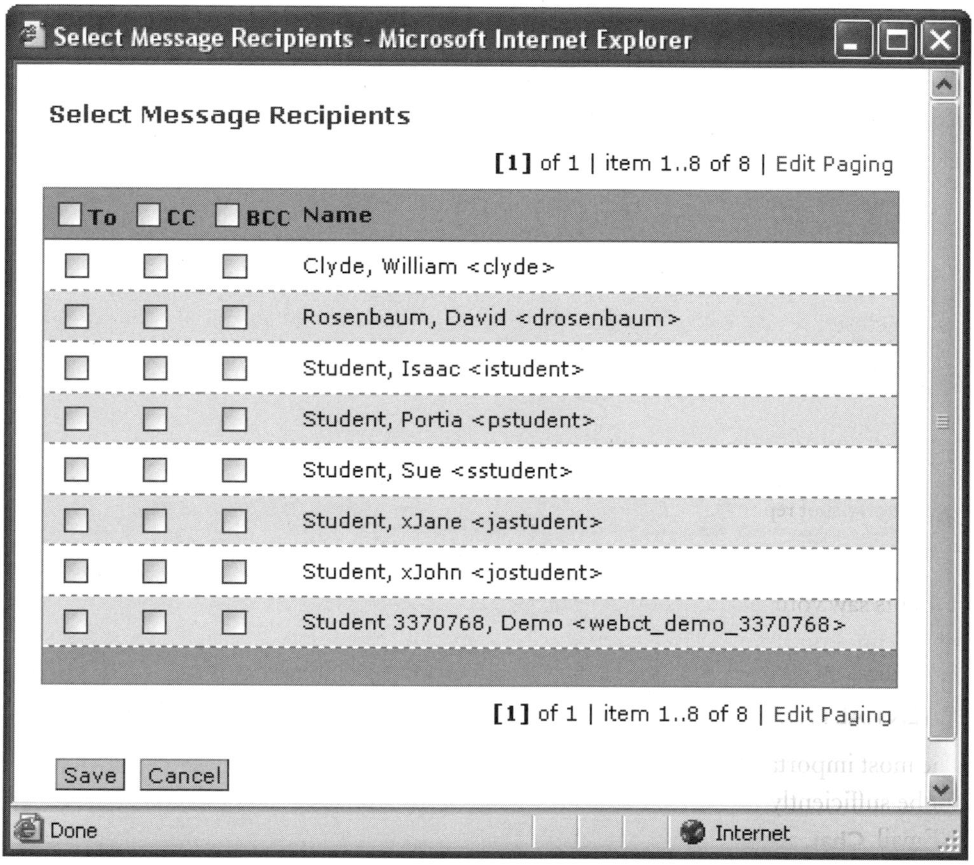

Fig. 1.4: Email options through a course management system. Microsoft Internet Explorer™ screenshot reprinted by permission from the trademark holder, Microsoft Corporation. WebCT Campus Edition and WebCT Vista are registered trademarks of WebCT, Inc.

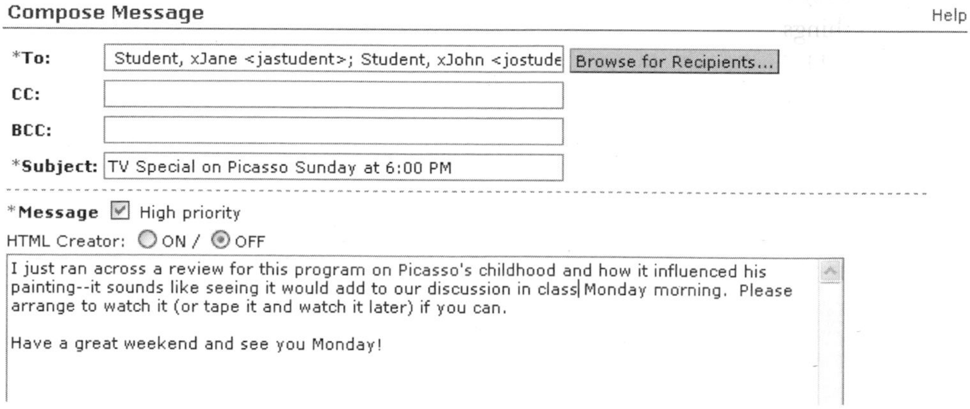

Fig. 1.5: Sending an Email through a course management system. WebCT Campus Edition and WebCT Vista are registered trademarks of WebCT, Inc.

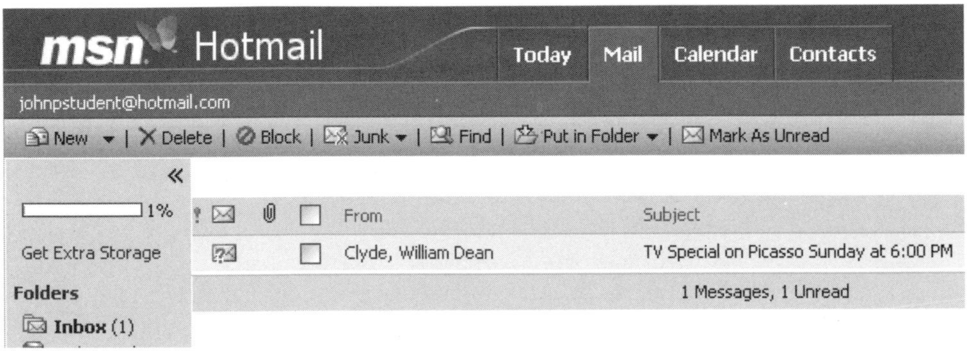

Fig. 1.6: Student receipt of an Email generated through a course management system. Microsoft Hotmail™ screenshot reprinted by permission of the trademark holder, Microsoft Corporation.

students saw your announcement. One solution is to do both—once the message is typed for an announcement it can easily be pasted into an Email.

POTENTIAL PITFALLS

The most important risk associated with these technology solutions is that students may not be sufficiently trained in their use. While many students may be sophisticated users of Email, **Chat**, and even **Threaded Discussions,** not all students are prepared to use these tools when they arrive on campus. Further, since the use of course management systems is not yet common in the K–12 environment, few college freshmen will have experience with them. As such, you must ensure that your students are comfortable with any tools you plan to use. Most university IT staffs offer training for students—many will even create sessions targeted to the needs of a specific class. One method of identifying whether students are ready to use a particular technology tool is to give small "test run" assignments as you get things going at the beginning of term. You might, for instance, ask them all to print out and bring to class the first announcement you post, just to make sure they can find it. Or you might send everyone an Email from the course management system and ask all to reply to you with their contact information or some other information it would be useful for you to have. Starting with something simple gives the students confidence in their ability to use the tools and helps you to identify any stragglers for further training.

Another potential pitfall results from the varying reliability of external Email services (this assumes campus Email is reliable, which is usually the case). Students may prefer to send or receive messages from an external Email service, such as AOL or Hotmail (as shown in figure 1.6), but not all of these external services are reliable, meaning that messages sent by you may not be received by them and vice versa. Further, university policy regarding privacy may prevent you from sending sensitive information (espe-

> **Chat**—software that gives two or more users the ability to communicate with each other at the same time, usually by typing messages that all participants in the Chat can see

cially feedback and grades) to an off-campus Email account not **<u>Authenticated</u>** by the university. The easiest way around these problems is to require that all Email communication for the course go through university Email accounts.

SCENARIO 3: Leveraging the Value of Good Questions (and Answers)

TRADITIONAL SOLUTIONS

Office hours often produce questions, answers, and discussion from which the whole class might benefit. Increasingly, student questions may also come to you in the form of Email, as discussed in Scenario 4 in this chapter. In any case, you may often wish that you could somehow record a good set of questions and your answers to share with the whole class.

The most obvious way of trying to leverage the benefits of a good conversation is to replicate it, or at least report it in class—though you may not deem this good use of class time given other demands on it. To the extent the conversation included drawings and/or calculations on paper, copies might be made and handed out to the class. And, of course, such encounters can be used to clarify your notes for the next time you teach the material.

Still, much of the value of the learning experience may have resulted from the student's desire for knowledge at the moment he or she was working through a problem. It would be nice if the reporting of the conversation could be archived in a way that would allow other students to access it whenever they were working through the same problem, which, again, may not be during class.

And then there is the whole series of other conversations in which students are learning from other students as they ask and answer questions in and out of class. (More ideas on facilitating collaborative learning such as this are found in Chapter 3.) It seems likely that you would want to capture these student-to-student question-and-answer sessions in your archive so that all students might benefit from these as well. But doing this by traditional means is all but impossible, because you don't even know about most of these conversations, much less have a chance to record them.

TECHNOLOGY ALTERNATIVES

Technology provides a simple and effective way of recording, organizing, and accessing these conversations. Threaded discussions are available in all course management systems and allow you to create an organized "online space" in which you and your students can record and develop these learning discussions. Creating a threaded discussion, like that in figure 1.7, involves choosing a name (Frequently Asked Questions, or FAQs, is one obvious choice with which most students will be familiar) and describing what students should expect to find (and post, if they are

> **Authenticated**—recognized by a computer or network with restricted access; usually accomplished by providing a user name and password, which the restricted access system compares to records it already holds regarding acceptable user name/password combinations

expected to contribute). When creating the threaded discussion you may also allow students to post anony-mously, to **Attach Files** to their postings, to edit or delete their postings, etc. If participation in this or any threaded discussion is to be graded (more on this in Chapter 8 on assessment), that fact should be included

> **Attach Files**—the ability to add a file containing a document, spreadsheet, presentation, video, etc., to an Email, a threaded discussion, or other message

in the description as well as in the syllabus. Once created, the threaded discussion will be presented to students as in figure 1.8.

By clicking on the hyperlinked discussion title (Frequently Asked Questions in the example in figure 1.8), students are taken to the discussion itself, in which no messages have been posted yet (figure 1.9). Clicking on the Add New Thread button at top left takes you to a template used to post the initial message (figure 1.10). Here is where you type in the question asked of you during office hours and the answer you would like to share with the class. You will also be able to attach files with pictures, spreadsheets, articles, etc., in support of the message, assuming you allowed that option when setting up the discussion (more on that in Chapter 3 under Scenario 1).

Once submitted, the message is added to the discussion, as shown in figure 1.11. By clicking on the hyperlinked title of the message ("More on David Hume's work on trade . . ."), students are taken to the message, to which they can reply by clicking on the Reply button (at lower right in figure 1.12) and typing their reply messages into a form like that in figure 1.13. Again, your students will be able to attach files in support of their messages as needed.

Once submitted, the reply will appear in the discussion under the message to which it refers (figure 1.14), extending this first "thread" of the threaded discussion, which can be several messages long (messages are sorted this way by default but can also be sorted by date and author).

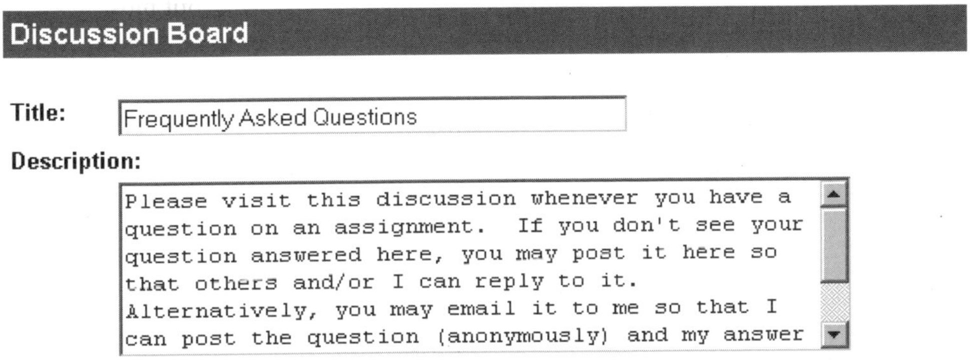

Discussion Board

Title: | Frequently Asked Questions |

Description:

```
Please visit this discussion whenever you have a
question on an assignment.  If you don't see your
question answered here, you may post it here so
that others and/or I can reply to it.
Alternatively, you may email it to me so that I
can post the question (anonymously) and my answer
```

◉ Smart Text   ○ Plain Text   ○ HTML

Fig. 1.7: Template for creating a threaded discussion in a course management system. Property of Blackboard. Used with the permission of Blackboard.

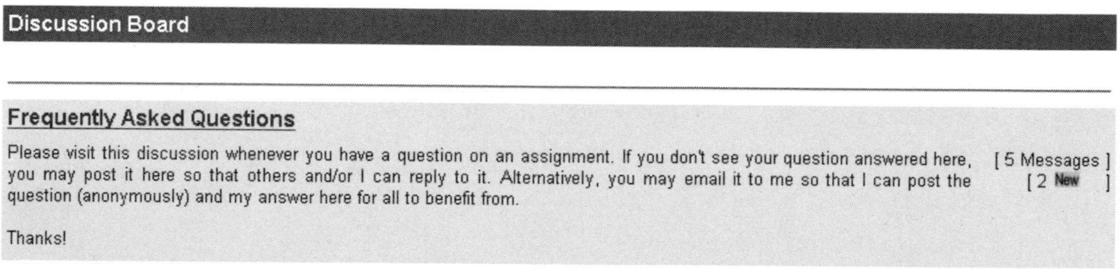

Discussion Board

Frequently Asked Questions

Please visit this discussion whenever you have a question on an assignment. If you don't see your question answered here,   [5 Messages]
you may post it here so that others and/or I can reply to it. Alternatively, you may email it to me so that I can post the   [2 New   ]
question (anonymously) and my answer here for all to benefit from.

Thanks!

Fig. 1.8: Title, description, and hyperlink (associated with the title) to a threaded discussion in a
course management system. Property of Blackboard. Used with the permission of Blackboard.

Discussion Board

To start a discussion thread, use the **Add New Thread** button below.

[Add New Thread]

VIEW UNREAD MESSAGES ▼   EXPAND ALL ⊞   COLLAPSE ALL ⊟
                                                                                                              SEARCH ⸮

                                                    ▼   SHOW OPTIONS

[Click Here for Archives]

Sort By: Default ▼

                                                                                                        (OK)

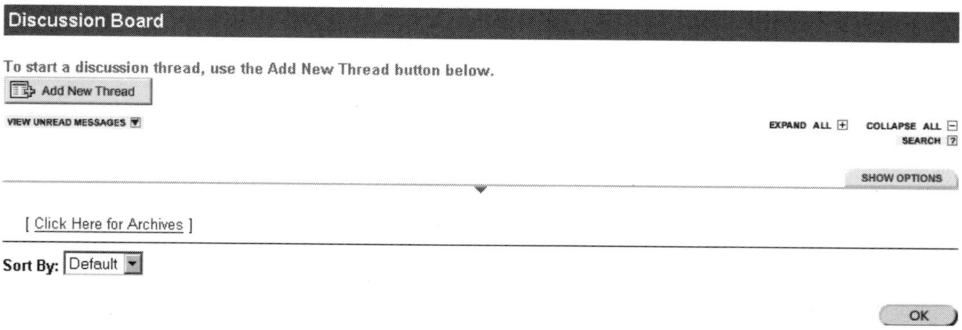

Fig. 1.9: A threaded discussion before the first message is posted. Property of Blackboard. Used with
the permission of Blackboard.

Create New Message

Current Forum: Frequently Asked Questions

Date: Tue May 28 2002 9:10 am

Author: Clyde, William

Subject: More on David Hume-'s work on trade balances

Message:
```
Q: I'm interested in finding out more about David Hume--
particularly his work
related to trade balances.  Could you suggest anything to point
me in the
right direction?
A:  TRY VISITING WWW.DAVIDHUME.ORG FOR A COLLECTION OF ARTICLES
AND REFERENCES.  THERE IS A WHOLE SECTION ON HIS WORK ON TRADE
BALANCES.  GOOD LUCK!
```

Options: ⦿ Smart Text ○ Plain Text ○ HTML

Attachment: [   ]   (Browse...)

                                              (Preview) (Cancel) (Submit)

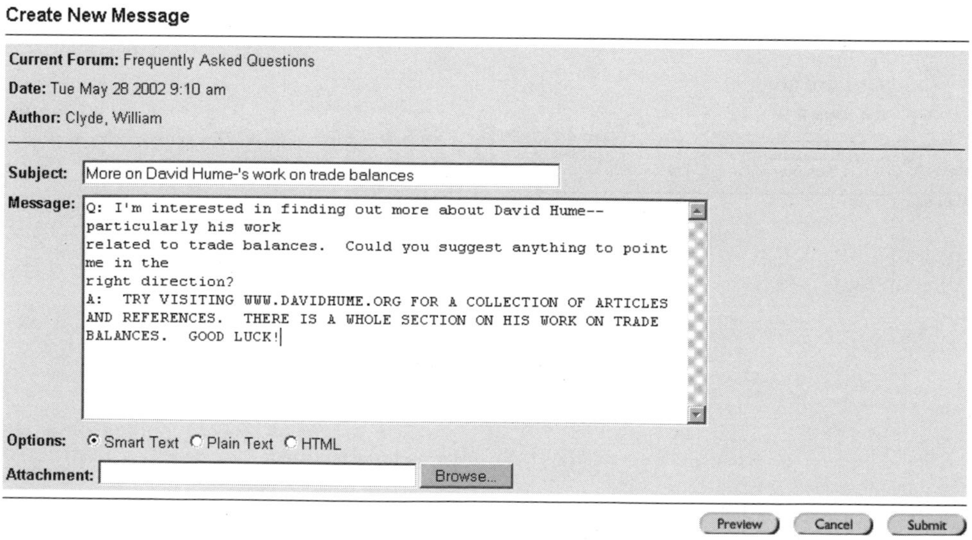

Fig. 1.10: Creating a message to be posted in a threaded discussion in a course management system.
Property of Blackboard. Used with the permission of Blackboard.

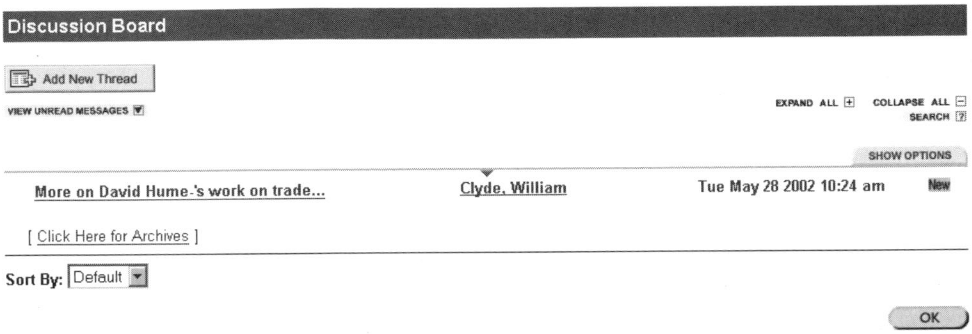

Discussion Board

Add New Thread

VIEW UNREAD MESSAGES ☑

EXPAND ALL ⊞   COLLAPSE ALL ⊟
SEARCH ？

SHOW OPTIONS

More on David Hume-'s work on trade...   Clyde, William   Tue May 28 2002 10:24 am   New

[Click Here for Archives]

Sort By: Default ▼

OK

Fig. 1.11: A threaded discussion after the first message is posted, beginning the first "thread." Property of Blackboard. Used with the permission of Blackboard.

Discussion Board

◄◄ Previous Message   Next Message ►►

Current Forum: Frequently Asked Questions
Date: Tue May 28 2002 10:24 am
Author: Clyde, William <william.clyde@quinnipiac.edu>
Subject: More on David Hume-'s work on trade balances

Q: I'm interested in finding out more about David Hume--particularly his work
related to trade balances. Could you suggest anything to point me in the
right direction?
A: TRY VISITING WWW.DAVIDHUME.ORG FOR A COLLECTION OF ARTICLES AND REFERENCES. THERE IS A WHOLE SECTION ON
HIS WORK ON TRADE BALANCES. GOOD LUCK!

Reply

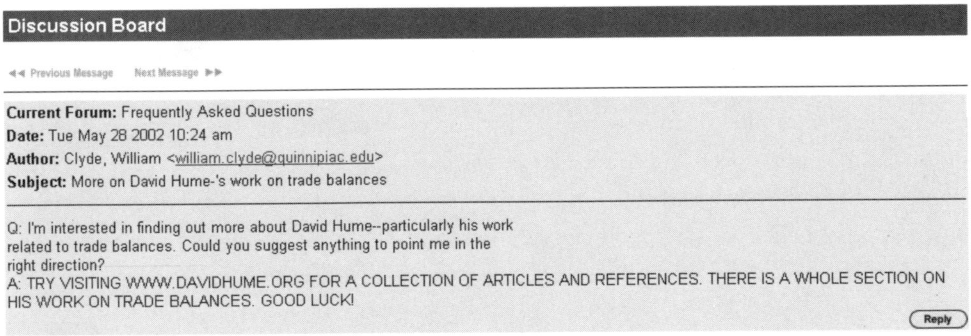

Fig. 1.12: Reader view of the message contained in the first posting. Property of Blackboard. Used with the permission of Blackboard.

Your Response:

Current Forum: Frequently Asked Questions
Date: Wed May 29 2002 12:51 pm
Author: Student, xJohn P.

Subject: Re: More on David Hume-'s work on trade balances
Message:

Options: ⦿ Smart Text ○ Plain Text ○ HTML
Attachment: Browse...

Preview   Cancel   Submit

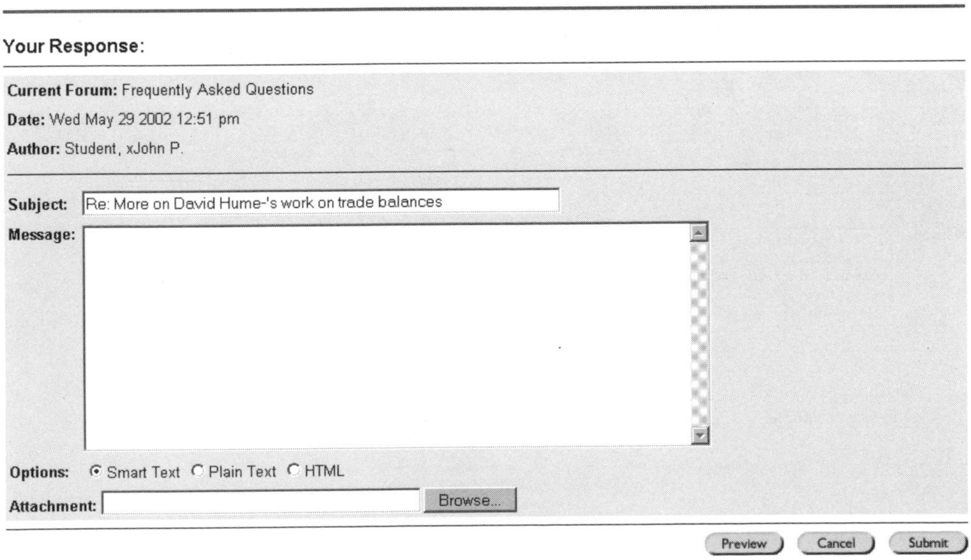

Fig. 1.13: Template for replying to a message posted in a threaded discussion. Property of Blackboard. Used with the permission of Blackboard.

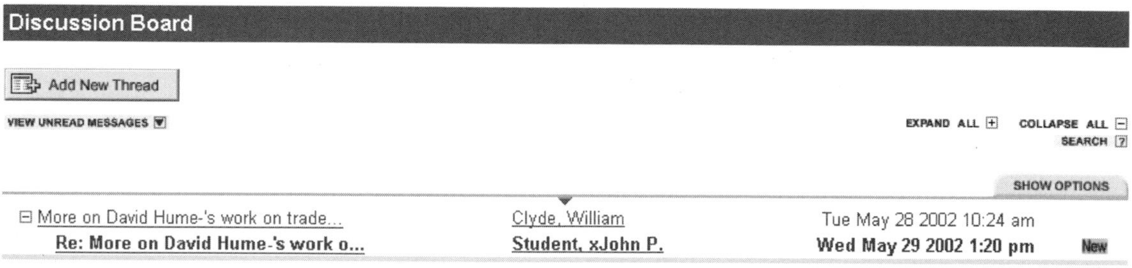

Discussion Board

🔲 Add New Thread			
VIEW UNREAD MESSAGES ▼		EXPAND ALL ⊞ COLLAPSE ALL ⊟	
		SEARCH ?	
		SHOW OPTIONS	
⊟ More on David Hume-'s work on trade...	Clyde, William	Tue May 28 2002 10:24 am	
Re: More on David Hume-'s work o...	Student, xJohn P.	Wed May 29 2002 1:20 pm	New

Fig. 1.14: A threaded discussion after the first message has been replied to, extending the first "thread." Property of Blackboard. Used with the permission of Blackboard.

At any point, anyone involved in the discussion can reply to any of the posted threads, or reply to any of the replies already posted. The threaded discussion used in this example also allows students to post questions directly as new threads, as shown in figure 1.15 (a student posted the message starting the new thread, "Help with Calculations in Lab 4?"), which may then be answered by other students (see Chapter 3 for more on facilitating collaboration) or the instructor.

POTENTIAL PITFALLS

Again, the most important concern with respect to successful use of threaded discussions relates to student preparation: all students must be able to access and post to the threaded discussion if it is to benefit everyone. A simple way to make sure that all students are ready to use this tool is to set up an "Introductions Discussion," as shown in figure 1.16, in which students are asked to introduce themselves to the class at the beginning of term.

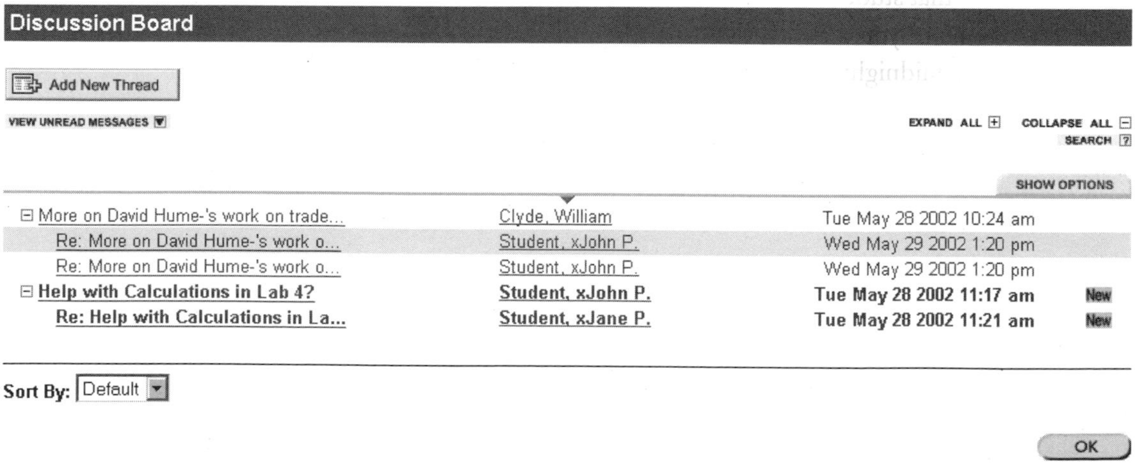

Discussion Board

🔲 Add New Thread			
VIEW UNREAD MESSAGES ▼		EXPAND ALL ⊞ COLLAPSE ALL ⊟	
		SEARCH ?	
		SHOW OPTIONS	
⊟ More on David Hume-'s work on trade...	Clyde, William	Tue May 28 2002 10:24 am	
Re: More on David Hume-'s work o...	Student, xJohn P.	Wed May 29 2002 1:20 pm	
Re: More on David Hume-'s work o...	Student, xJohn P.	Wed May 29 2002 1:20 pm	
⊟ Help with Calculations in Lab 4?	Student, xJohn P.	Tue May 28 2002 11:17 am	New
Re: Help with Calculations in La...	Student, xJane P.	Tue May 28 2002 11:21 am	New

Sort By: Default ▼

OK

Fig. 1.15: Student creation of new threads in a threaded discussion. Property of Blackboard. Used with the permission of Blackboard.

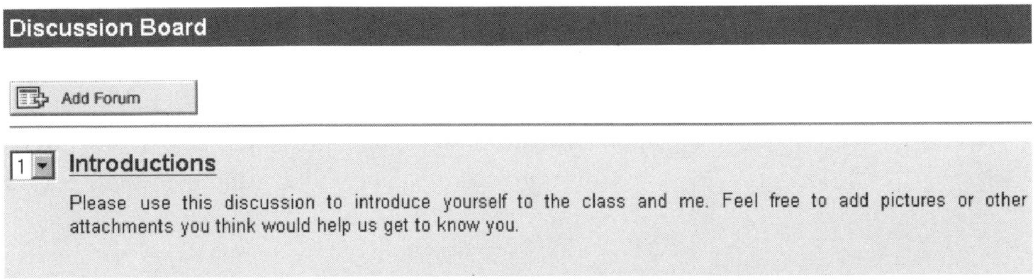

Discussion Board

🗐 Add Forum

`1 ▾` **Introductions**

Please use this discussion to introduce yourself to the class and me. Feel free to add pictures or other attachments you think would help us get to know you.

Fig. 1.16: Using a threaded discussion to allow students to introduce themselves and get comfortable with using a threaded discussion. Property of Blackboard. Used with the permission of Blackboard.

This can help build class community while it lets you identify any students in need of further training (those who don't post to the discussion).

Another potential concern is that you might be inundated with questions and that managing the threaded discussion might take large amounts of your time. It is true that using technology can foster increased student contact, and student expectations must be managed, as discussed under Potential Pitfalls in Scenario 4 below. In our experience, however, using threaded discussions to foster and share discussion of frequently asked questions actually provides more for students while requiring no more—and perhaps less—of you. First, to the extent that questions posted to the discussion are truly common questions, you are answering them each only once instead of several times, and your answers are available to students around the clock once you have posted them. Second, to the extent that some questions posted to the discussion are unusually insightful and would not commonly have been asked, all students benefit from the insight. Third, it is possible that student questions posted to the discussion may be answered by other students before you are even aware of them. It is not uncommon for student questions posted at midnight to be answered minutes later by other students.

SCENARIO 4: Students Contacting You Between Classes

TRADITIONAL SOLUTIONS

There are many reasons students might want to contact you between classes—to let you know they are unable to attend class, to seek clarification of concepts or assignments, and to seek advising/mentoring. Office hours are the primary mechanism for such contact in most institutions. But with growing pressures on time, faculty increasingly have trouble keeping their office hours, and students' schedules often do not allow them to stop by during specified hours. Ad hoc meetings are often called to accommodate conflicts, but these involve special scheduling—and frustration when one of the two parties misses the meeting. Phone calls, or sometimes "phone tag," fill some of this need for contact be-

> **Copy and Paste**—the ability to highlight data (text, an image, a file, etc.), save a copy of it to the digital clipboard, and then paste that data somewhere else; this ability is available in most applications

tween classes. The phone is well suited to brief messages, clarifications, and personal interaction, but it is deficient with respect to discussion of topics that require writing or drawing. Notes passed under the door or through campus mail allow detail but not rapid iteration.

TECHNOLOGY ALTERNATIVES

Two of the methods (Email and threaded discussions) that technology gives us for accommodating this need for contact between classes have been discussed above. Increasingly, students choose to Email "office hours"–type questions to their instructors, meaning that the request for additional information on David Hume dealt with in Scenario 3 might well have come to the instructor in the form of Email (figure 1.17).

Such a request may actually be easier for you to post to a threaded discussion (rather than if you had received the question by phone or in person) because the question is already typed. You need only type your answers in your reply Email to the student and then **Copy and Paste** the question (without reference to the student unless you receive permission from him or her) and your answer to the threaded discussion discussed and shown in Scenario 3.

Email is also a good solution when a student needs to leave you a short message, such as that she will miss class, as in figure 1.18.

Virtually all Email systems provide a feature that allows you to easily collect, account for, and access Email submitted by your students: they let you set up rules by which your mail will be sorted or organized (by whom it's from, by subject, etc.) into folders created

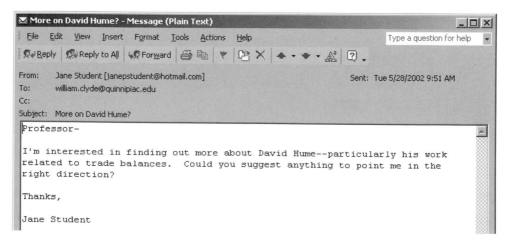

Fig. 1.17: Student Email to an instructor, asking "office hour" type of question. Microsoft Outlook™ and Microsoft Hotmail™ screenshot reprinted by permission from the trademark holder, Microsoft Corporation.

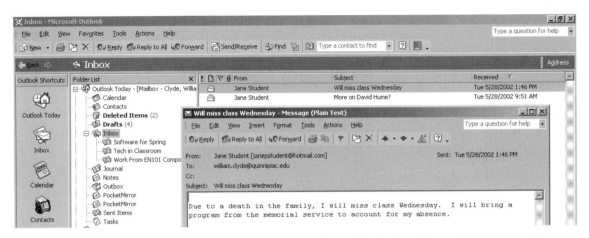

Fig. 1.18: Student Email making the instructor aware that the student will miss class. Microsoft Outlook™ and Microsoft Hotmail™ screenshot reprinted by permission from the trademark holder, Microsoft Corporation.

and named by you. The first step is to create a folder with a name that makes sense to you. In Outlook, for instance, you create a new folder by clicking on "File" at top left in figure 1.19, then clicking on "Folder," then "New Folder," to open a box that lets you name your new folder (shown in figure 1.20).

Once created, your new folder appears in the "Inbox" in the Folder List, as shown toward the left in figure 1.21. All Email from students in your class can then be automatically sorted or organized by creating rules that move all messages from your students to this newly created folder, as shown at right in figure 1.21. ("Ways to Organize Inbox" is opened by clicking on "Tools" at top left, and then choosing "Organize" from the pull-down menu.)

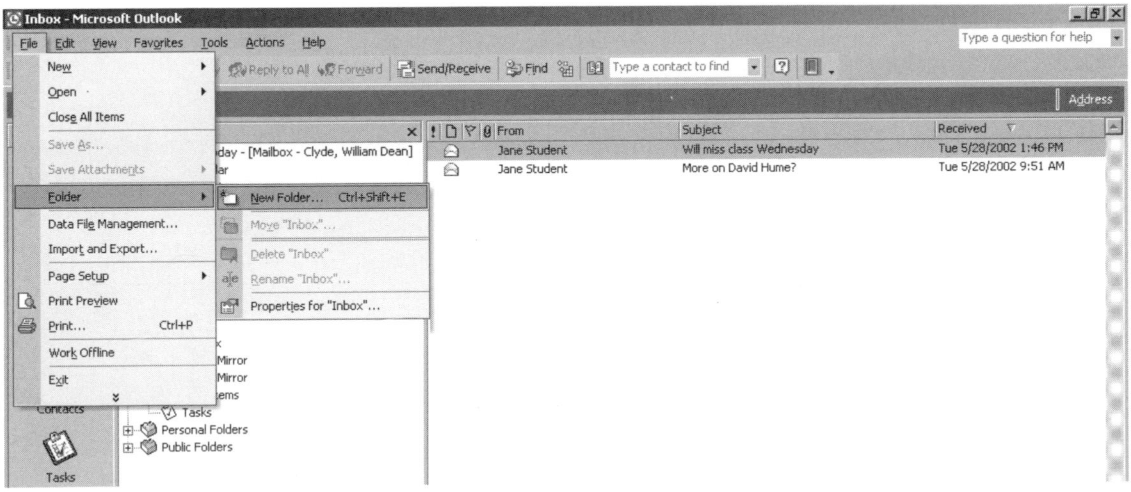

Fig. 1.19: Creating a new folder in which to organize your Email in Outlook. Microsoft Outlook™ screenshot reprinted by permission from the trademark holder, Microsoft Corporation.

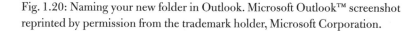

Fig. 1.20: Naming your new folder in Outlook. Microsoft Outlook™ screenshot reprinted by permission from the trademark holder, Microsoft Corporation.

Knowing that all messages from your students are moved to your new class folder, as shown in figure 1.22, allows you to quickly see whether your students have sent any new messages and to find any old messages from them you might need to refer to.

Another easy yet powerful way to allow students to contact you between classes is to hold "virtual office hours" using a Chat session, as shown from the instructor's view in figure 1.23.

In most course management systems, the Chat is available only when the instructor opens it (as when you open your door for office hours), so it is important that you schedule this online meeting with your students beforehand. Methods of getting the word out include announcements and Email through the course management system, as discussed in Scenario 1 above. Once the Chat tool is open, the instructor and all participating students are presented with a space for typing greetings, questions, answers, etc. (In figure 1.23 the instructor is the bottom line, in which is written "Sure. First let me get the curves up on the whiteboard above.") Anything typed there can be changed until the typist hits the Enter key, at which point the message is added to the Chat in the box just above the typed message. The Chat features in most course management systems also provide the

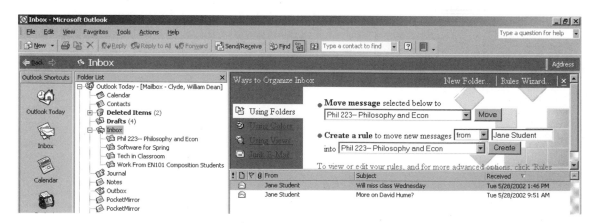

Fig. 1.21: Creating a rule that will automatically sort Email from your students into your new folder in Outlook. Microsoft Outlook™ screenshot reprinted by permission from the trademark holder, Microsoft Corporation.

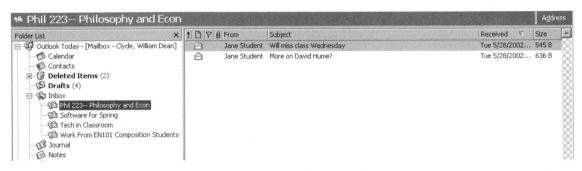

Fig. 1.22: Student Emails accumulating in your new folder in Outlook. Microsoft Outlook™ screenshot reprinted by permission from the trademark holder, Microsoft Corporation.

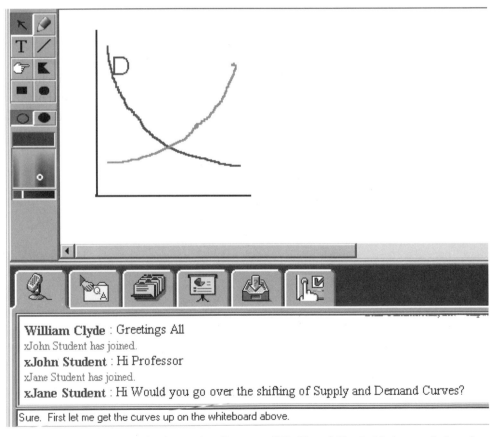

Fig. 1.23: Instructor's view of a chat session. Property of Blackboard. Used with the permission of Blackboard.

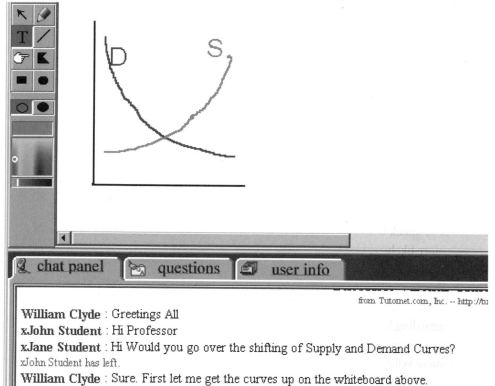

from Tutornet.com, Inc. -- http://tu

William Clyde : Greetings All
xJohn Student : Hi Professor
xJane Student : Hi Would you go over the shifting of Supply and Demand Curves?
xJohn Student has left.
William Clyde : Sure. First let me get the curves up on the whiteboard above.

Fig. 1.24: Student's view of a chat session. Property of Blackboard. Used with the permission of Blackboard.

instructor with an electronic whiteboard, on which figures can be drawn, equations written, etc., to facilitate the conversation. More advanced features allow the instructor to show spreadsheets, presentations, and other material in this space as well. The student view of the Chat (shown in figure 1.24) shows all of the conversation and whiteboard drawings but is usually somewhat simpler than the instructor's view (note there are fewer and more clearly labeled tabs between the whiteboard and the conversation in the student view than in the instructor view).

POTENTIAL PITFALLS

Student comfort with these technologies is, as always, an important concern if these tools are to provide effective solutions for all of your students. While many students spend hours a week in Chat sessions, others may never have entered one. If you have access to a computer lab or if your students all have laptops, an in-class Chat session, in which each student is required to contribute, can be a nice way to confirm everyone's ability to use Chat and to break the ice at the beginning of term: it is well known that students who are

Expectations of Students and Instructor:
I have tried to build a series of learning activities that will help you master, apply, experience, and appreciate many of the important terms, calculations and concepts in investments as well as develop a variety of general business skills. During the course, you should expect that I will:
    -Return email within 24 hours if received during the (Monday through Friday) workweek,
    -Not return email over the weekend, but will return it the following Monday AM,
    -Return feedback on submitted work within a week.
As a student participant in this course, it is expected that you come to the course with a desire to learn about the subject and to use the course activities to that end. I anticipate that the activities for each week should take you about 9 hours a week—3 in class and 6 outside of class. Specifically, it is expected you will:
    -Submit only your own work on all individual assignments (though you are encouraged to compare and discuss ideas with other students),
    -Submit all work on time unless pre agreed with the instructor,
    -Strive to truly master material for the Mastery Quizzes, and not just to pass the quizzes,
    -Work responsibly and collegially on team/class projects.
Please complete the Expectations Agreement to indicate that you understand and agree to try by live up to these expectations.

Fig. 1.25: Course Syllabus excerpt outlining expectations of students and instructor

reluctant to speak up in class may be more willing to speak out in a Chat session—and may be more likely to speak in class after having established themselves in a Chat.

Another important concern is that you will be overwhelmed by student contact between classes. For faculty at institutions with teaching-centered missions, this increased student contact may be welcomed to a point, but it is important for everyone that expectations regarding between-class communication be established and agreed upon from the beginning. An easy way to do this is to lay out what is expected of you and your students in the course syllabus, as in figure 1.25.

This example includes the added feature of requiring the students to complete an online Expectations Agreement in the form of the quiz shown in figure 1.26. Such quizzes are easy to create in course management systems, which also automatically grade them and record those grades in online grade books. Creation and use of such assessments is discussed in detail in Chapter 8.

SCENARIO 5: Students Submitting Work

TRADITIONAL SOLUTIONS

The traditional methods of collecting student work include

- collecting it in class,
- having students place it under your door,
- having students send it to or place it in your campus mailbox, and
- leaving it with a designated secretary.

One problem with all of these is in accounting for which students have handed in work and which have not. Collecting assignments in class is the most straightforward, especially if all students hand in the assignment on time and you keep track of who handed it in. Unfortunately, there always seem to be a few stragglers. Even if you have a "no make-ups" policy, you will probably have exceptions for documented sickness, death in the

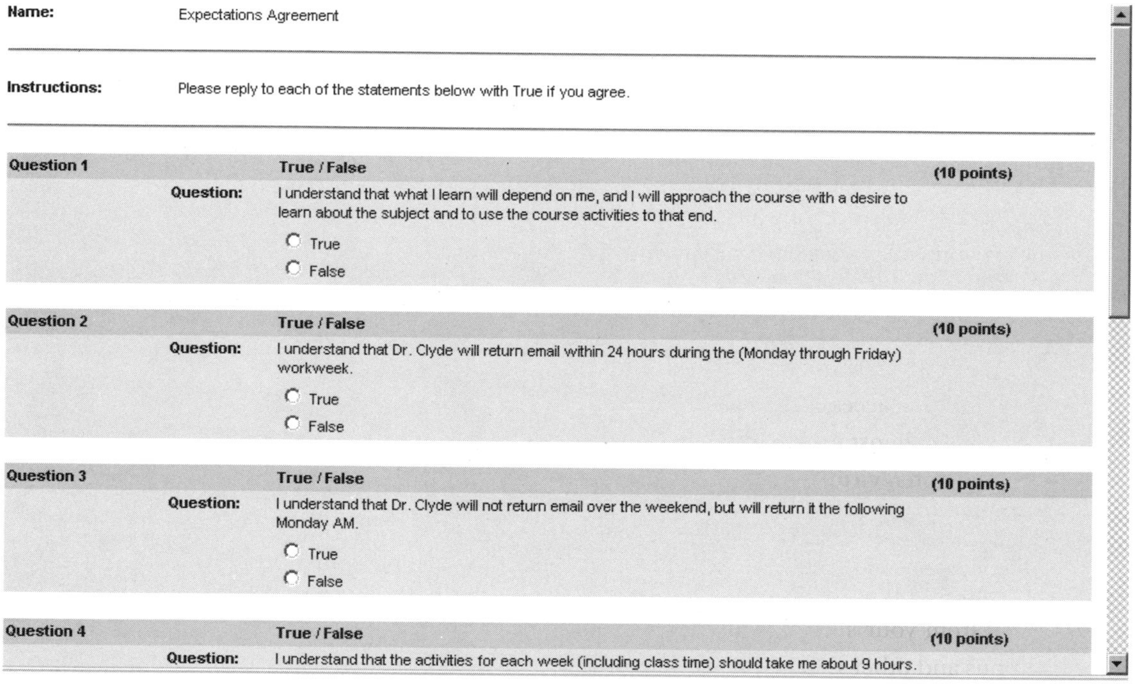

Name:	Expectations Agreement

Instructions:	Please reply to each of the statements below with True if you agree.

Question 1   **True / False**   (10 points)

Question: I understand that what I learn will depend on me, and I will approach the course with a desire to learn about the subject and to use the course activities to that end.

○ True
○ False

Question 2   **True / False**   (10 points)

Question: I understand that Dr. Clyde will return email within 24 hours during the (Monday through Friday) workweek.

○ True
○ False

Question 3   **True / False**   (10 points)

Question: I understand that Dr. Clyde will not return email over the weekend, but will return it the following Monday AM.

○ True
○ False

Question 4   **True / False**   (10 points)

Question: I understand that the activities for each week (including class time) should take me about 9 hours.

Fig. 1.26: Online quiz used to record student agreement with expectations of students and the instructor. Property of Blackboard. Used with the permission of Blackboard.

family, etc., and one or two students may be allowed extensions on each assignment. Unless you are very organized and disciplined, keeping track of who those one or two students are and making sure their assignments are filed with the others once handed in (instead of stuffed in a textbook or in your briefcase with other papers) may put your accounting in question—and with it the integrity of your grading system. And what about the student who says he/she handed the assignment in but you don't have it? Could another student have removed it from the pile? Could it somehow have ended up in the papers for the committee meeting you attended just after class?

In any case, in-class collection is not a solution when you will not be around (as described in the scenario) when the assignments are to be handed in. In that scenario you need one of the other three collection methods listed above. Of these, the last (leaving it with a designated secretary) is the most reliable, though it depends on the reliability—and availability—of someone to collect and account for assignments as they come in. A shortcoming of these last three methods is that you have to go to where the assignments were left. Best case, this may mean a (perhaps long) drive to work. Worst case, you are at a conference with some time on your hands between meetings that would be ideal for grading, but you have no way of getting the assignments.

TECHNOLOGY ALTERNATIVES

Fortunately, technology allows you to collect assignments in ways that provide both accountability and accessibility. You may, for instance, tell your students that the assignment is to be Emailed to you. So long as you save your Email, receiving an assignment in this fashion means you will always have a copy you can find—even if you missed it initially you can trace it by searching for mail from the student in question. Since Email can be accessed from anywhere in the world, it also provides

> **Drop Box**—a feature of a course management system that allows students to post messages or files to a space accessible only to the instructor; once an item is posted, the posting student cannot edit or remove the item. A digital drop box is usually used as a space in which students can submit assignments online, and all student assignments are collected there for retrieval by the instructor

literally global accessibility—an assignment submitted via Email in Connecticut is available to you almost instantly in New York, London, or Delhi. As discussed in Scenario 4 of this chapter, virtually all Email systems provide another feature that allows you to set up rules by which your mail will be sorted into folders created and named by you (see Scenario 4 above for details on how to set up and use the feature).

Setting up sorting/organizing rules at the beginning of a semester will mean that Email from your students will never be overlooked as you sort through the barrage of campus and other Email you may receive, and you will always have an accessible record of everything they've sent you. (You can also use this feature to automatically delete Email from unwanted sources.)

Another method of collecting assignments that provides accountability and accessibility is the **Drop Box**, which is a feature of virtually all course management systems (such as Blackboard and WebCT). Upon accessing this feature, the student is presented with a list of files he or she has previously submitted to the Drop Box (so he or she can see what has been submitted and when). No work has as yet been submitted in the example in figure 1.27.

By clicking on the Send File button, the student opens a template (figure 1.28) into which is written the title of the submission and the comments, which can be very long and might actually be the assignment itself.

A file from the student's computer can be added to the submission—usually this is a

Digital Drop Box

Add File   Send File

No files found.

OK

Fig. 1.27: Accessing the Digital Drop Box. Property of Blackboard. Used with the permission of Blackboard.

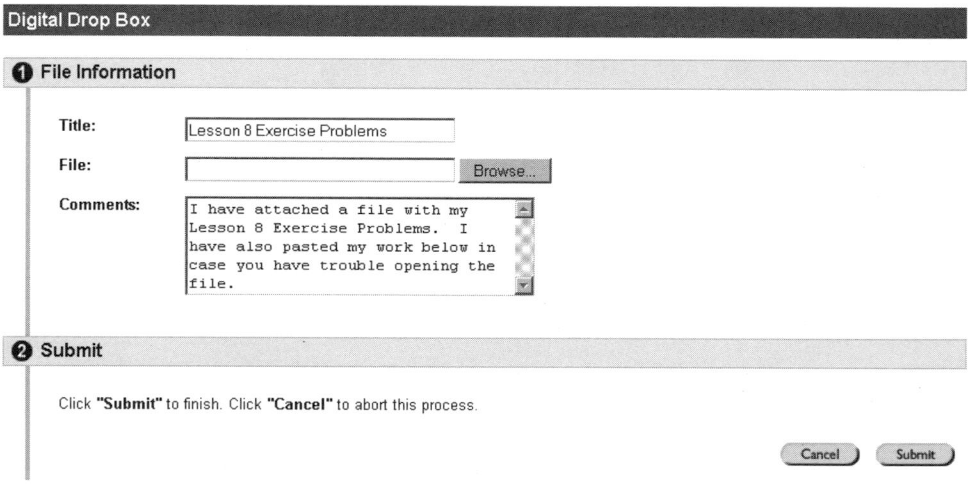

Digital Drop Box
1 File Information
Title:
Lesson 8 Exercise Problems
File:
Browse...
Comments:
I have attached a file with my Lesson 8 Exercise Problems. I have also pasted my work below in case you have trouble opening the file.
2 Submit
Click "Submit" to finish. Click "Cancel" to abort this process.
Cancel
Submit

Fig. 1.28: Using a template to prepare a submission to the Digital Drop Box. Property of Blackboard. Used with the permission of Blackboard.

document, spreadsheet, presentation, graphic, video, etc., that is itself the submitted assignment. This file is added to the submission by clicking on the Browse button (near the center in figure 1.28) to open a new window in which the student searches for, highlights, and opens the file (by clicking at lower right), as shown in figure 1.29.

This process yields a completed submission template (the space for the file is now filled in with the location of the file being added to the submission), as in figure 1.30.

Choose file
Look in:
English Assignments
Lesson 8 Exercise Problems
My Recent Documents
Desktop
My Documents
My Computer
My Network Places
File name:
Lesson 8 Exercise Problems
Files of type:
All Files (*.*)
Open
Cancel
Cancel
Submit

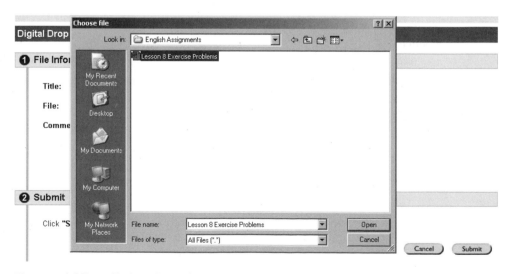

Fig. 1.29: Adding a file from the student's computer to a submission to the Digital Drop Box. Property of Blackboard. Used with the permission of Blackboard.

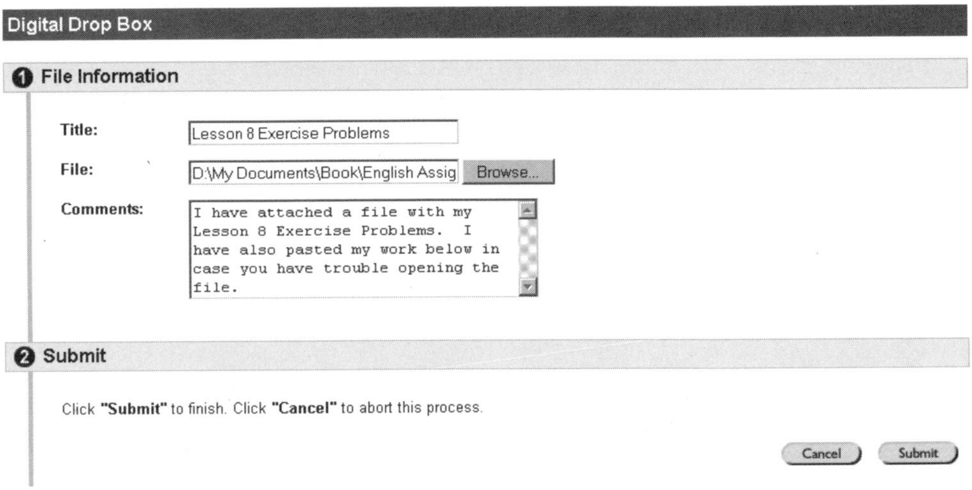

Fig. 1.30: Completed template for submitting an assignment to the Digital Drop Box. Property of Blackboard. Used with the permission of Blackboard.

Once completed, the submission shows up in both the student's and the instructor's Drop Boxes (figure 1.31).

The file associated with the submission can be opened by either the student or the instructor by clicking on the hypertexted title for the submission ("Lesson 8 Exercise Problems" in the example above). All assignments submitted by all students remain in the Drop Box throughout the term (unless removed by the instructor) and can usually be sorted chronologically or by student. To the instructor, the Drop Box represents an easy way to collect assignments against any deadline, and it provides accountability in terms of when who submitted what and in terms of access wherever there is access to the Web (and privacy, since no one but the instructor can view the student submissions).

Receiving assignments in electronic form also allows the instructor to use electronic feedback techniques such as changes tracking, annotations, or comments, which are discussed in detail in Chapters 6 and 8.

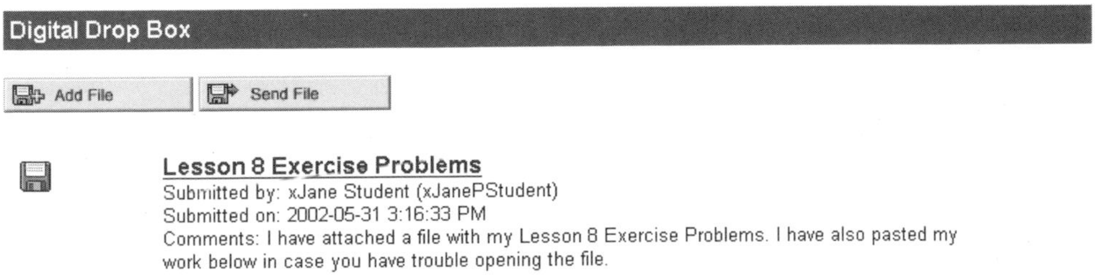

Fig. 1.31: Submission to the Digital Drop Box as it appears to student and instructor. Property of Blackboard. Used with the permission of Blackboard.

POTENTIAL PITFALLS

Again, a primary concern in having students submit work electronically is making sure they know how to use the technology. As discussed in the Potential Pitfalls sections for Scenarios 3 and 4, it is best to monitor student use of the technology (Drop Box, in this case) closely the first time it is used to identify students who need additional training.

Another issue related to electronic submission of work has to do with personal preferences of the grader. While it is true that electronic submission provides greater access, accountability, and potentially valuable feedback tools, these advantages must be weighed against the need to be online to access the submissions (at least long enough to download them onto your computer) and the need to open and close each file/assignment to grade it (or at least to print it out for grading) instead of just picking up the next paper on the pile. Depending on the assignment and the preferences of the grader, the latter may limit the attractiveness of electronic submission for a given assignment or the course as a whole.

CHAPTER 2

Distributing Course
Materials to Students

SCENARIO 1: Handing Out Your Syllabus

You put a lot of effort into designing your course syllabus. It includes objectives, expectations, timelines, descriptions of projects, and policies—all important resources for your students. Yet you feel a little guilty using so much paper to make copies, especially when it seems that your students never have the syllabus when they need it.

SCENARIO 2: Adding Readings at the Last Minute

You are standing at the copy machine five minutes before your class begins, having just discovered a reading that you'd like to give to your students today. There are three people ahead of you in line to use the copier, which just ran out of paper.

SCENARIO 3: Providing Access to Supplementary Material

You have some articles and other handouts that your students will need over the course of the semester and want to make sure everyone has access to them when they need them.

SCENARIO 4: Making Up Canceled Classes

Having canceled a class, you must negotiate the lost time. Normally you show up at the next class and try to pick up the pieces.

SCENARIO 5: Distributing Graphics, Videos, and Audio Materials

You have some illuminating photographs, video footage, and audio recordings that you usually share with your students in class. You would like for your students to be able to study them further.

SCENARIO 1: Handing Out Your Syllabus

TRADITIONAL SOLUTIONS

A new semester means updating, copying, and disseminating your syllabus. Each semester you find better ways to organize your courses and their learning objectives. But the additional pages add guilt as you send a lengthening file to the copiers, so you try to revise, squeezing in the vitals without wasting paper. You make enough copies to hand it out on the first day of class and also bring a few spare copies. You hand out the copies the first day of class and spend most of the session reviewing the syllabus.

TECHNOLOGY ALTERNATIVES

You are probably already using a word-processing program to create and save your syllabus. Doing so not only means that you can always make a copy, and that next semester's syllabus may be only a few minor revisions away, it also means that your syllabus is already in an electronic form ready to send by Email or **Post** to course Web pages. Doing so may allow you to better use the first day of class. Students could review your syllabus prior to the first day and bring a printout with them to class, along with their questions. You can also refer students to the electronic copy of your syllabus later in the semester when they may have lost the paper copy.

Course Management Systems allow you to easily send Email (with attached files, such as your syllabus) to some or all of the students in your class (see Chapter 1, Scenario 1). Here we explain how to send a file to your students via stand-alone (non–course management system) Email.

Begin by creating and addressing a new Email message. Most Email applications have some redundancy built in so that you can do any task in three or more ways. One common way to create a new message is to look under the "File" menu (shown at upper left in figure 2.1). To do so, place your **Cursor** on the word "File" and **Click**; often a menu will drop without your clicking. Once the **Drop-Down Box** has appeared, slide the cursor down to "New" and click. The drop-down menu may present some challenges to those with less-than-steady mouse manipulation. Another possibility is the presence of an **Icon** of a new message—an envelope, perhaps. Place your cursor on the icon, click once, and a new message box appears. In any case, click on the new message option.

In creating the new message (by clicking on the big white space below the "Subject" line and typing), keep it simple: Email messages that contain simple information and simple, easy-to-understand file names are most efficient.

Cursor—the shape or symbol controlled by the mouse and used to point to items appearing on the screen

Clicking—depressing a mouse button, usually when the cursor is over a specific onscreen object; unless otherwise indicated, clicking means left-clicking

Drop-Down Box—a list of subheadings, features, instructions, capabilities, etc., that appears just below the onscreen item to which it refers; sometimes the user has to click on the item to make the drop-down box appear, and sometimes the box appears when you move the cursor over the item

Icon—a small onscreen picture, usually hyperlinked or otherwise associated with a Web page, start-up of a software application, or other resource in such a way that clicking or double-clicking on it gives the user access to that associated resource

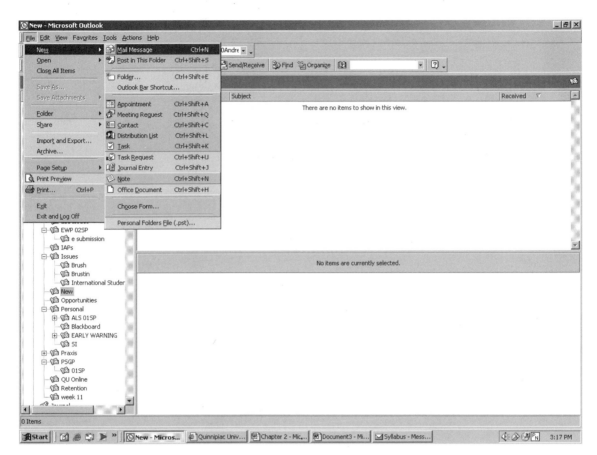

Fig. 2.1: Using the toolbar to create a new Email message. Microsoft Outlook™ screenshot reprinted by permission from the trademark holder, Microsoft Corporation.

Once the new Email message box pops up, as shown in figure 2.2, you can type in the Email address of any and all people you want to send it to—either in the white space next to "To" (for the primary receivers of the message), or in the white space next to "Cc" (for those you want to know about the message but who have no responsibilities associated with it).

After finishing the addressing and the body of the message, it's time to attach the file—your syllabus in this case. Like creating a new message, there is usually more than one way to attach a file. The drop-down menu across the top of the message may have a word like "Insert" or "Attachment." When you see one of these options, place your cursor on that menu button and click. This may result in other menu options; move the cursor to select the "file" option and click, as seen in figure 2.3. Once again, an icon option can simplify this process by eliminating some cursor clicks.

Now you will need to pick the file you want to attach to the Email message. If you have been using the computer to create and save your syllabi, a copy exists somewhere on the computer you've been using; now you have to find it. This process is the same as

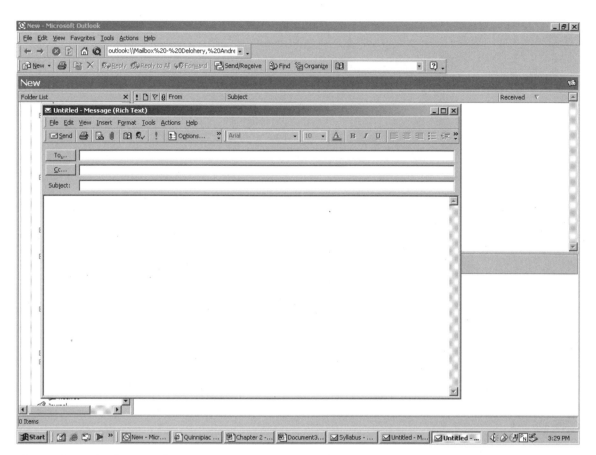

Fig. 2.2: A new Email message box. Microsoft Outlook™ screenshot reprinted by permission from the trademark holder, Microsoft Corporation.

opening the file. But instead of opening the file, you will be telling the computer to attach a copy of it to the Email. Place your cursor over the file, click once to highlight the file, and then click on the Insert (or Attach) button, in this case found at lower left in the Insert File **Pop-Up Box** (figure 2.4).

After you've attached the file you can send the Email. If you like, you can open the document from the Email to make certain you have attached the right file—and that it properly attached (it is common for people to send an Email referring to an attached file that they forgot to, or did not successfully, attach; opening the attached file to check it before sending messages will prevent you from doing that). In effect, you will be opening a copy of the document you are sending. Simply place your cursor on the file icon in the message and **Double-Click**. The document will open, and you can review it. Then close

Pop-Up Box—a box that appears, and can be manipulated, as layered above the other objects on the screen; sometimes a pop-up box appears as part of a process the user is executing, providing additional detail or choices. Increasingly, pop-up boxes appear with advertisements while the user views pages on the Web

Double-Click—to left-click twice in rapid succession to do something like open a file or start a software program

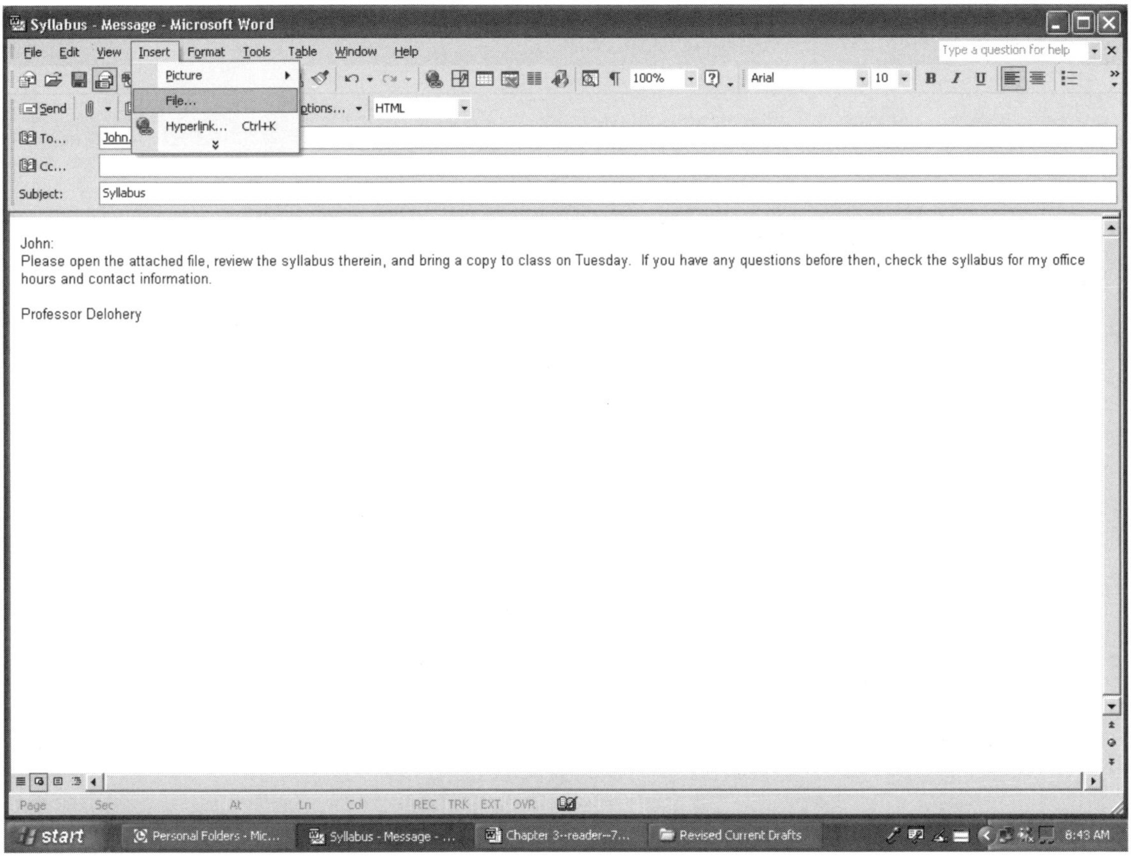

Fig. 2.3: Using the toolbar to attach a file. Microsoft Word™ and Microsoft Outlook™ screenshot reprinted by permission from the trademark holder, Microsoft Corporation.

the document and send the Email by clicking on "Send" (in the upper left of the message box in figure 2.5).

Another way to get the syllabus to your students is by posting it to a course management system. As indicated in the Introduction to this book, surveys indicate that course management systems, like WebCT and Blackboard, are available at the vast majority of colleges and universities. These tools organize many features from the traditional classroom and place them, electronically, at the students' fingertips (as indicated by the buttons at left in figure 2.6). One advantage is the ability to post (display) material you want your students to access. Students accessing this shared course page will be able to read whatever you post. They don't have to bring a paper copy to class, and they won't lose it. In addition, you can embed in your syllabus links to other resources on the Web. Students can use your syllabus as a starting point toward research or simply as a way to obtain a broader perspective on their primary material. You can also link your syllabus to

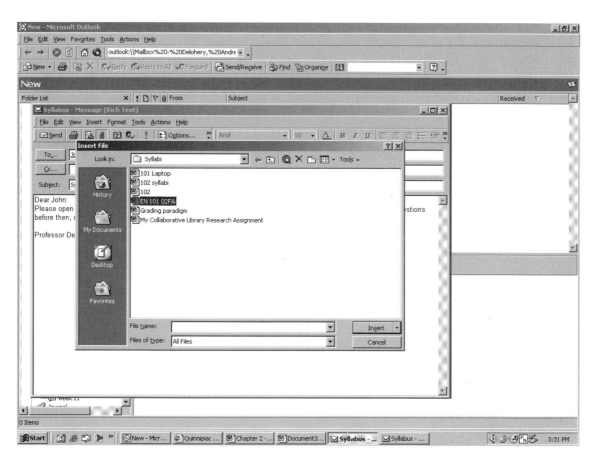

Fig. 2.4: Finding the file to attach. Microsoft Outlook™ screenshot reprinted by permission from the trademark holder, Microsoft Corporation.

Web pages that discuss your school's institutional and departmental policies, providing easy access to information that merits your students' attention.

An added benefit to using a course management system is that it organizes information for your students in a consistent fashion. They won't misplace important information, such as Email messages. Students grow frustrated, and as a result they pay less attention to course work and have less interest in using technology as a learning tool. With a course management system the organization is done for them, making access to information easier.

Most course management systems offer specific pages for posting your syllabus. For example, Blackboard and WebCT have buttons (at left in figure 2.6) that are labeled "Syllabus" and link directly to your posted syllabus. In some cases you can have the link go to a copy of the syllabus in a file (which can be Word, PowerPoint, Excel, or others), while in other cases the link will go directly to text you have saved to the page itself. Figure 2.7 shows an example of each: a link to a file is shown as the first item (with the underlined

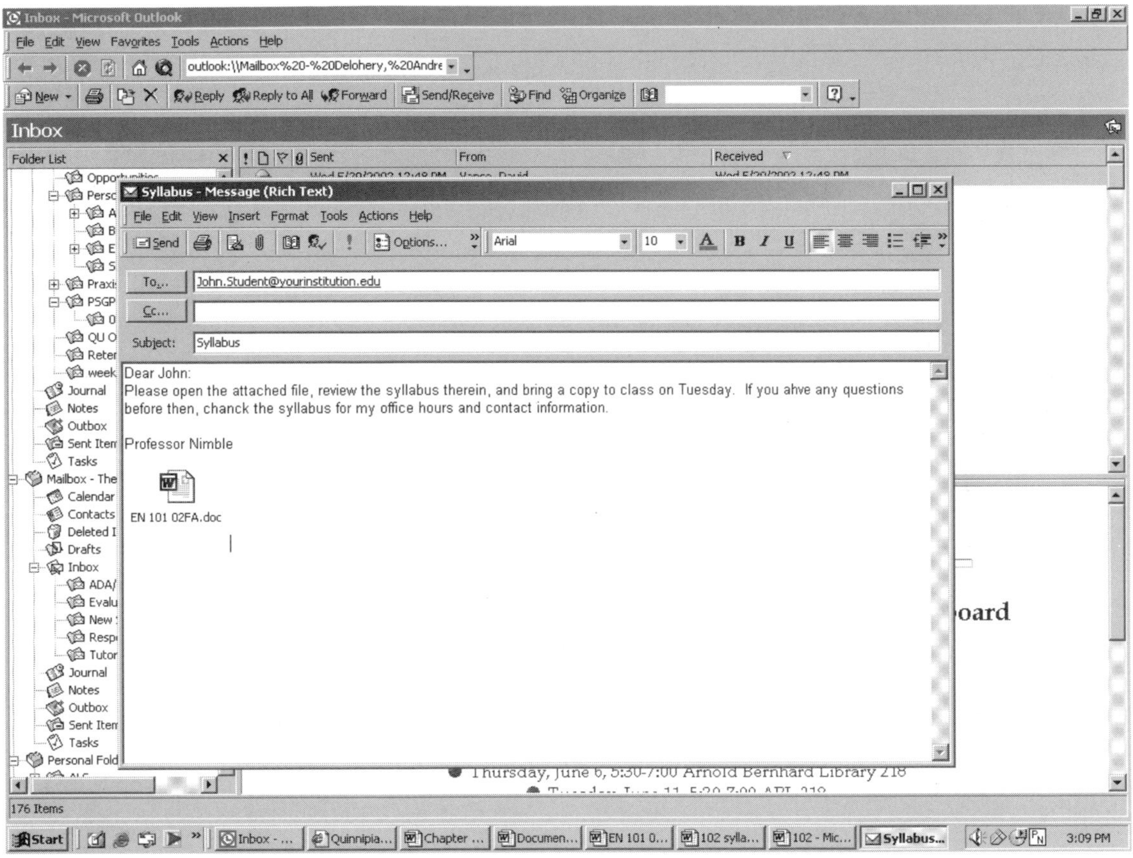

Fig. 2.5: A view of a message with a file attached, ready to be sent. Microsoft Outlook™ screenshot reprinted by permission from the trademark holder, Microsoft Corporation.

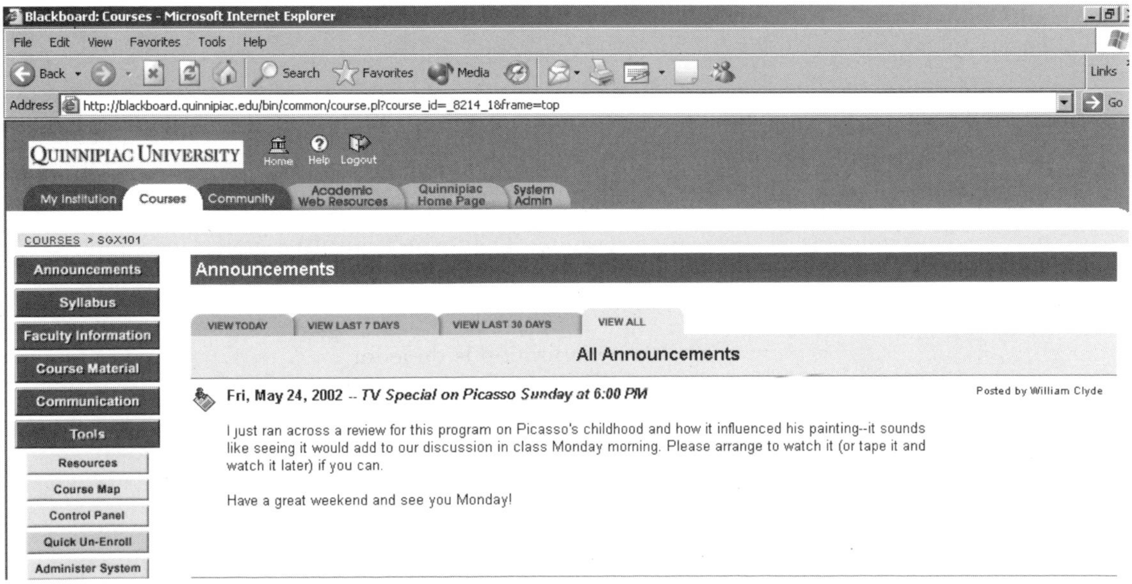

Fig. 2.6: An example of a course home page in a course management system. Property of Blackboard. Used with permission of Blackboard. Microsoft Internet Explorer™ screenshot reprinted by permission from the trademark holder, Microsoft Corporation.

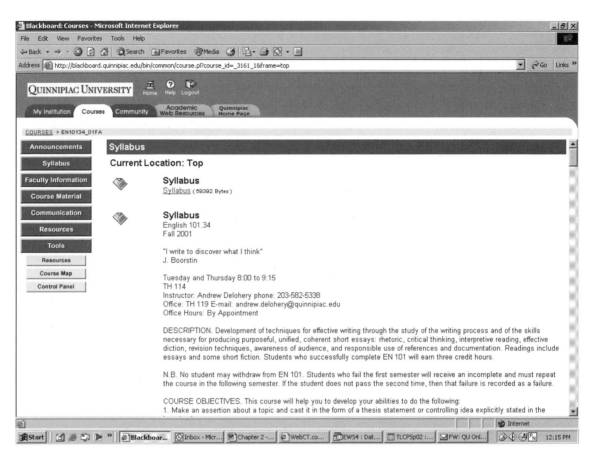

Fig. 2.7: A sample syllabus page in a course management system. Property of Blackboard. Used with permission of Blackboard. Microsoft Internet Explorer™ screenshot reprinted by permission from the trademark holder, Microsoft Corporation.

"Syllabus" being the hyperlink to that file), followed by a copy of the entire text displayed on the syllabus Web page.

In order to post material you need to access the template that allows you to input such material—in this case, your syllabus. In WebCT, the index of pages that allow you to input and manage the course Web pages is called the "Designer Map," as seen in figure 2.8. In Blackboard, it's called the "Control Panel," as seen in figure 2.9.

From these pages you can add content, view students' use, create quizzes, and select other helpful options. To post your syllabus you will need to click on the appropriate link (in this case that named "Syllabus") to show you a page like that shown in figure 2.10. Your students will not have access to the controls on these pages.

After opening the link you may have options for organizing. As discussed above, and shown in figure 2.7, you can post the syllabus as a file, or you can create a folder and place the syllabus in that folder. In Blackboard, these controls are located on the left of the screen

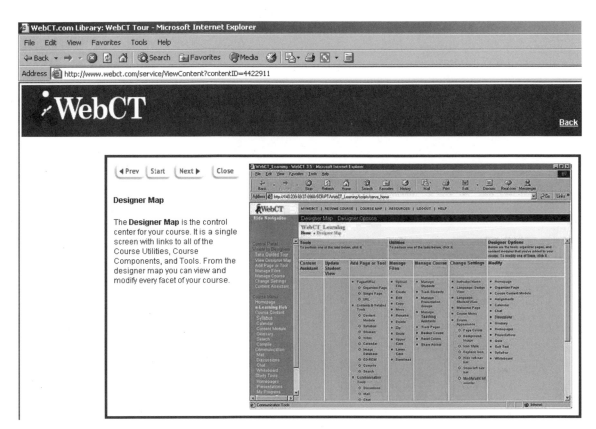

Fig. 2.8: A view of WebCT's Designer Map. Microsoft Internet Explorer™ screenshot reprinted by permission from the trademark holder, Microsoft Corporation. WebCT Campus Edition and WebCT Vista are registered trademarks of WebCT, Inc.

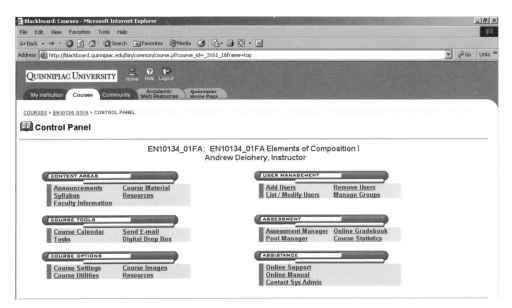

Fig. 2.9: A view of Blackboard's Control Panel. Property of Blackboard. Used with the permission of Blackboard. Microsoft Internet Explorer™ screenshot reprinted by permission from the trademark holder, Microsoft Corporation.

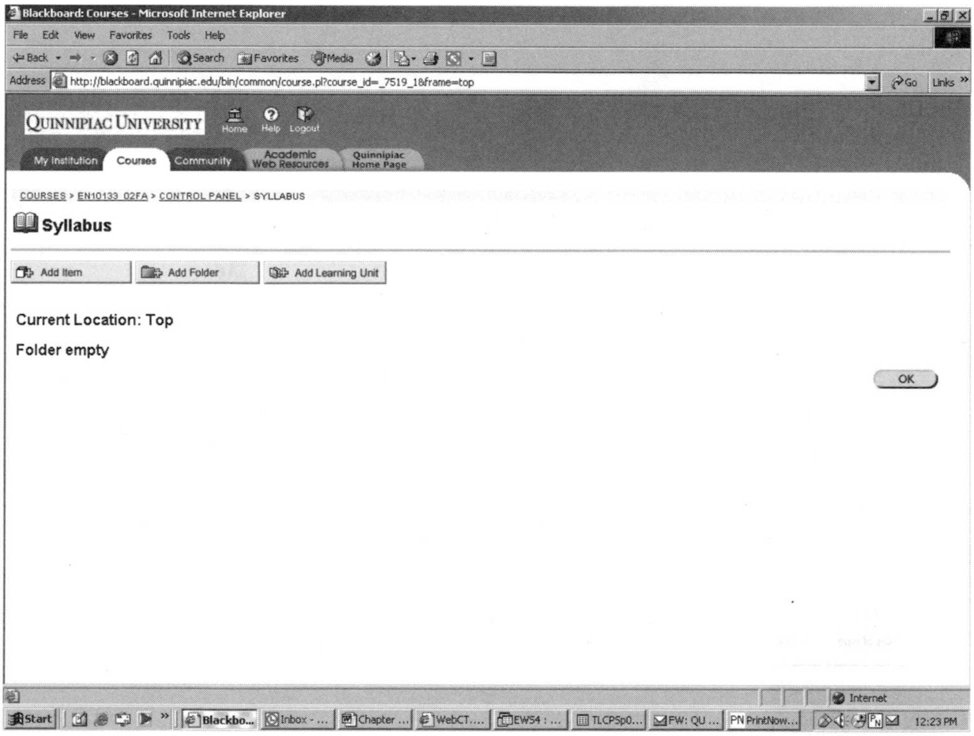

Fig. 2.10: A view of the organizing options when attaching the syllabus. Property of Blackboard.
Used with permission of Blackboard. Microsoft Internet Explorer™ screenshot reprinted by permission from the trademark holder, Microsoft Corporation.

(just below the boldface "Syllabus"), as seen in figure 2.10. Most students prefer the simplest access—the fewer clicks of the mouse, the better. Adding information to these tools is very much like attaching a file to an Email message. By clicking the appropriate button you will **Browse** your files for the right file to post. Usually a pop-up box appears that allows you to browse your files, as seen in figure 2.11. Double-click on the file containing the syllabus (or single click on it to highlight it and then click on "Open" at lower right in the pop-up box), and it will be copied to the syllabus page of the course management system.

After reviewing the file you can submit it for posting. Now it will be available to your students whenever they need it, as seen in figure 2.12.

If you wish to post the syllabus as displayed text in the course management system instead of as a file (remember that figure 2.7 shows the syllabus posted both as a file and as displayed text), you simply type the text (or, more likely, copy and paste the text from the word-processing document containing the syllabus) into a text box like that shown in figure 2.13. Adding this to the posting of the syllabus as a file shown in figure 2.12 will result in a syllabus page looking like that shown in figure 2.7.

Browse—to view a list of files and/or folders of files, or to view the contents of a file or group of files

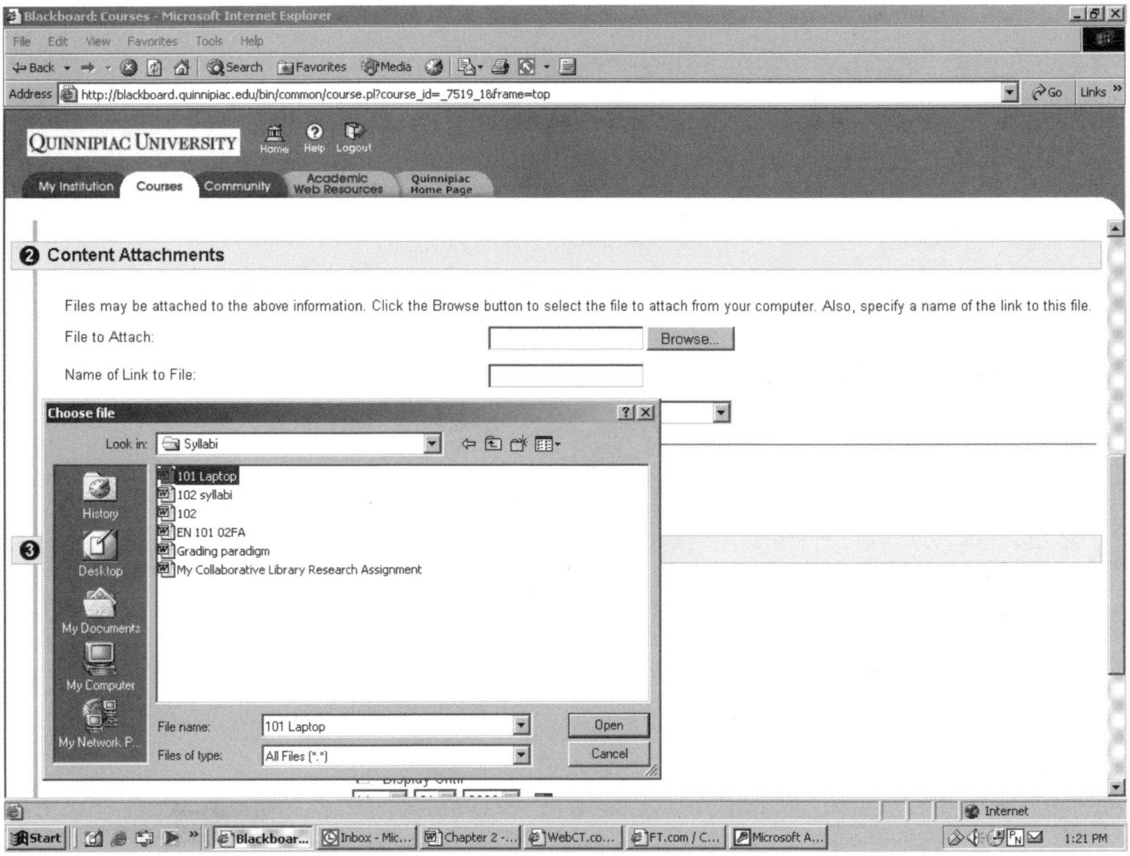

Fig. 2.11: A browsing box used to find the file you want to post. Property of Blackboard. Used with permission of Blackboard. Microsoft Internet Explorer™ screenshot reprinted by permission from the trademark holder, Microsoft Corporation.

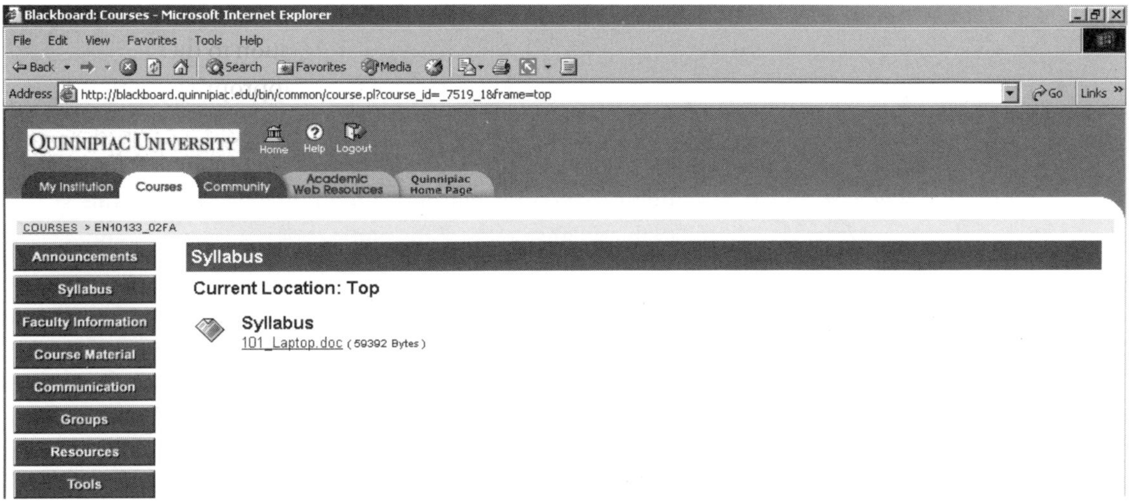

Fig. 2.12: Student view of the posted syllabus. Property of Blackboard. Used with permission of Blackboard. Microsoft Internet Explorer™ screenshot reprinted by permission from the trademark holder, Microsoft Corporation.

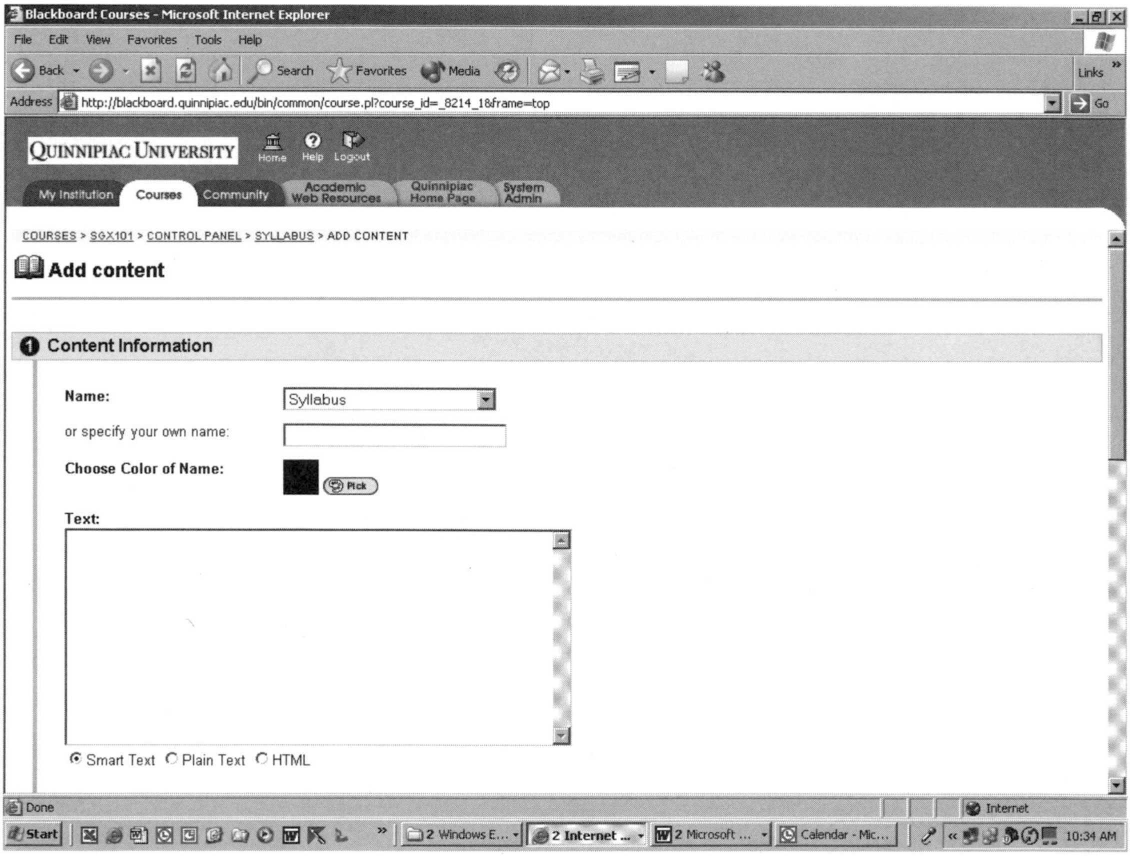

Fig. 2.13: Template for posting the syllabus as displayed text. Property of Blackboard. Used with permission of Blackboard. Microsoft Internet Explorer™ screenshot reprinted by permission from the trademark holder, Microsoft Corporation.

POTENTIAL PITFALLS

It is important to avoid confusing files names. As mentioned above, simple is better, so get in the habit of naming the files as intuitively as possible. For example, "EN 101 Syllabus" makes clear to your audience the contents of the file. This name, however, may be too simple for your records. You probably have a copy of each semester's syllabus and have named them by semester. So something a bit more date-specific might serve all parties. For example, "EN 101 Syllabus 02SP" might allow you send files without renaming and resaving each time you send.

Failing to successfully attach the file to an Email causes frustration and lost time. As mentioned above, this is quite common, usually the result of simply forgetting to attach the file. Whatever the cause, it means you will need to send an "oops" Email with the attachment. This omission can be avoided by getting into the practice of opening the attached file before sending the message (as described above)to make sure it has success-fully attached. This practice will also solve the following potential problem.

Attaching the wrong file to an Email also causes frustration and lost time. Prior to sending the file, you can open it to make sure it is the correct version. The process of nam-ing files to save on your computer takes time and can have a learning curve. Despite cre-ating folders and arranging material that seems to be organized at the moment, you may have trouble finding or recognizing the file at a later date. So the mistakes that may attend the normal learning curve of efficient archiving can be mitigated by checking the file be-fore sending it.

Another potential problem in using this technology will occur if students are not able to open their Email accounts. If your institution offers Email to its students, then this ser-vice may be subject to things like bursar holds or other institutional barriers. To be fair, students may have technical problems with their computer or its applications that will mean a trip to the help desk. It is necessary, however, that students invest some time in learning to use Email. Frequently, students cannot receive messages because their mail-boxes are full.

Also a potential concern when using Email is that Email messages, like printed hand-outs, run the risk of being ignored. Often students will put the handout in their notebooks and not look at it again until you mention it. Sending too many Emails or sending Emails that are not clearly labeled may overwhelm or confuse students. Make sure you label them appropriately. Also, as with printed material, students take their cue from your own at-tention to the material. Simply giving them material does not mean they will read it. Hav-ing sent the material, be prepared to follow up on it in class or use it in an assignment. Ma-terial must have merit.

A potential concern, whether Emailing or posting your file, is whether students have the software to access that type of file. On occasion, students may be using different soft-ware than you are for basic applications. For example, students may try to open a Micro-soft Word file using the WordPerfect application—in general, this should work fine, but on occasion it may cause problems. Again, making sure students are aware of differences in software is helpful. You can, however, do one more thing to limit the likelihood of prob-lems. Try saving the file you want to send in "RTF"—Rich Text Format. This may limit your formatting (fonts, etc.), but it is more universal, lending itself to several applications. To save your document as an RTF file, check your options when you save the document. Word has a pull-down box at the bottom of the "save as" window that allows you to choose the type of file you want to use when saving the text on the screen. A view of this is seen in figure 2.14. Pull down the menu, highlight the type of application you want to use, and save the document.

When posting your materials to course Web pages it is important to make sure that your students are able to find and access your pages. As with Email, some students will

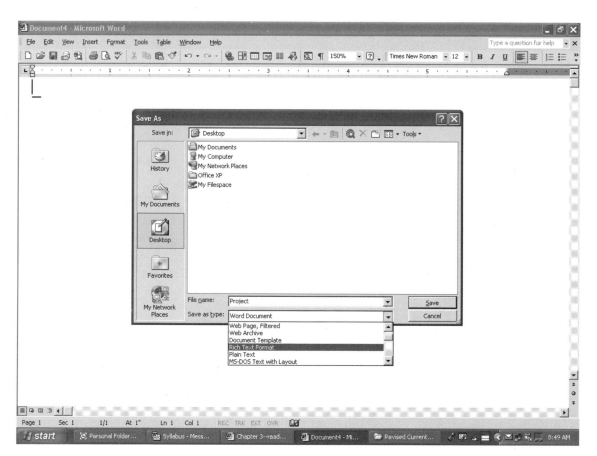

Fig. 2.14: A view of the "Save as type" option in Word. Microsoft Word™ screenshot reprinted by permission from the trademark holder, Microsoft Corporation.

experience problems with their computers or Email accounts, or may have other tech-nology-oriented issues. They may not be able to access the course page. This means a trip to the help desk to make sure the programs are working well. It may also mean that they are not on your roster. Student access to most course management systems is informed by your roster; if a student has enrolled late or is not on the roster, the name may not have been loaded into your course page. In our experience, fully half of the students claiming technical problems—"I can't get into the course management system"—have been expe-riencing problems with their own learning curve. This difficulty can be preempted by en-suring that students receive adequate training—either institutionally, or specifically for your class.

Both of these processes—sending the syllabus by Email and posting it to the course page of a course management system—are similar to other applications discussed in this chapter and elsewhere in this book. The ability to attach a document and send it to students lends itself to a great many other possible applications.

SCENARIO 2: Adding Readings at the Last Minute

TRADITIONAL SOLUTIONS

> **Listserv**—software for managing Email lists in which users can subscribe (to become part of a list and receive Email sent to the list) and unsubscribe (to remove themselves from the list); listservs are often used by organizations to send messages and information to members

Many times you have an epiphany just before class, thinking that if you could just get your students a copy of this article, this poem, this outline, this chart, the whole lecture would fall into place. Perhaps you've just received something in your Email from a colleague, or from a **Listserv,** or you've found a link to a journal article already in electronic format. Perhaps in reviewing your lecture notes you remember an outline you developed last semester that will help with the lecture. Now you take your copy and hurry to the copier before class begins. Even if the copier is working and has no line of professors before it, you still need to wait while the copier makes enough copies for your class.

TECHNOLOGY ALTERNATIVES

As discussed above, you may send materials to your students as displayed text or in attached files in Email messages sent through either a course management system or a stand-alone Email system. Email is easy to send, and many stand-alone Email systems allow you to keep track of who received what information, when they received it, and what they did with it—which can be useful if you want to know whether they received it before class. In Outlook, for example, you can request a read receipt for your message. Adding this feature to an Email message you are sending is as easy as clicking on "Tools" (in the menu at top), then on "Options" (in the resulting drop down), and then (in the pop-up box shown in figure 2.15) clicking on the box next to "Request a read receipt for this message" to put a check mark in it, and then clicking on "Close" to close the pop-up box. When the recipient of your message either opens it or deletes it—whichever happens first—you are sent a brief message indicating the actions of the recipient. A read receipt lets you know how many students have actually opened your message, giving you a better idea of which students will be prepared for class.

As shown in Scenario 1 above, you can copy the text of a file, in whole or in part, which will allow you to place the information right into the body of the Email. You can also attach a copy of the file to the Email as an attachment. Students can then save the information where they want and can print out copies as they need them. You don't have to worry about getting to the copier and making sure you have enough copies to go around.

If the last-minute discovery you want your students to see is a Web site, you simply type (or copy and paste) the Web address of the site into the text of the Email message.

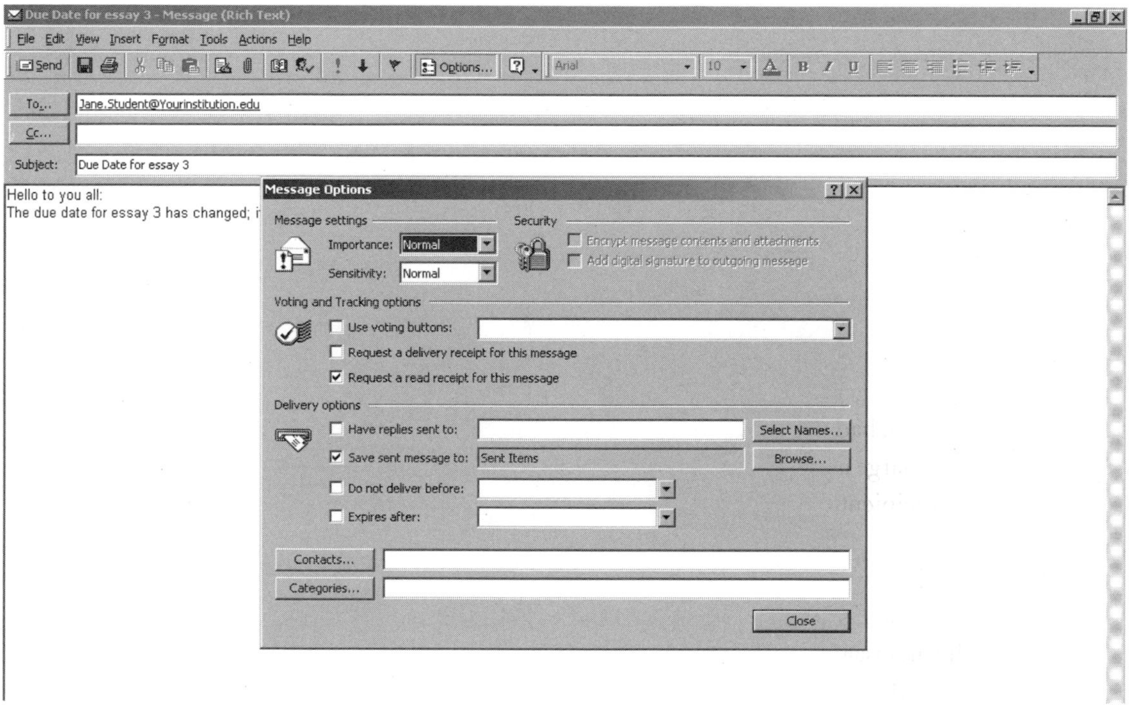

Fig. 2.15: A view of Email message options. Microsoft Outlook™ screenshot reprinted by permission from the trademark holder, Microsoft Corporation.

The code behind the prose text should also travel with the copied material, thus placing a link directly into your Email (meaning it will show up as underlined text in a different color). If the link does not transfer, your students can copy the text of the link from your message into the browser they are using and hit Enter or Return on their keyboards to be taken to the Web site you want them to see. Students will have access to the material whenever they have access to a computer and the Internet.

Another way to get materials to your students at the last minute is to post them in the course management system in a way similar to that shown in Scenario 1 for posting a syllabus. Follow the process outlined above.

POTENTIAL PITFALLS

The potential pitfalls discussed in Scenario 1 above apply to this scenario as well. In addition to those issues, there are issues related to copyright and to the use of Email read receipts.

Copyright issues are growing increasingly important and complicated. Copying material from the Web, and, in an increasing number of cases, copying student work, should be informed by research into copyright laws as they apply to electronic sources (the material in the Appendix will get you started). When in doubt, make sure you give credit.

Regarding Email read receipts, be advised that, while this is a very good tool, it stays applied once you have selected it. This means that a read receipt will be returned for every person to whom the message has been sent. A read receipt for individual messages is not taxing, but if you send a message to a long list of people or use a **Distribution List** to send a single Email, you will be sent a read receipt for every person on the list.

> **Distribution List**—a premade list of Email addresses, usually available to users of an Email system, for sending Email to groups of people; in an academic environment, there are probably distribution lists for "All Faculty," "All Students," "All Staff," and subgroups within these groups

The twenty to thirty receipts you would receive by requesting a read receipt on a message to your class are manageable. But if you decide to send the same message to several class lists or use a larger list, you will greatly increase the number of receipts in your inbox. Once you have had this happen you are not likely to forget to disengage this option when sending to a large number of people. In addition, be aware that certain preview panes may allow the recipient to see the content of a message without actually opening it. If the recipient reads the message in such a preview pane and then deletes it, your receipt may indicate that the recipient did not read the message. Also, as technology develops, the recipient of the Email is being offered the option of sending a receipt or ignoring the request. When the messsage is opened, a pop-up box appears, offering various options. If you are using the read receipt option you may want to tell your students that you expect receipts.

SCENARIO 3: Providing Access to Supplementary Material

TRADITIONAL SOLUTIONS

Over the course of a given semester, you offer students reserve material. Usually these materials are books, copies of journal articles, or videotapes that you place on reserve in the library. Placing material on reserve means collecting it yourself, arranging with a librarian to make it available to your students, and then retrieving it at semester's end. It also means wear and tear on your personal resources, only one student at a time can use it, and the student will have to go to the library to begin with.

Sometimes you prefer to copy journal articles for students, giving them a packet or two over the course of the semester. Depending on secretarial support available to you, if you chose to copy the material and hand out packets, you may have increased your workload. You must gather the material, make copies, organize, collate, staple, and then bring it all to class. Then you will have to make a few more copies for next class to accommodate the people who were not there or who forgot or lost their copies.

TECHNOLOGY ALTERNATIVES

Hyperlinks allow you to direct your students toward specific sources on the Internet. Rather than making yet another handout, carrying it to class, handing it out, and then doing it again for those who were absent or who misplaced their copies, you can simply give students the link in your syllabus. As you compose your syllabus in Microsoft Word you can identify the very place you'd like to place a link. It may be that you already include something about your institution's academic integrity policy, or perhaps an institutionalized finals policy. These documents may already exist on the Web. By linking to them you have cut the space devoted to them on the syllabus, and you have put that much more onus on the student for navigating and understanding the material.

As you are developing your syllabus, look for opportunities to link to pertinent information. A link to your institution's honor code or academic integrity policy may be helpful. Having found the opportune spot in your syllabus, highlight the text you want to be the link, as seen in figure 2.16.

Again, many software packages have built-in redundancies that offer more than one way to access functions. In Microsoft Word, two quick ways are right at the top of the screen. One is to pull down the "Insert" menu and highlight the hyperlink option, as seen in figure 2.17.

Another quick way to access the insert hyperlink option is to click on the "Insert Hyperlink" icon, located in the row of icons at the top of the screen. Either method will bring you to the "Insert Hyperlink" options, as seen in figure 2.18.

Once you've reached the options you will have a variety of choices. You can browse the Web or review the browsing you have done. You can insert an Email address that will

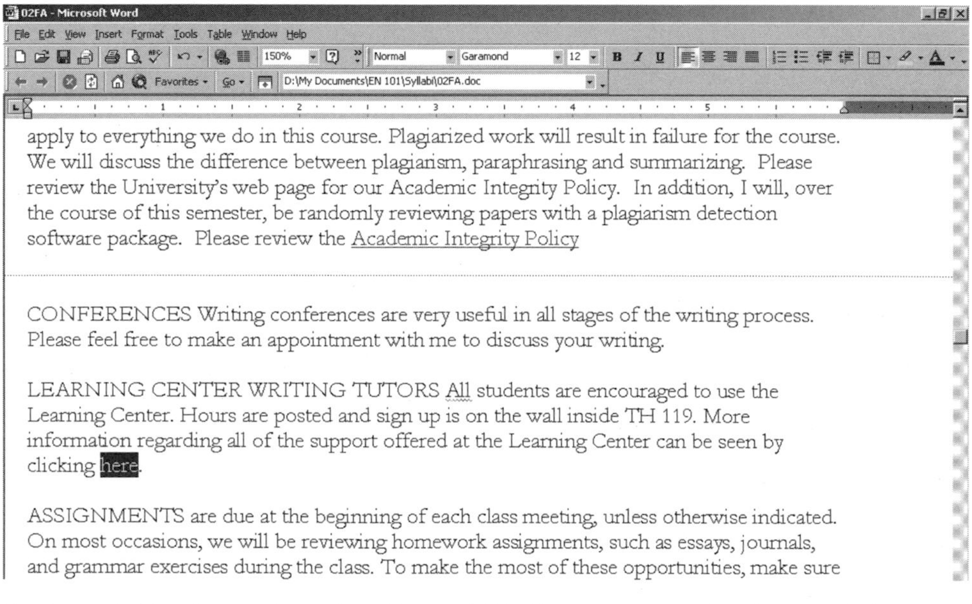

Fig. 2.16: Highlighting text for the link. Microsoft Word™ screenshot reprinted by permission from the trademark holder, Microsoft Corporation.

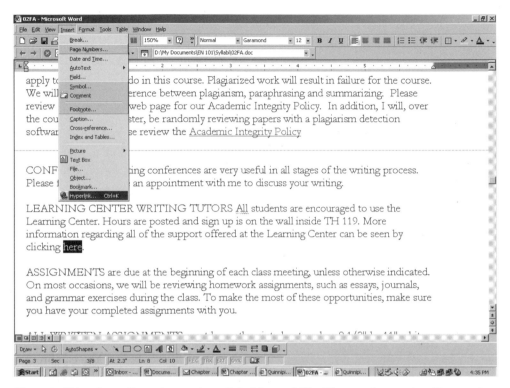

Fig. 2.17: Using the toolbar to insert a hyperlink. Microsoft Word™ screenshot reprinted by permission from the trademark holder, Microsoft Corporation.

open into a new message for the user. Some experimentation is needed to find the best option for your needs.

Another way to distribute learning materials to your students involves using a course management system, such as Blackboard or WebCT. Such an environment offers the ability to put "reserve" material in front of students to use at their convenience. Once the reserve material is in the appropriate format, you can post a copy to your course page. Students can access this information any time their computers are connected to the Internet.

It is important that the material you hope to post be in an electronic format. For example, the syllabus that you Emailed in the previous scenario was in electronic format as a text document. You may want to post a spreadsheet in Excel or a presentation in PowerPoint. As long as the material is saved to your computer, you should be able to post it to the course page. Perhaps you have a journal article or a book chapter that is not saved in your computer but is on paper. If this is the case, you should chat with staffers in your information technology department or library to learn about having the material scanned and saved in an appropriate format, such as a Microsoft Word file, jpeg, tif, or pdf (see Appendix for copyright issues related to this process). Each of these files can be sent

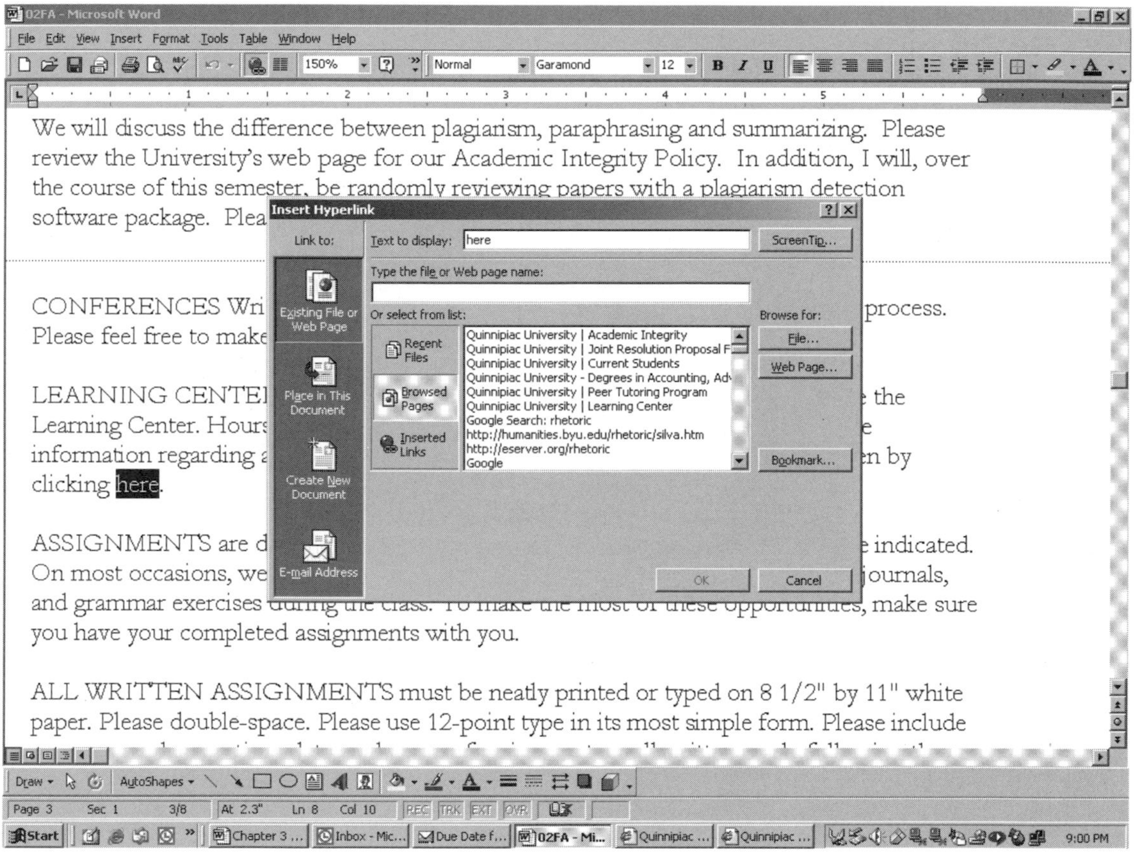

We will discuss the difference between plagiarism, paraphrasing and summarizing. Please review the University's web page for our Academic Integrity Policy. In addition, I will, over the course of this semester, be randomly reviewing papers with a plagiarism detection software package. Plea

CONFERENCES Wri   process.
Please feel free to make

LEARNING CENTE   the
Learning Center. Hour
information regarding a   n by
clicking here.

ASSIGNMENTS are d   indicated.
On most occasions, we   journals,
and grammar exercises during the class. To make the most of these opportunities, make sure
you have your completed assignments with you.

ALL WRITTEN ASSIGNMENTS must be neatly printed or typed on 8 1/2" by 11" white
paper. Please double-space. Please use 12-point type in its most simple form. Please include

Insert Hyperlink dialog box:

Text to display: here

Type the file or Web page name:

Or select from list:
- Quinnipiac University | Academic Integrity
- Quinnipiac University | Joint Resolution Proposal F
- Quinnipiac University | Current Students
- Quinnipiac University - Degrees in Accounting, Ad
- Quinnipiac University | Peer Tutoring Program
- Quinnipiac University | Learning Center
- Google Search: rhetoric
- http://humanities.byu.edu/rhetoric/silva.htm
- http://eserver.org/rhetoric
- Google

Fig. 2.18: Options for inserting a hyperlink. Microsoft Word™ screenshot reprinted by permission from the trademark holder, Microsoft Corporation.

to you via Email and saved to your computer. Text files are usually smaller and more easily saved and opened.

Once you have your file(s) in the appropriate format, you are ready to post the material. You'll need to have enough knowledge of your course management system to get to the page that allows you the options of posting. In Blackboard it's called the Control Panel and is located in the menu bar to the left. Again, this button is on the course home page, as seen in figure 2.6. Place your cursor over the Control Panel button and click.

The Control Panel page allows you to manage the content of the course. Blackboard offers an organizational style that clearly labels course material. A view of the control panel page can be seen in figure 2.9. Place your cursor over the link that says "Course Material" and click.

You'll see your course material page, but of special note are the three buttons that allow you to add material. These buttons can be seen in figure 2.19. If you will be attaching several files to support one assignment, you may want to consider organizing

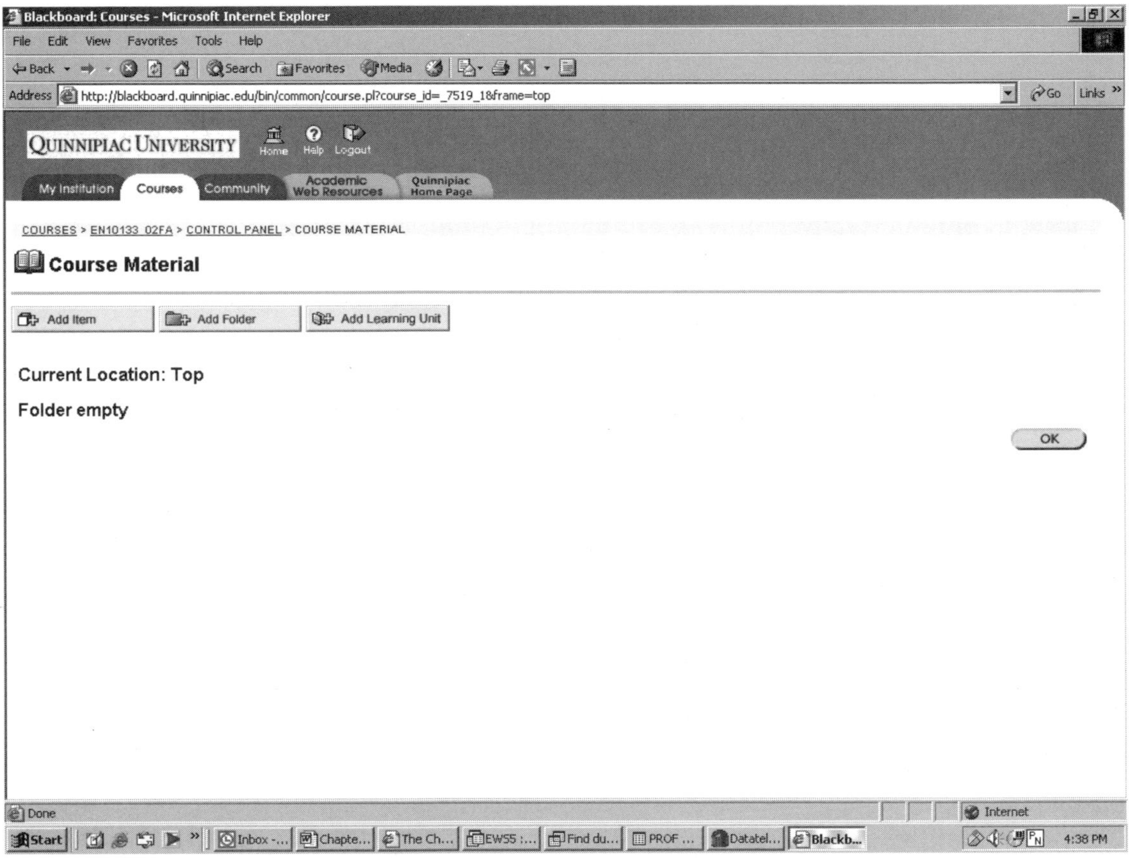

Fig. 2.19: Options for attaching a file in Blackboard. Property of Blackboard. Used with the permission of Blackboard. Microsoft Internet Explorer™ screenshot reprinted by permission from the trademark holder, Microsoft Corporation.

them in a folder labeled for that assignment. After you click on the appropriate button, a window will open; figure 2.20 shows this window that will allow you to browse (search) your computer for the file you wish to post. Select the file by clicking on it, and your next view will be an example of how the page will look when you post it. This review option, as seen in figure 2.21, allows you to check your file before posting it.

Course management systems provide two distinct advantages. Everyone has access to the material, and that material is always in the same place. Unless you, the instructor with access to the control panel, move the files around, students should be able to become comfortable in accessing the information.

One last way to get resource materials to your students is to Email it—as discussed in Scenario 1 regarding sending your syllabus, you can Email other files to them as well. Follow the discussion in Scenario 1, noting that the text file containing your syllabus can easily be a jpeg containing a graphic, an Excel file containing a spreadsheet, or a file containing a video clip.

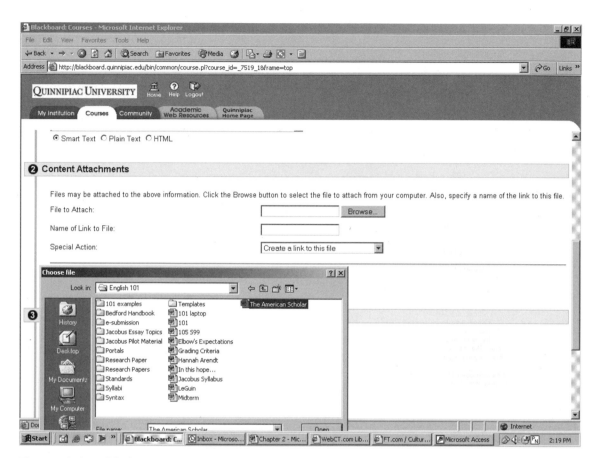

Fig. 2.20 A view of the browsing pop-up. Property of Blackboard. Used with the permission of Blackboard. Microsoft Internet Explorer™ screenshot reprinted by permission from the trademark holder, Microsoft Corporation.

POTENTIAL PITFALLS

When using hyperlinks, make sure that the links are not too subtle. While students do come with some degree of Web savvy, they may miss a link buried in prose. You may consider making an obvious statement: "To find out more information on this topic, click here." Then insert the link.

When posting resources to the course Web pages, organization is terribly important, and that organization should be as intuitive as possible. Given your familiarity with the material you will post and the connections among the material, your logical arrangement may not speak to your students. Try to group material by assignment or by learning objective or by some other relatively clear (if not obvious) criterion. Try to require as few clicks as possible to access the material.

Organization is also important when you choose to Email materials to your students, but it puts the responsibility on your students instead of you. Emailing files means that

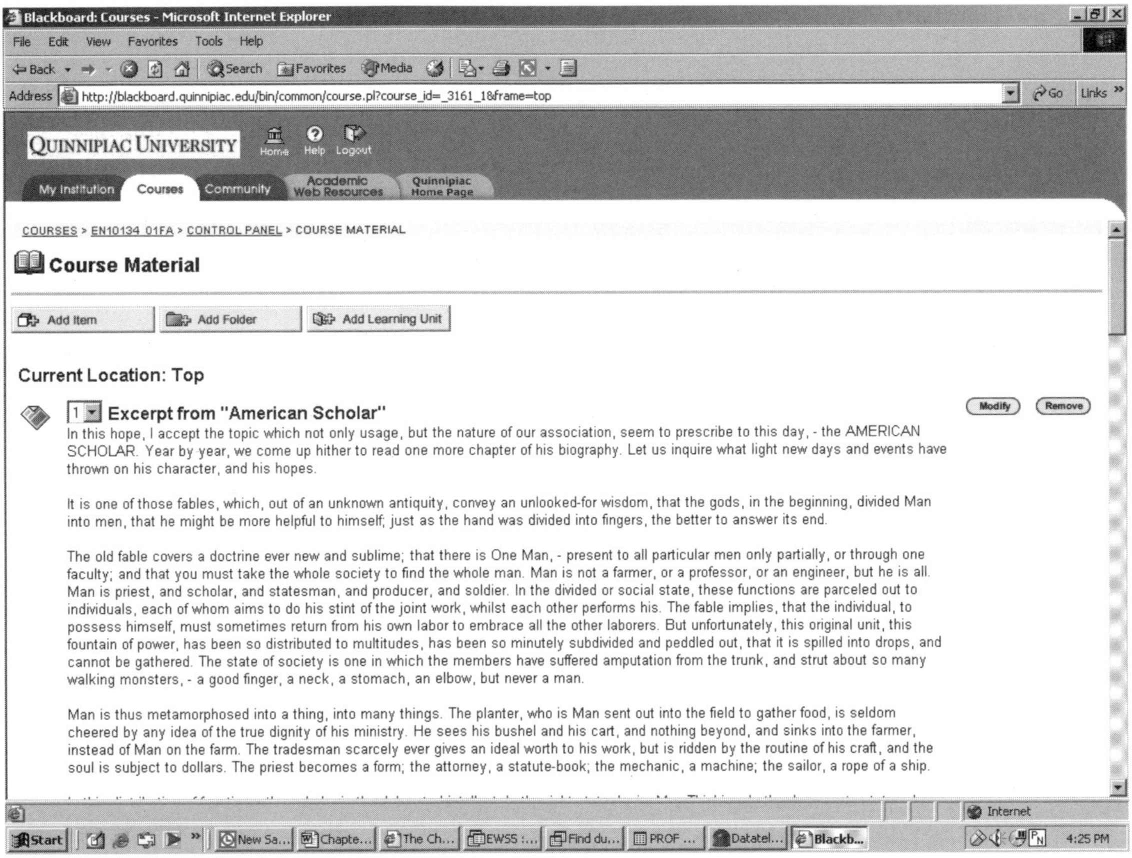

Fig. 2.21: An opportunity to review the file while still in the control panel. Property of Blackboard. Used with the permission of Blackboard. Microsoft Internet Explorer™ screenshot reprinted by permission from the trademark holder, Microsoft Corporation.

your students must organize the material for themselves. If you are going to give them the pieces of the puzzle in this fashion you may want to spend time in class discussing how you expect this material to be used and how often the students will need it. If the supplementary material is listed and linked in the schedule or the syllabus, or posted to the course management system, the student can rely on your organization rather than on his or her own system.

SCENARIO 4: Making Up Canceled Classes

TRADITIONAL SOLUTIONS

A sense of stress often accompanies the realization that you will be missing a class. If you have to cancel, you must make calls to the department secretary to post a sign on the door or write a message on the board. Unless you've planned the cancellation, the loss of the class time affects your semester's schedule. And, of course, a canceled class disrupts the class dynamic; there's a skip in the rhythm you have worked to develop.

Usually a canceled class is water under the bridge. Yes, we console ourselves with the idea that students will use the extra day or days to work on their current assignment or to get ahead—or to catch up—with the reading. It may be, however, that you thought ahead and prepared a phone tree with which to share the task of contacting everyone in class and revising assignments or homework. But even with this phone tree we often lose the class time and have to make it up from the remaining time in our schedule.

TECHNOLOGY ALTERNATIVES

If you are going to miss class unexpectedly, there are usually two things that need attention. If you've decided to cancel class, you have to tell someone. If the cancellation is beyond your control, you still may have to tell your students. In any case, however, you'd proba-bly like to redirect their efforts so as to lose as little steam as possible. You can certainly send them an Email message, but now you can also attach a variety of files to that mes-sage, perhaps the handouts you were going to distribute or the essay to be used in a work-shop. You could also direct their attention to specific Web sites, embedded in the files or copied to the Email, for their review prior to the next class. The opportunities are endless. The practical issue is how to contact them. Scenario 2 of Chapter 1 lays out ways of doing that using the Announcements and Email features in a course management system, while what follows lays out how to do it using a stand-alone Email system, namely, Outlook.

At the beginning of each semester, tell your students that they need to check their Email. Also, make sure you make some mention of Email and its use in your syllabus. One challenge you may face is obtaining the Email addresses of your students. If you've made a habit of corresponding with your students via Email, you may have some record of their addresses in your Inbox. A few clicks of cut and paste, and you can create an impromptu distribution list from your records. You may also have copies of Email addresses in your Sent Items Folder, although you would have had to set this feature earlier. You may not have all the Email addresses, but if you can reach half of the class, you can ask them to for-ward the Email to others in the class. If enough people forward the message, everyone should receive a copy. If you are working with an institutional software package, a copy of your class roster or simply remembering a few names can get the information out. With institutional software, Email addresses are usually formulaic. If you have a copy of your class roster, you can send out the message. Even without the roster, the first few letters of the last name may enable you to use the "check names" function or a search function to find the right name. In Outlook, select the To button, located in the top left of the screen. This button opens a search function, seen in figure 2.22, which allows you to type in a few letters of the student's last name and attempts to match those letters to the names on file. A double-click on the correct name automatically addresses the Email to that address.

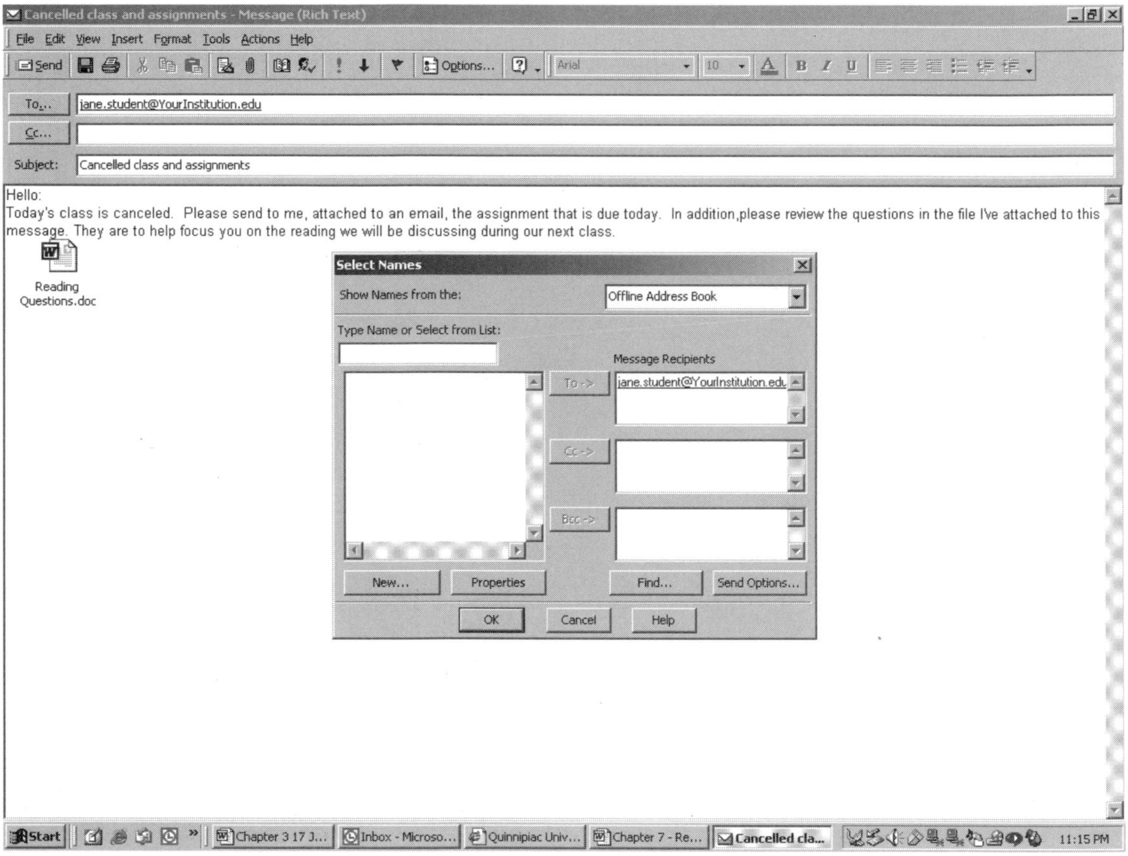

Fig. 2.22: Selecting names in Outlook. Microsoft Outlook™ screenshot reprinted by permission of the trademark holder, Microsoft Corporation.

Now, if you are able to use this select function, you can save significant time by continuing to select students' names to add to the list of message recipients. In the best case, you would have already created a list that you saved. But if you have not, adding the rest of your students by selecting in this fashion is the next best thing (figure 2.23). If you feel that you are missing someone, ask that the students receiving this message send it along to other members of the class as well.

POTENTIAL PITFALLS

Distribution lists take a few minutes to create. Even before the semester begins, try to create a distribution list for each class. Yes, you will have people adding and dropping your class, but in reality, more will stay than will leave or show up. And it's much better to invest the time early and create the tool. You will probably use it more often that you think.

Creating a distribution list can be accomplished in several ways. One way is to ask all

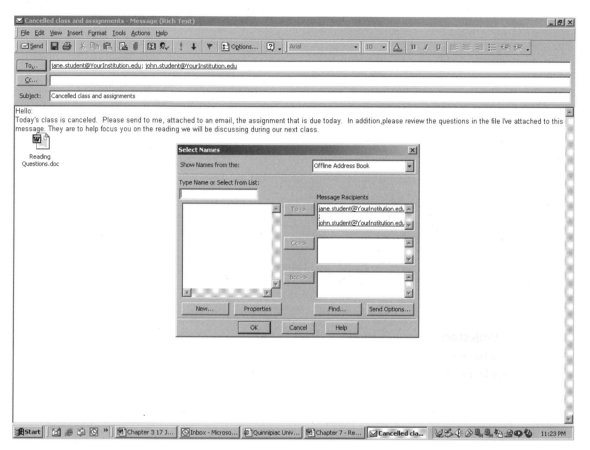

Fig. 2.23: Adding more students' names to the same Email message. Microsoft Outlook™ screenshot reprinted by permission of the trademark holder, Microsoft Corporation.

of your students to send you an Email. Then, copy the senders' Email addresses to a list of addresses of students in that section. You may find it best to arrange your distribution lists by course section, as you may wish to send information to one section and not to another. When you need to use this list, open the file, copy the list, and paste it into the address box of the new Email. Saving the list in a word document usually works fine. If your institution provides Email accounts to its community, the task is quite simple.

SCENARIO 5: Distributing Graphics, Videos, and Audio Materials

TRADITIONAL SOLUTIONS

One issue to consider is when the audiovisual items will be used. If you are going to ask students to use them on their own time, you need to provide access to the material. Sometimes you may include graphs or charts as teaching adjuncts. Other times a video or a soundtrack may be appropriate. The charts and graphs you can usually reproduce, which means copying them yourself—with its attendant problems—or thinking far enough ahead to arrange for someone else to copy them. Assigning a video, cassette tape, CD, or DVD usually means a trip to the library to begin the task of placing the material on reserve. Students will go to the library and, one at a time, use these resources to prepare for class.

Now, to use these resources during class, you must have enough paper copies to hand out. Or perhaps you are a fan of overhead projections, which means making transparent copies. Videos and audios are accompanied by their own challenges. You have to bring the item to be played and make sure that the player is in the classroom. So, you call media services (typically forty-eight hours ahead), to make sure that the overhead projector (with a working bulb) and screen will be in the room. Or that the television/VCR cart will be hooked up and ready to go. Or that the tape player has been delivered.

TECHNOLOGY ALTERNATIVES

In fact, most of the traditional solutions to the scenario listed above depend on technology. The alternatives discussed in this section will bring in course management systems and **Video Projectors**. In order to save graphics, videos, or audios onto a computer (so that they can be posted in a course management system), these elements must be converted to a digital format if they are not in that form already. The audiovisual or media services departments in most institutions are capable of performing these conversions. In addition to arranging for someone to do the conversion, you will need to make sure that your license to use the graphic, audio, or video allows you to digitize it. When you contact the source of the item to check on your licensing, in many cases you will discover that the item is offered and licensed in a digital format, which will solve both problems at once.

With a digital version of your item you have a lot more flexibility in how you can use it (though, again, you must make sure that whatever you do is consistent with the terms of copyright law and your licensing). The first thing you will probably want to do is post all of the files containing these resources into your course Web pages in your course management system, as discussed in Scenario 3 of this chapter. You may want to organize these resources into folders by categories, as shown in figure 2.24, or give your students access to the resources through weekly Web pages for your course, as discussed in Chapter 5.

In either case, once these resources are posted to your course pages in the course management system, your students will have access to them whenever they are using the Internet. Figure 2.25 shows links to three video files containing dance sequences being studied in a course. Students simply double-click on the link for the video file they want to view, wait a couple of seconds while the file downloads and opens (large files will take longer if students are using dial-up connections to access the Internet), and watch the video clip. They can view a video repeatedly to study whatever idea you are focusing on,

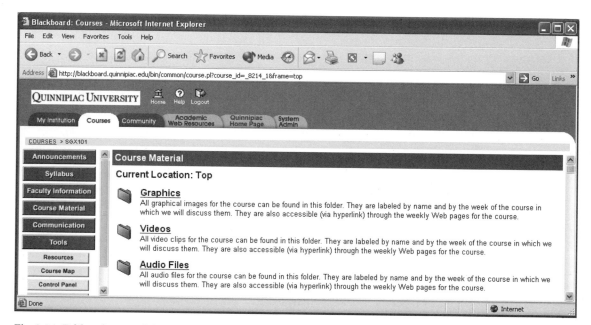

Fig. 2.24: Folders for organizing course resources in a course management system. Property of Blackboard. Used with the permission of Blackboard. Microsoft Internet Explorer™ screenshot reprinted by permission from the trademark holder, Microsoft Corporation.

and students who missed the class in which the video was introduced can easily do make-up work. The same process and accessibility holds for audio or image files.

Once your materials are posted in the course management system, you always have access to them in class, so long as your classroom has a computer and a video projector. Many institutions have made large-scale investments in video projection, equipping many of their classrooms with these devices, and most also have portable video projec-

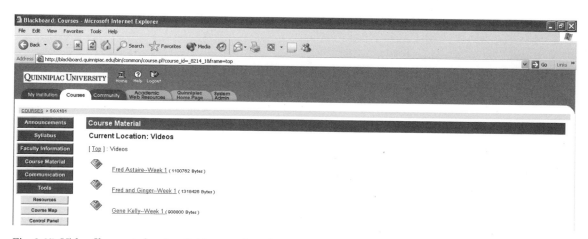

Fig. 2.25: Video files posted and available to students in a course management system. Property of Blackboard. Used with the permission of Blackboard. Microsoft Internet Explorer™ screenshot reprinted by permission from the trademark holder, Microsoft Corporation.

tors that can be brought into any classroom on request. With a computer and a video projector in the classroom you can show your students how to navigate to your course resources. Linking your audiovisual materials this way means that you never have to remember to bring them to class and that you can always refer to materials from previous weeks (or to material in future weeks) without having to carry the whole semester's materials with you to every class.

POTENTIAL PITFALLS

Besides making sure that your students can access your course pages in your course management system, there are two other concerns.

First, you need to make sure that the digital files you are using are in standard formats and that the computers your students use will have the software needed to open and access material in those files. This is generally not a problem because formats are pretty well standardized and software for running the standard image, audio, and visual file formats is automatically loaded on most computers.

The second potential concern relates to video projection equipment: you need to make sure that your classroom either has it built in or delivered, that a computer is either built in or can be delivered (unless you have a laptop to bring to class), and that you know how to use the projector to show students your materials. This is a simple matter of planning, but it is important that you do it to ensure that everything will go smoothly.

CHAPTER 3 Promoting Collaborative Learning

SCENARIO 1: Fostering and Extending In-Class Collaboration

> You want the class to discuss a case, article, problem, etc. You wish that you could have wider class participation than you often do and that you could have a better record of contributions of each student than your memory often affords. You are often frustrated that class ends just as the discussion is heating up.

SCENARIO 2: Facilitating Work on Group Projects Outside of Class

> Your students are working on group projects (cases, papers, presentations, etc.) that require collaboration outside of class. The students all have tight (and different) schedules and have a hard time getting together often enough to get the work done.

SCENARIO 3: Building Networks of Collaboration for Learning from Peers

> You know that your students often have questions regarding class projects and assignments. You also know that they frequently receive help with these questions from other students (in addition to receiving help from you) when they can find them. You would like to facilitate and monitor this flow of support between students.

SCENARIO 4: Fostering Peer Feedback

> You often ask a peer to read over your writing to provide feedback, and you would like to promote a similar activity among your students.

SCENARIO 5: Assessing and Managing Team Performance

> You have students working in groups. You fear that one or two students in each group are carrying the weight and want to be able to assess that and manage it.

Research on the importance of social interaction and collaboration in learning has a long history. Dewey and Piaget both argued that social interaction is central to learning.[1]

Recent studies (Slavin, Evans, Topping, Nichols and Miller, Newstead and Evans, Vye et al., and Tang,[2] among others) have found that students working in groups on projects and problems can learn more, produce better work, and spend more of their time in **Higher-Order Learning Activities** than can comparable students working by themselves. In particular, it has been found that students working alone spend their time gathering and organizing information on the basic issues of an assignment while students working in groups go beyond these activities, spending time sharing, comparing, analyzing, criticizing, supplementing, and applying each other's information and ideas.

> **Higher-Order Learning Activities**—referring to a taxonomy of learning such as that presented by B. S. Bloom (1956), in which learning is classified into levels or orders, usually with knowledge of basic facts and definitions at the first level and the abilities to apply, critique, and synthesize ideas at higher levels

The main problem associated with group assignments is that, due to social norms and disparate grade expectations among group members, groups are often dominated by one or two of their members who, in the extreme, may leave other group members out of decision making, or even the project as a whole. What's worse, it seems common that the same students tend to dominate every group they are in, meaning that the same students can be left in the role of follower—or left out entirely. And, because only one assignment is handed in by the entire group, it is often hard to tell whether the learning displayed is shared by all or by only a few of the group members. These are serious concerns that prevent many faculty members from exploring the potential benefits of collaborative learning.

The technology solutions suggested below can be used to facilitate collaborative work, limit the negative impact of social norms, and account for the relative contributions of group members.

SCENARIO 1: Fostering and Extending In-Class Collaboration

TRADITIONAL SOLUTIONS

In-class collaboration, whether discussion, casework, problem solving, or another activity, can present many challenges. It can be difficult to ensure that everyone is prepared for fruitful participation (more on that in Scenario 1 of Chapter 8), difficult to get the conversation going, difficult to achieve widespread and even participation, difficult to accurately account for participation (if that is part of student evaluation), and frustrating when class ends just as things seem to be picking up. Fostering in-class collaboration may de-

pend largely on the skill and art of the faculty member, but there are many traditional solutions for solving some of these problems.

One common way of fostering in-class collaboration and interaction is to begin such
projects in small groups (groups of four to six are probably most common). Sometimes
the in-class group discussion is a springboard for a group assignment, but it is also a way
to get full class discussion started. Shy students are usually more willing to speak up in
smaller groups, and notes taken in these small group discussions can be reported to the
class as a whole, providing specific, personalized material for class discussion.

Another strategy for getting ideas flowing is to ask each student to write down his or
her ideas on a topic, question, or problem to be discussed. The instructor can either wan-
der around noting ideas to share with the class, or ask students to share what they've written. Either way, students have had time to reflect, and more students may give more confident and better answers than if they were not given time to think and write.

These strategies can help foster better in-class collaboration, but they do not aid instructors in accurately evaluating student contributions, nor do they help extend a good
discussion once class is over.

TECHNOLOGY ALTERNATIVES

Fortunately, technology offers at least two tools that can foster widespread and thoughtful in-class collaboration, provide accountability regarding the contributions of each student, and allow flourishing in-class collaborations to commence before class begins and
be extended after it ends.

The first of these is **Chat** (see Scenario 4 of Chapter 1 for another example of the
use of Chat). Chat allows several people to type messages, each of which is visible to the
other participants as soon as its author submits it by hitting the Enter key. Messages appear in the Chat in the order in which they were submitted, meaning messages tend to be
short (a sentence or two) to keep participants in the conversation. An **Instant Messenger**
is a specialized Chat in which generally only two people can participate. Many forms of
Chat are available through course management systems (such as WebCT and Blackboard), other software specialized for education, and a wide variety of free Internet
sites. Students who claim technophobia are often still avid participants in Chat sessions,
sometimes seeming more at ease in virtual conversations than they do in real ones.
This is cause for concern by many—face-to-face human interaction is foundational,
and developing live communication skills is an important part of a good education. But
students' widespread comfort with virtual conversations through Chat and Instant
Messengers provides an opportunity for helping de-
velop these critical live communication skills.

Instant Messenger—software that allows
two or more users to exchange messages
immediately; as in a phone conversation, all
participants in an Instant Messenger session
must be online at the time of the exchange

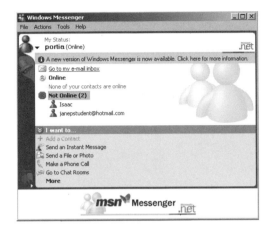

Fig. 3.1: Windows Messenger is a tool for Chat and Instant Messenger. Microsoft Windows Messenger™ screenshot reprinted by permission from the trademark holder, Microsoft Corporation.

A typical example of a free source of Chat on the Internet is Windows Messenger, which is shown in figure 3.1. On the screen you can see

- Your name (Portia in this case),
- Which of your contacts (teammates) are currently Online (none in this case),
- Which of your contacts are Not Online (Isaac and JanePStudent in this case),
- And choices below as to actions you can take (Add a Contact, Send an Instant Message, etc.).

Contacts can be added by clicking on Add a Contact. This allows you to identify your new contact by his or her Email address (johnpstudent@hotmail.com in figure 3.2).

Upon submission of this form, your new contact is added to your list of contacts (as shown in figure 3.3, another contact who is Not Online).

As teammates come online to participate in the virtual conversation they move from the list of contacts who are not online to the list of contacts who are online (note that Isaac has come online in the example shown in figure 3.4).

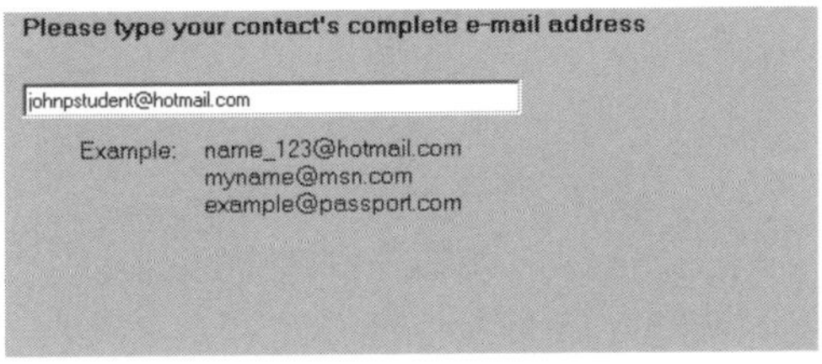

Fig. 3.2: Adding contacts in Windows Messenger. Microsoft Windows Messenger™ screenshot reprinted by permission from the trademark holder, Microsoft Corporation.

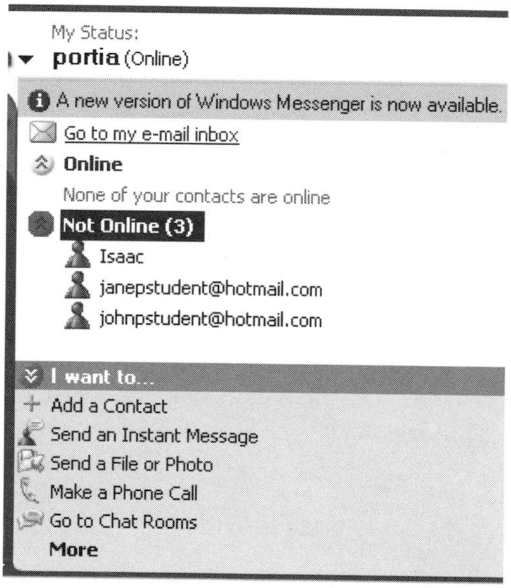

Fig. 3.3: Windows Messenger after another contact has been added. Microsoft Windows Messenger™ screenshot reprinted by permission from the trademark holder, Microsoft Corporation.

Once teammates are online they can send Instant Messages or move to a Chat room, which might look like the screen in figure 3.5. Participants in this online conversation type their messages in the box at the bottom of the screen ("I think the accent over the 'e' is just so you say . . ." is the message Portia is preparing to send), which is not visible to other participants until the writer of the message hits the Enter key (or clicks on the Send button).

Fig. 3.4: Windows Messenger after another contact has come online. Microsoft Windows Messenger™ screenshot reprinted by permission from the trademark holder, Microsoft Corporation.

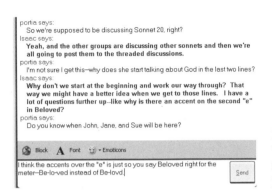

Fig. 3.5: An ongoing Chat session. Microsoft Windows Messenger™ screenshot reprinted by permission from the trademark holder, Microsoft Corporation.

Experience suggests that students are often more thoughtful, focused, and candid in online discussions than they are in face-to-face discussions—even if they are all in the same room when they are participating in the virtual conversation. If these online conversations are taking place in the classroom, a **Video Projector** can be used to easily project any of the team conversations onto a screen at the front of the class so that everyone can observe any of the online conversations that the instructor finds especially instructive. Whether participants are in the same room or miles apart, the instructor can pop in and out of the group conversations, monitoring their progress if desired.

By beginning a class discussion with fifteen minutes of online group discussions, and monitoring each of these discussions, you can quickly discover many starting points for the class discussion. Better still, you can require that each group have a fifteen-minute Chat on the topic before they come to class and have them post these Chats to a threaded discussion, as shown in figure 3.6. Finally, if the discussion is flowing fast when class ends, students can continue the discussion online, and post it to a threaded discussion for all to see if desired.

As discussed in Scenario 3 of Chapter 1, a threaded discussion is an organized online space in which you and your students can record, organize, and store interactions and information. Threaded discussions like that in figure 3.6 can be thought of as traditional outlines:

- the initial message posted to start each thread is justified farthest left and is like a large Roman numeral entry in an outline (initial messages in figure 3.6 are, "An Ode to the Starters," "Swinging for the Right Field Fence," "Double Play!," and "The Old and the New"),
- a reply to the initial message in a thread appears below that initial message, indented one level, and is like a capital letter entry in an outline (there are two replies to the initial message "An Ode to the Starters" in figure 3.6, each titled, "Re: An Ode to the Starters"—one just below the initial posting and one just above the next initial posting),

- a reply to any message appears below that message and is indented one level from the message being replied to (the first reply to "An Ode to the Starters" has two replies (the first titled "Re: An Ode to the Starters" and the second titled "Starters Redux"), and the first of these has a reply titled "A different Start?"]
- most threaded discussions allow threads to contain many levels of replies, each indented from the prior level.

Messages with files attached are usually designated with paper clips (only three messages in figure 3.6 do not have attachments), and messages not yet read by you are usually designated both by appearing in bold and with some kind of label ("New" at right in figure 3.6).

A threaded discussion can help foster collaboration in at least two ways: as a place for storing and accessing Chat discussions that have already taken place, and as a vehicle for collaborative discussions in its own right. In either case the discussion needs to be created using a template like that in figure 3.7. In addition to having space to type the threaded discussion's title and description you will usually be able to decide whether your students will be able to

- post anonymously (see Potential Pitfalls in Scenario 2 of Chapter 8),
- edit or remove messages they've posted (this can cause mayhem on a long thread),
- attach files to postings, and/or
- create initial messages (new threads) in the discussion (at times you may want to allow students to create initial messages; at other times you may want to ensure the organization of the discussion by posting all of the initial messages yourself).

Once the threaded discussion is created, your students will be able to access it by clicking on its **Hyperlinked** title ("Discussion of Sonnets from the Portuguese" in figure 3.8) on a page indexing the threaded discussions for your course, to discover the discussion

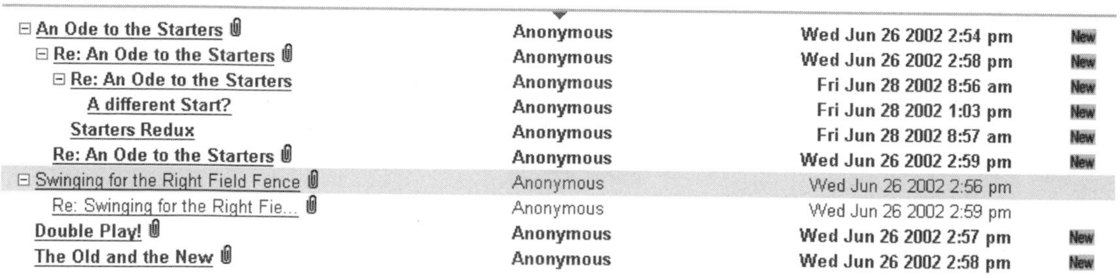

⊟ An Ode to the Starters 🔗	Anonymous	Wed Jun 26 2002 2:54 pm	New
⊟ Re: An Ode to the Starters 🔗	Anonymous	Wed Jun 26 2002 2:58 pm	New
⊟ Re: An Ode to the Starters	Anonymous	Fri Jun 28 2002 8:56 am	New
A different Start?	Anonymous	Fri Jun 28 2002 1:03 pm	New
Starters Redux	Anonymous	Fri Jun 28 2002 8:57 am	New
Re: An Ode to the Starters 🔗	Anonymous	Wed Jun 26 2002 2:59 pm	New
⊟ Swinging for the Right Field Fence 🔗	Anonymous	Wed Jun 26 2002 2:56 pm	
Re: Swinging for the Right Fie... 🔗	Anonymous	Wed Jun 26 2002 2:59 pm	
Double Play! 🔗	Anonymous	Wed Jun 26 2002 2:57 pm	New
The Old and the New 🔗	Anonymous	Wed Jun 26 2002 2:58 pm	New

Fig. 3.6: A threaded discussion with multiple threads and replies. Property of Blackboard. Used with the permission of Blackboard.

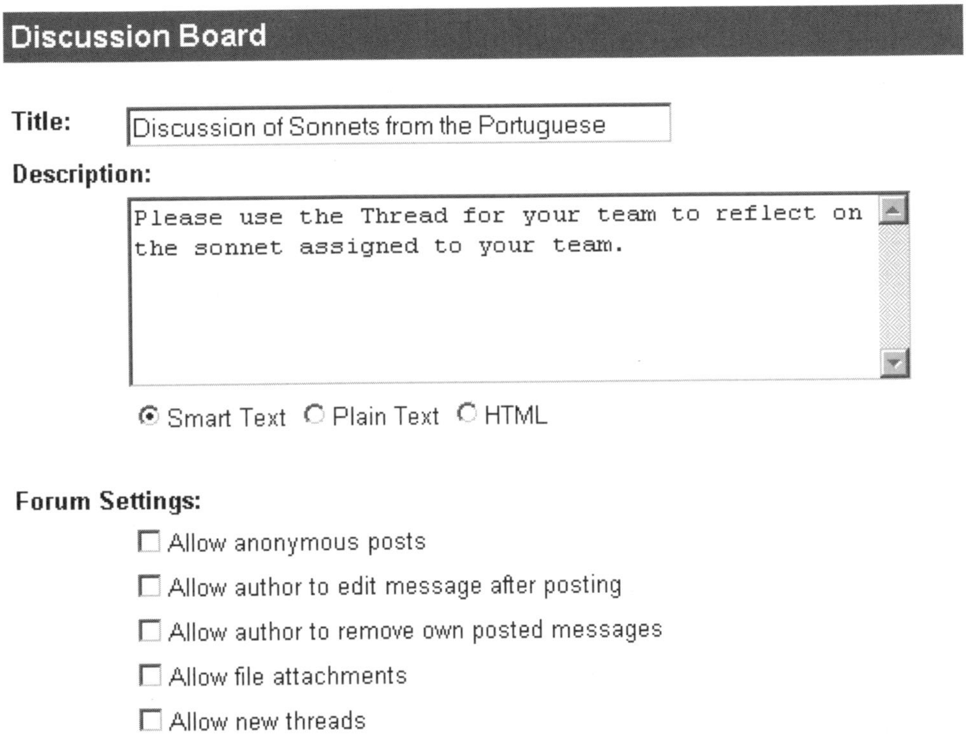

Discussion Board

Title: | Discussion of Sonnets from the Portuguese |

Description:

> Please use the Thread for your team to reflect on
> the sonnet assigned to your team.

◉ Smart Text   ○ Plain Text   ○ HTML

Forum Settings:

☐ Allow anonymous posts

☐ Allow author to edit message after posting

☐ Allow author to remove own posted messages

☐ Allow file attachments

☐ Allow new threads

Fig. 3.7: Template for creating a threaded discussion. Property of Blackboard. Used with the permission of Blackboard.

itself. Since students have not been given the ability to create new threads in the example, the blank discussion board leaves them with nothing to do until you post an initial message (figure 3.9).

Your view of the discussion at this point would be as shown in figure 3.10. By clicking on the Add New Thread button at left in figure 3.10 (note that students do not have that button in their view), you will be presented with a standard message creation template, like that in figure 3.11.

Once you have posted initial messages ("Team 1 . . .," "Team 2 . . .," "Team 3 . . .," and "Team 4 . . ." in figure 3.12) students can view them by clicking on a message title.

The message titled "Team 4—Sonnet 20" (figure 3.13) actually has no message but simply creates an initial posting to which Team 4 can post replies—it becomes that team's space for collecting and developing their work and discussion. By clicking on Reply in that initial posting (at lower right), a student is presented with the template (figure 3.14) for replying to the initial message. In this case the reply is a copy of the Chat discussed at the beginning of this section. When the student clicks the Submit button, the reply is posted under, and indented from, the message to which it is replying (figure 3.15).

This application of a threaded discussion permits a Chat conversation to be stored in a way that is organized and accessible to students in the class. But it is also common to

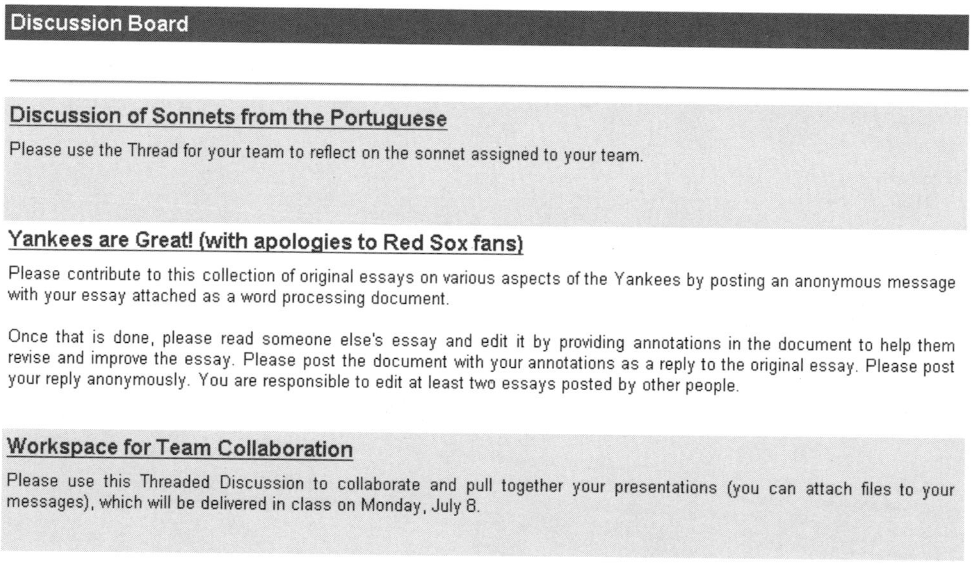

Discussion Board

Discussion of Sonnets from the Portuguese

Please use the Thread for your team to reflect on the sonnet assigned to your team.

Yankees are Great! (with apologies to Red Sox fans)

Please contribute to this collection of original essays on various aspects of the Yankees by posting an anonymous message with your essay attached as a word processing document.

Once that is done, please read someone else's essay and edit it by providing annotations in the document to help them revise and improve the essay. Please post the document with your annotations as a reply to the original essay. Please post your reply anonymously. You are responsible to edit at least two essays posted by other people.

Workspace for Team Collaboration

Please use this Threaded Discussion to collaborate and pull together your presentations (you can attach files to your messages), which will be delivered in class on Monday, July 8.

Fig. 3.8: Index of threaded discussions for a course. Property of Blackboard. Used with the permission of Blackboard.

Discussion Board

Creation of new threads is not permitted, so there is nothing here for you to do.

VIEW UNREAD MESSAGES ▼   EXPAND ALL ⊞   COLLAPSE ALL ⊟
                                                                                         SEARCH ?

                                                                              SHOW OPTIONS

Sort By: Default ▼

OK

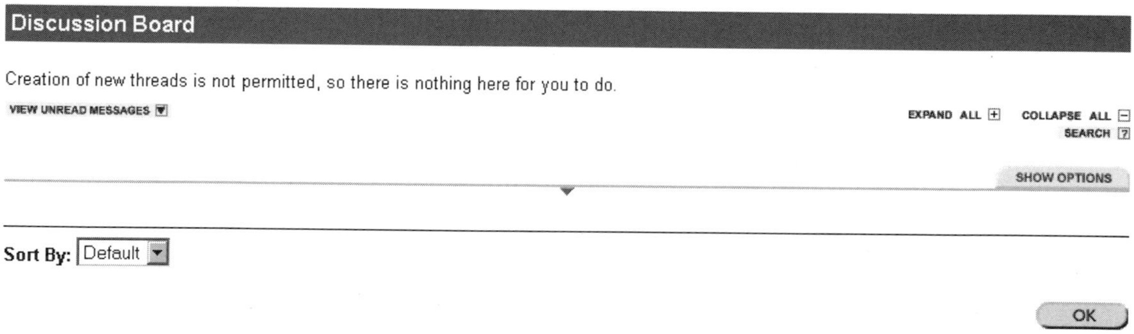

Fig. 3.9: Student view of a threaded discussion in which they are not allowed to create new threads. Property of Blackboard. Used with the permission of Blackboard.

Discussion Board

To start a discussion thread, use the Add New Thread button below.

Add New Thread

VIEW UNREAD MESSAGES ▼   EXPAND ALL ⊞   COLLAPSE ALL ⊟
                                                                                         SEARCH ?

                                                                              SHOW OPTIONS

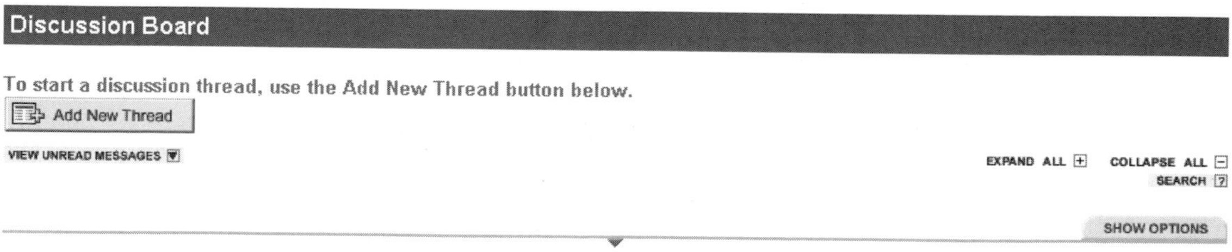

Fig. 3.10: Instructor view of a threaded discussion in which no threads have yet been created. Property of Blackboard. Used with the permission of Blackboard.

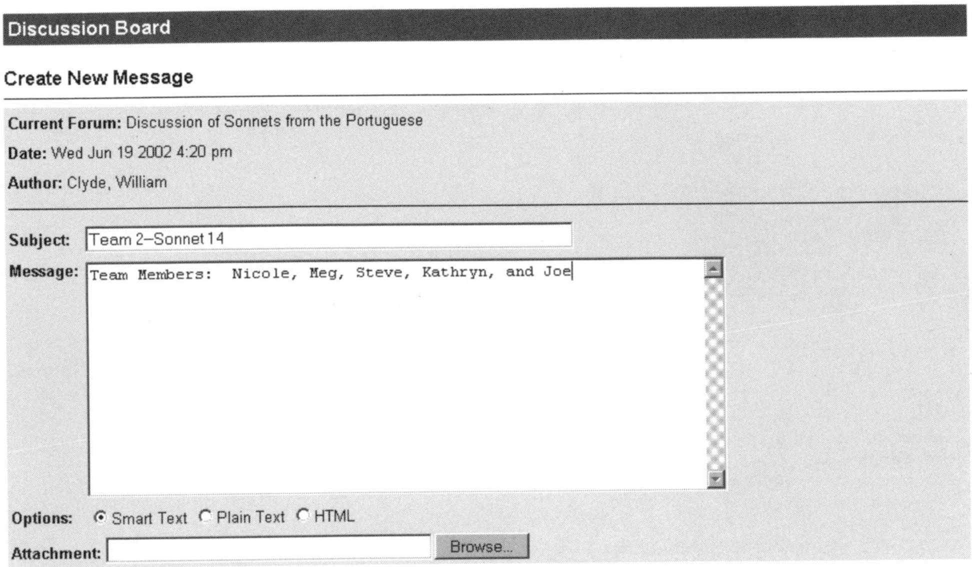

Discussion Board

Create New Message

Current Forum: Discussion of Sonnets from the Portuguese

Date: Wed Jun 19 2002 4:20 pm

Author: Clyde, William

Subject: Team 2–Sonnet 14

Message: Team Members: Nicole, Meg, Steve, Kathryn, and Joe

Options: ⦿ Smart Text ○ Plain Text ○ HTML

Attachment: [   ] Browse...

Fig. 3.11: Template for posting a message in a threaded discussion. Property of Blackboard. Used with the permission of Blackboard.

Discussion Board

VIEW UNREAD MESSAGES ▼

EXPAND ALL ⊞   COLLAPSE ALL ⊟
SEARCH ?

SHOW OPTIONS

Team 1--Sonnet 6	Clyde, William	Wed Jun 26 2002 11:24 am	New
Team 2--Sonnet 14	Clyde, William	Wed Jun 26 2002 11:24 am	New
Team 3--Sonnet 29	Clyde, William	Wed Jun 26 2002 11:25 am	New
Team 4--Sonnet 20	Clyde, William	Wed Jun 26 2002 11:26 am	New

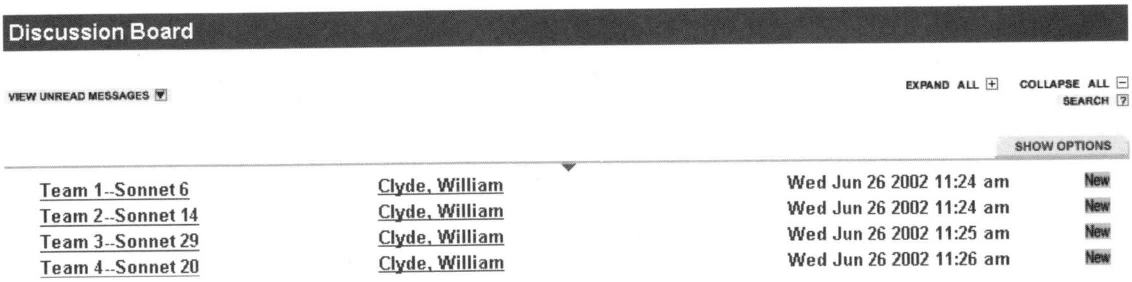

Fig. 3.12: Threaded discussion after four initial messages, or new threads, have been posted. Property of Blackboard. Used with the permission of Blackboard.

Discussion Board

◄◄ Previous Message   Next Message ►►

Current Forum: Discussion of Sonnets from the Portuguese

Date: Wed Jun 26 2002 11:26 am

Author: Clyde, William <william.clyde@quinnipiac.edu>

Subject: Team 4--Sonnet 20

(Reply)

◄◄ Previous Message   Next Message ►►

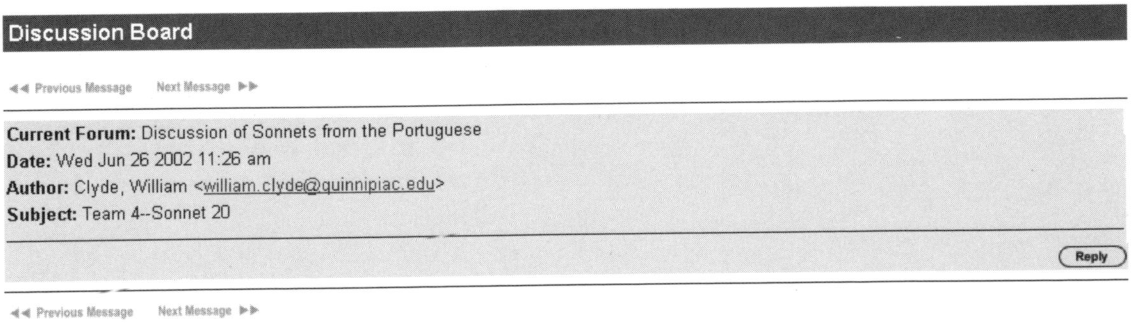

Fig. 3.13: Blank initial message creating an online space in which a team can collect its developing work. Property of Blackboard. Used with the permission of Blackboard.

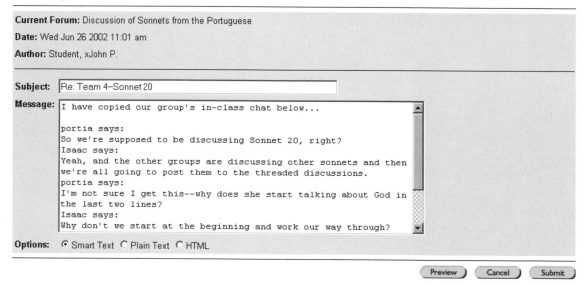

Fig. 3.14: Using a template to post a Chat that has already taken place. Property of Blackboard. Used with the permission of Blackboard.

have the conversation itself take place as a sort of **Asynchronous Chat** in the threaded discussion. Participants in such a discussion would reply to the initial message for their team with comments or questions (as in figure 3.16) that they would have contributed as entries in the Chat conversation if that medium were being used.

Participants would participate in the conversation by replying to others' postings in the threaded discussion (as opposed to sending messages in the Chat session), potentially resulting in extended threads like those shown in figure 3.17.

Chat and threaded discussions can be used in class or out of class to foster collaboration in small groups or full classes. Each can allow students to contribute to a conversation wherever they are, and to be identified by name or to remain anonymous in their postings. Since Chat allows the whole conversation to be visible (or at least to be accessed by simply **Scrolling**) at all times, it surpasses threaded discussion in facilitating fluid conversations. It is a medium most students are very familiar and comfortable with and well versed in. Chat can be thought of as a typed conference call. Like a phone call, Chat's shortcomings are that participants in Chat need to meet online at the same time, and that conversations

Asynchronous Chat—a Chat session that takes place over hours, days, or even weeks instead of over a few minutes, and in which all participants may not be online and participating at the same time (as would be true in a Synchronous Chat) but will check in and out, reading contributions that others have added since the last visit, and replying and contributing at each visit

Scrolling—used whenever the item (page, document, or image) being viewed is too large to fit on the screen; scrolling up and down or right and left lets the user see other parts of the item

Discussion Board			

VIEW UNREAD MESSAGES ▾   EXPAND ALL ⊞   COLLAPSE ALL ⊟
                                                    SEARCH ?

SHOW OPTIONS

Team 1--Sonnet 6	Clyde, William	Wed Jun 26 2002 11:24 am	New
Team 2--Sonnet 14	Clyde, William	Wed Jun 26 2002 11:24 am	New
Team 3--Sonnet 29	Clyde, William	Wed Jun 26 2002 11:25 am	New
⊟ Team 4--Sonnet 20	Clyde, William	Wed Jun 26 2002 11:26 am	
Re: Team 4--Sonnet 20	Student, xJohn P.	Wed Jun 26 2002 11:55 am	New

Fig. 3.15: Threaded discussion after a reply to an initial thread has been posted. Property of Blackboard. Used with the permission of Blackboard.

in Chat are usually not automatically saved (though Chat features in course management systems generally have **Archive** capabilities).

Threaded discussions, on the other hand, are more like communicating by putting notes on each other's desks—with the added convenience that the notes are being automatically organized by topic as they accumulate. The advantages relative to Chat are that

- participants do not need to meet online at the same time—the conversation can take place over several hours, days, or even weeks as participants check in to the discussion, and
- an organized record of the conversation is automatically kept and available to all participants at all times.

The main disadvantage of a threaded discussion relative to Chat is that it is less conducive to a flowing conversation—each message and each reply to it must be opened separately and replied to with a new, separate message if a reply is desired.

As suggested above, marrying the two by starting a conversation in Chat and then copying it to a threaded discussion can provide the best of both worlds: a conversation that builds momentum in Chat and then is saved and organized and can be continued over time in a threaded discussion.

POTENTIAL PITFALLS

The main concern with respect to using Chat and threaded discussion is that all students have access to these tools and are competent in their use. Even students who seem to be techno-whizzes can have significant blind spots, and it is always better to assess and build student abilities early in the semester. Start-of-term threaded discussions in which you and your students introduce yourselves, for instance, can break the ice, begin to build a class community, and give everyone a chance to try out a threaded discussion before the real assignments start. Likewise, you can open a Chat session during your office hours in the first week of classes and ask that all students check in to the Chat

Archive—a feature of many components of a course management system that allows the instructor and sometimes the student to record and save a digital copy of an online event such as a Chat session

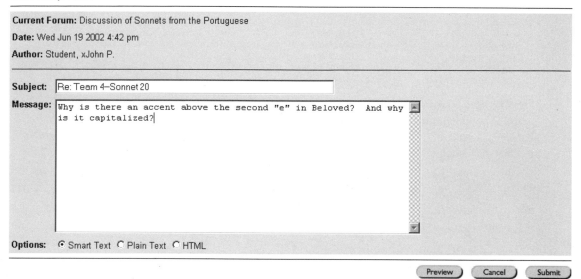

Discussion Board

Your Response:

Current Forum: Discussion of Sonnets from the Portuguese

Date: Wed Jun 19 2002 4:42 pm

Author: Student, xJohn P.

Subject: Re: Team 4–Sonnet 20

Message: Why is there an accent above the second "e" in Beloved?   And why
is it capitalized?

Options: ⦿ Smart Text   ◯ Plain Text   ◯ HTML

Preview   Cancel   Submit

Fig. 3.16: Using a threaded discussion to do an asynchronous Chat session. Property of Blackboard. Used with the permission of Blackboard.

Discussion Board

VIEW UNREAD MESSAGES ▼   EXPAND ALL ⊞   COLLAPSE ALL ⊟
                                                                             SEARCH ?

                                                                         SHOW OPTIONS

Team 1--Sonnet 6	Clyde, William	Wed Jun 19 2002 4:44 pm	
Team 2--Sonnet 14	Clyde, William	Wed Jun 19 2002 4:53 pm	
Team 3--Sonnet 29	Clyde, William	Wed Jun 19 2002 4:54 pm	
⊟ Team 4--Sonnet 20	Clyde, William	Wed Jun 19 2002 5:10 pm	
⊟ Re: Team 4--Sonnet 20	Student, xJohn P.	Wed Jun 19 2002 5:14 pm	
⊟ **Beloved**	**Student, Portia P.**	**Wed Jun 19 2002 5:25 pm**	New
⊟ **Re: Beloved**	**Student, xJohn P.**	**Wed Jun 19 2002 5:26 pm**	New
⊟ **Re: Beloved**	**Student, Portia P.**	**Wed Jun 19 2002 5:35 pm**	New
⊟ **Re: Beloved**	**Student, xJohn P.**	**Wed Jun 19 2002 5:36 pm**	New
⊟ **Re: Beloved**	**Student, Portia P.**	**Wed Jun 19 2002 5:37 pm**	New
Re: Beloved	**Student, xJohn P.**	**Wed Jun 19 2002 5:38 pm**	New
The last two lines	**Student, Portia P.**	**Wed Jun 19 2002 5:27 pm**	New

Fig. 3.17: An extended thread resulting from an asynchronous Chat between two students using a threaded discussion. Property of Blackboard. Used with the permission of Blackboard.

to confirm that they are able to. To the extent that you or your students need training with these tools, IT staff are usually able to provide it, given sufficient lead time.

SCENARIO 2: Facilitating Work on Group Projects Outside of Class

TRADITIONAL SOLUTIONS

One of the most common student concerns regarding group projects is finding enough times for all group members to meet to complete a project. Strategies for dealing with this concern are generally neither universally applicable nor satisfying, and the burden is usually left on the student team to "work it out." One strategy is to assign groups for the term and ask each group to set aside a weekly out-of-class meeting time so that work and social schedules for the semester might be built around those meeting times in the same way those schedules are built around classes. Setting aside such a time can increase commitment to the team and can be an important part of the team-building process, but part-time students and students working full-time jobs may have little flexibility for additional meetings, even if scheduled at the beginning of term.

Another traditional way of facilitating out-of-class collaboration is to create a folder or journal for each group that remains on reserve in the library. In it group members collect, organize, and edit their projects. This can reduce the number of actual meetings needed, but it requires that students travel to the library whenever they wish to make contributions to the group.

TECHNOLOGY ALTERNATIVES

The main technology tool for facilitating work on group projects is the threaded discussion available in all course management systems. Creating a discussion can give your student groups space online in which to collect, organize, and edit their projects—and contributions can be made and seen by all group members whenever they have access to the Internet. The threaded discussion being set up in figure 3.18 could give students as much detail on the assignment as you wish. It requires that each student's name be associated with his or her messages (anonymous posts are not allowed), and it does not allow students to remove or edit messages after they are sent (removing the possibility that an important draft might be accidentally deleted). In addition, students may attach files to their posted messages (which is almost always important, since the project is likely to be a word-processing document, a presentation, a spreadsheet, or other file). The discussion reserves the right to create new threads for you as the instructor.

Once the discussion is created it will be added to the outline of discussions for your class, and you can create one thread (which can be used as a workspace) for each group

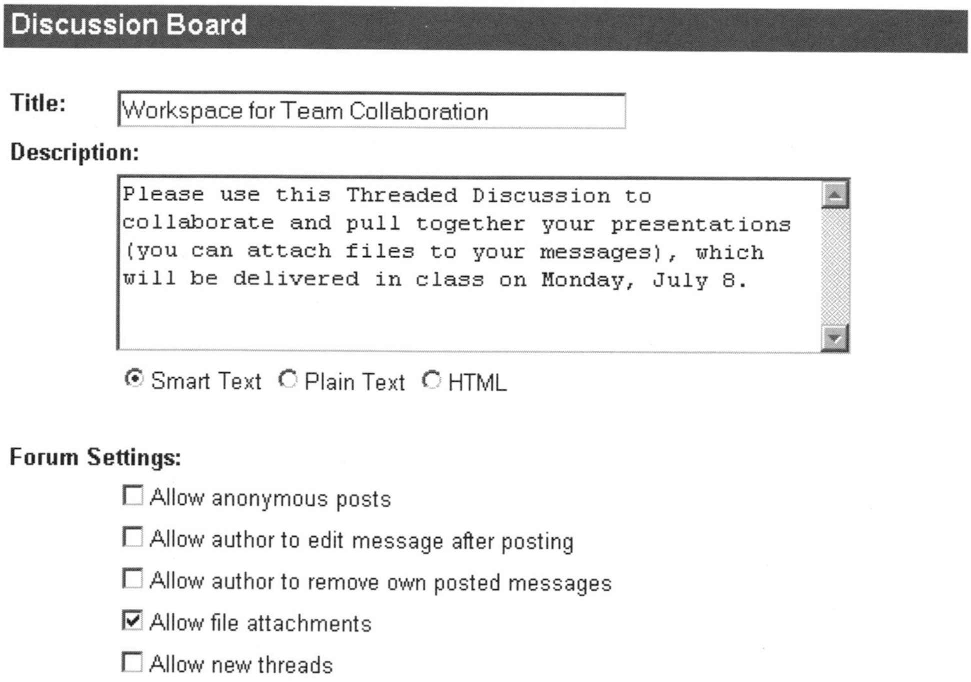

Discussion Board

Title: Workspace for Team Collaboration

Description:

Please use this Threaded Discussion to
collaborate and pull together your presentations
(you can attach files to your messages), which
will be delivered in class on Monday, July 8.

◉ Smart Text   ○ Plain Text   ○ HTML

Forum Settings:

☐ Allow anonymous posts

☐ Allow author to edit message after posting

☐ Allow author to remove own posted messages

☑ Allow file attachments

☐ Allow new threads

Fig. 3.18: Setting up a threaded discussion as a workspace to facilitate collaboration. Property of Blackboard. Used with the permission of Blackboard.

by following the procedures illustrated in figures 3.10 through 3.12. As indicated in Scenario 1, these initial messages can be blank, simply creating online space for each group to collect its work by replying to its initial message, or they can list group members and include any other group-specific information you wish to provide. While it is possible to create a private threaded discussion for each group in a way that prevents other groups from seeing its work, the discussion in this example is not set up that way. Unless you set up private threaded discussions, you must remember that anything you include in a message to one group can be seen by the other groups in the class.

In any case, your students will be presented with the title and description of the discussion, which lets them enter the discussion with a thread created by you. Figure 3.12 shows a threaded discussion with threads started for four student teams. Figures 3.13 through 3.17 illustrate the procedures by which students would post to this space. A team member using the discussion for Scenario 2 might post a message like that in figure 3.19.

As postings are added by other team members, the thread for Team 4 becomes filled with the contributions of all team members (as in figure 3.20), any of which can be accessed by any team member at any time.

Students should be encouraged to organize their group space (or thread), especially when they are working on large projects that will involve posting many messages to their

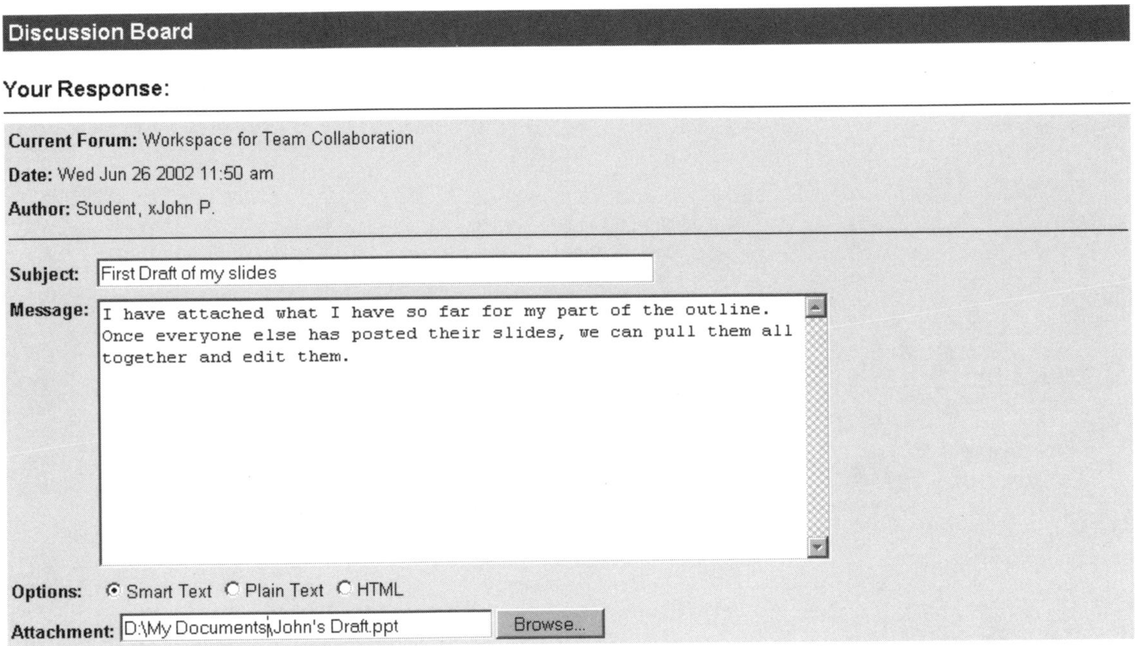

Discussion Board

Your Response:

Current Forum: Workspace for Team Collaboration

Date: Wed Jun 26 2002 11:50 am

Author: Student, xJohn P.

Subject: First Draft of my slides

Message:
```
I have attached what I have so far for my part of the outline.
Once everyone else has posted their slides, we can pull them all
together and edit them.
```

Options: ⦿ Smart Text ○ Plain Text ○ HTML

Attachment: D:\My Documents\John's Draft.ppt   Browse...

Fig. 3.19: A student posting using a threaded discussion as a space for facilitating work on a group project. Property of Blackboard. Used with the permission of Blackboard.

thread (Team 4 in figure 3.20). If, for instance, instead of posting the first drafts of their components directly to the Team 4 thread, the group members created a sub-thread for collecting the first drafts and then posted all of the first drafts of their components as replies to that sub-thread, their discussion space would begin to take on an organization like that in figure 3.21, making it easier for group members to find what they were looking for and follow the development of the project.

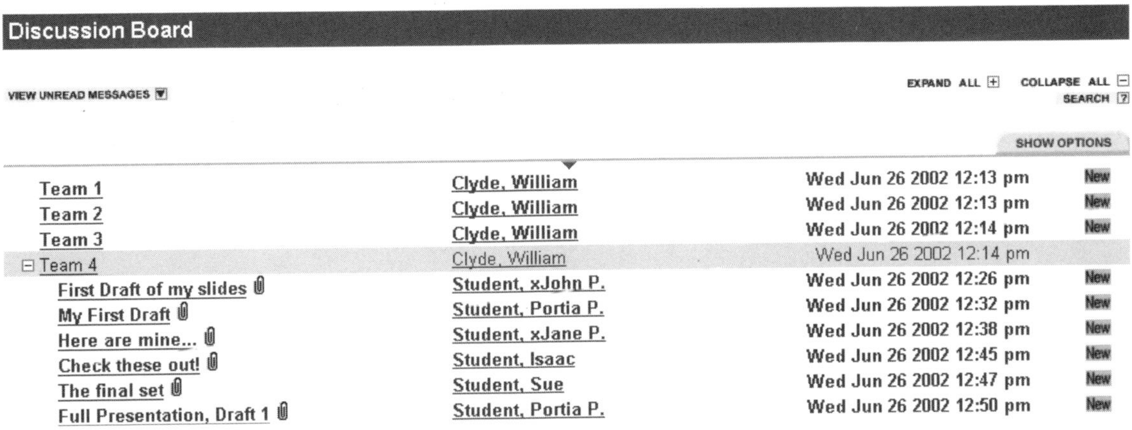

Discussion Board

VIEW UNREAD MESSAGES ▼   EXPAND ALL ⊞   COLLAPSE ALL ⊟
                                                                            SEARCH ?

                                                                SHOW OPTIONS

Team 1	Clyde, William	Wed Jun 26 2002 12:13 pm	New
Team 2	Clyde, William	Wed Jun 26 2002 12:13 pm	New
Team 3	Clyde, William	Wed Jun 26 2002 12:14 pm	New
⊟ Team 4	Clyde, William	Wed Jun 26 2002 12:14 pm	
First Draft of my slides 📎	Student, xJohn P.	Wed Jun 26 2002 12:26 pm	New
My First Draft 📎	Student, Portia P.	Wed Jun 26 2002 12:32 pm	New
Here are mine... 📎	Student, xJane P.	Wed Jun 26 2002 12:38 pm	New
Check these out! 📎	Student, Isaac	Wed Jun 26 2002 12:45 pm	New
The final set 📎	Student, Sue	Wed Jun 26 2002 12:47 pm	New
Full Presentation, Draft 1 📎	Student, Portia P.	Wed Jun 26 2002 12:50 pm	New

Fig. 3.20: A group thread with contributions of several team members posted. Property of Blackboard. Used with the permission of Blackboard.

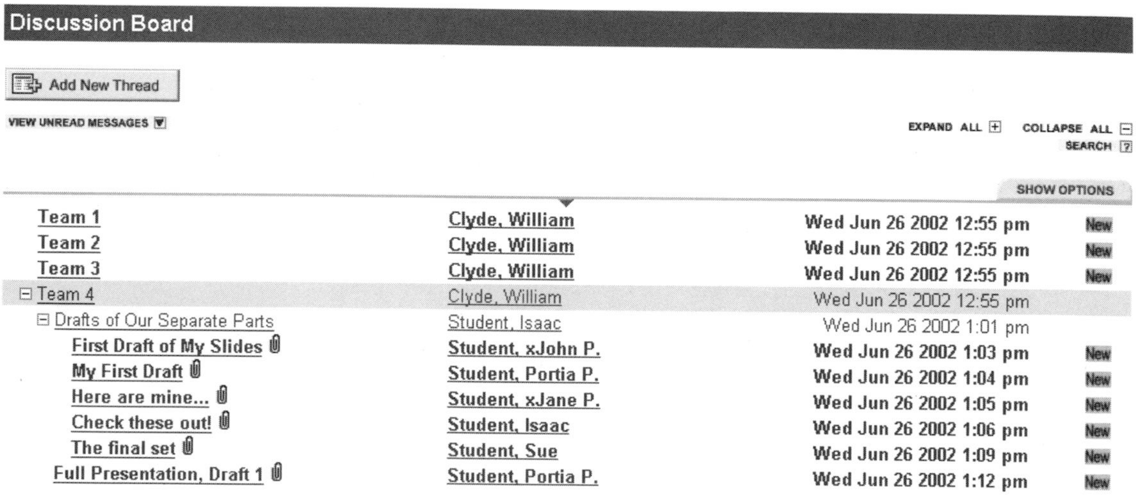

Discussion Board

📑 Add New Thread

VIEW UNREAD MESSAGES ▼   EXPAND ALL ⊞   COLLAPSE ALL ⊟
                                                                          SEARCH ?

			SHOW OPTIONS
Team 1	Clyde, William	Wed Jun 26 2002 12:55 pm	New
Team 2	Clyde, William	Wed Jun 26 2002 12:55 pm	New
Team 3	Clyde, William	Wed Jun 26 2002 12:55 pm	New
⊟ Team 4	Clyde, William	Wed Jun 26 2002 12:55 pm	
⊟ Drafts of Our Separate Parts	Student, Isaac	Wed Jun 26 2002 1:01 pm	
First Draft of My Slides 📎	Student, xJohn P.	Wed Jun 26 2002 1:03 pm	New
My First Draft 📎	Student, Portia P.	Wed Jun 26 2002 1:04 pm	New
Here are mine... 📎	Student, xJane P.	Wed Jun 26 2002 1:05 pm	New
Check these out! 📎	Student, Isaac	Wed Jun 26 2002 1:06 pm	New
The final set 📎	Student, Sue	Wed Jun 26 2002 1:09 pm	New
Full Presentation, Draft 1 📎	Student, Portia P.	Wed Jun 26 2002 1:12 pm	New

Fig. 3.21: A group thread with two organizing sub-threads. Property of Blackboard. Used with the permission of Blackboard.

POTENTIAL PITFALLS

The main concerns regarding this technology solution are the same as those discussed in Scenario 1: that students have access to computers that are online so that they can access threaded discussions and that students are competent in their use. As discussed in Scenario 1, basic learning activities and competence assessment early in the semester can ensure that your class is ready to use threaded discussions for a wide range of class activities, and it is important that access and competence are not simply assumed.

SCENARIO 3: Building Networks of Collaboration for Learning from Peers

TRADITIONAL SOLUTIONS

Peer assistance in learning is valuable because it contributes to

- the learning students, by adding extra resources (their classmates) who may be more available than you are when help is needed,
- the teaching students, by offering opportunities to gain better understanding of material by trying to explain it,
- a general perception that students can contribute to and share responsibility in their learning.

It would be helpful, however, to have the ability to monitor this "peer help network" to see whether the explanations and solutions being shared are substantially correct and that peer help has not degenerated into assignment sharing.

The main way to facilitate such student-to-student help using traditional activities is by using class time to allow students to solve problems in small groups or as a class. Such activities include the instructor as observer, or perhaps note taker, interrupting only when the discussion or solution seems significantly off track or confusing.

TECHNOLOGY ALTERNATIVES

In Scenario 3 of Chapter 1 we proposed using a threaded discussion titled "Frequently Asked Questions" (FAQs) to share with the class good questions your students ask during office hours or by Email (along with your answers to those questions). This medium allows you to post questions without identifying the students asking the questions and then facilitates follow-up questions and discussion, as shown in figure 3.22.

In addition to allowing you to post questions and answers, a FAQs discussion can be used by your students to develop a peer help network in which students post their questions so that they can be answered by other students (or by you when you are available).

A student using the discussion might post a message like that in figure 3.23, which would be added to the discussion outline (shown in figure 3.24) and accessible to everyone in the class.

Any student wanting to observe and perhaps answer the question would click on the title ("Help with Calculations in Lab 4?") to open the message (shown in figure 3.25), and then click on Reply to provide some suggestions or an answer, as in figure 3.26. Once this reply is posted the discussion would look like the one in figure 3.27.

The question and answer—or answers, as a given question will often draw several answers, each more refined or offering corrections or caveats to earlier answers—can be accessed and studied by your students and you at any time, becoming a semester-long resource.

Contributions to such a peer help network can be hindered by students' fear that their questions will make them look stupid—a fear that also keeps them from asking questions in class. This concern can be alleviated in the threaded discussion by allowing stu-

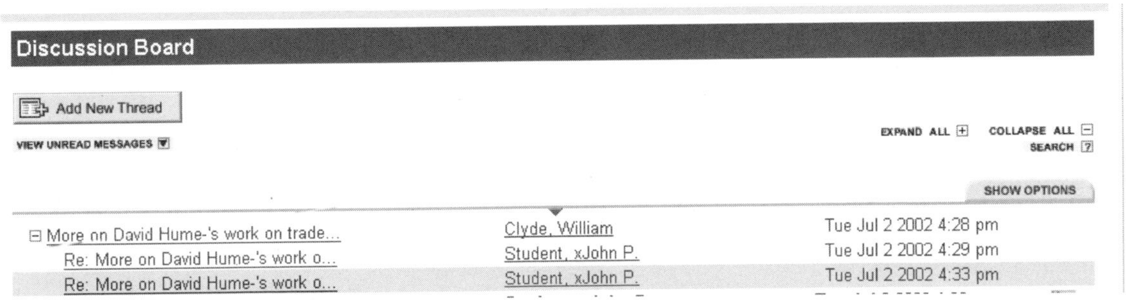

Fig. 3.22: Using a threaded discussion to post Frequently Asked Questions (FAQs). Property of Blackboard. Used with the permission of Blackboard.

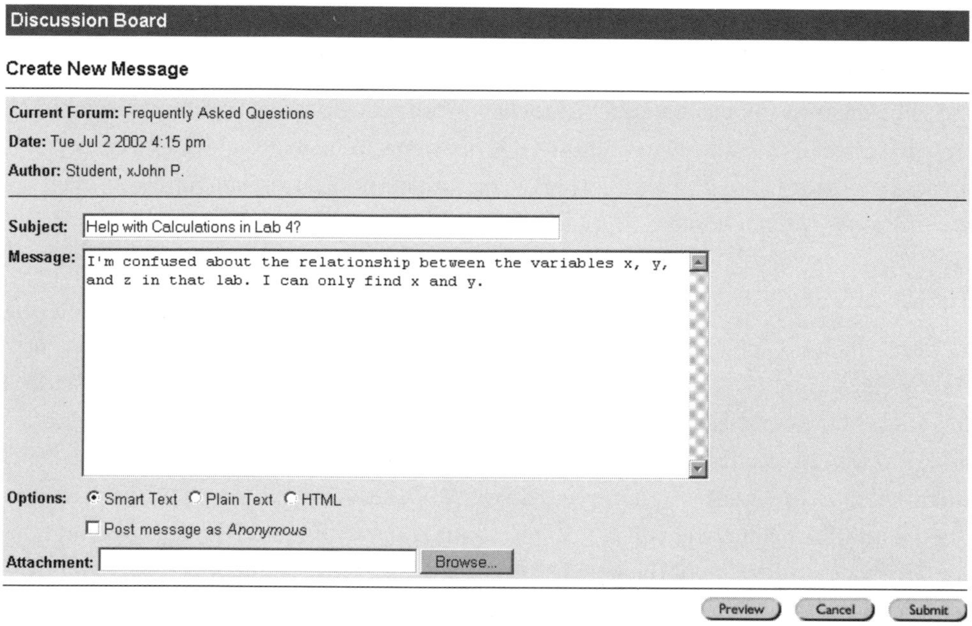

Create New Message

Current Forum: Frequently Asked Questions
Date: Tue Jul 2 2002 4:15 pm
Author: Student, xJohn P.

Subject: | Help with Calculations in Lab 4?

Message: | I'm confused about the relationship between the variables x, y, and z in that lab. I can only find x and y.

Options: ● Smart Text ○ Plain Text ○ HTML
☐ Post message as *Anonymous*

Attachment: | | Browse...

(Preview) (Cancel) (Submit)

Fig. 3.23: Student posting a question to the FAQs discussion for a course. Property of Blackboard. Used with the permission of Blackboard.

Discussion Board

Add New Thread

VIEW UNREAD MESSAGES ▼

EXPAND ALL ⊞   COLLAPSE ALL ⊟
SEARCH ⁇

SHOW OPTIONS

⊟ More on David Hume-'s work on trade...	Clyde, William	Tue Jul 2 2002 4:28 pm	
Re: More on David Hume-'s work o...	Student, xJohn P.	Tue Jul 2 2002 4:29 pm	
Re: More on David Hume-'s work o...	Student, xJohn P.	Tue Jul 2 2002 4:33 pm	
Help with Calculations in Lab 4?	**Student, xJohn P.**	**Tue Jul 2 2002 4:32 pm**	**New**

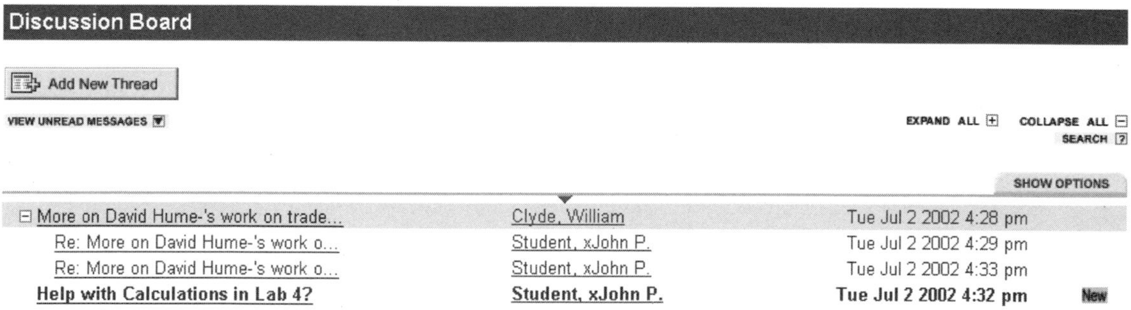

Fig. 3.24: The student posting from Fig. 3.23 added to the FAQs discussion. Property of Blackboard. Used with the permission of Blackboard.

Discussion Board

◄◄ Previous Message   Next Message ►►

Current Forum: Frequently Asked Questions
Date: Tue Jul 2 2002 4:32 pm
Author: Student, xJohn P. <johnpstudent@hotmail.com>
Subject: Help with Calculations in Lab 4?

I'm confused about the relationship between the variables x, y, and z in that lab. I can only find x and y.

(Reply)

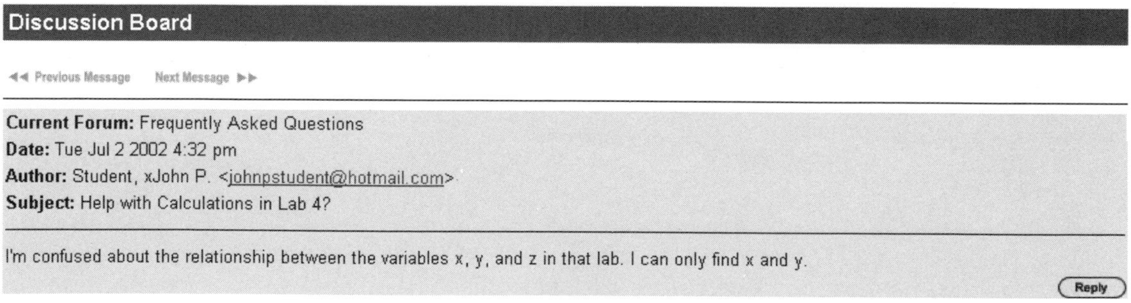

Fig. 3.25: Student view of the question posted by the student in Fig. 3.23. Property of Blackboard. Used with the permission of Blackboard.

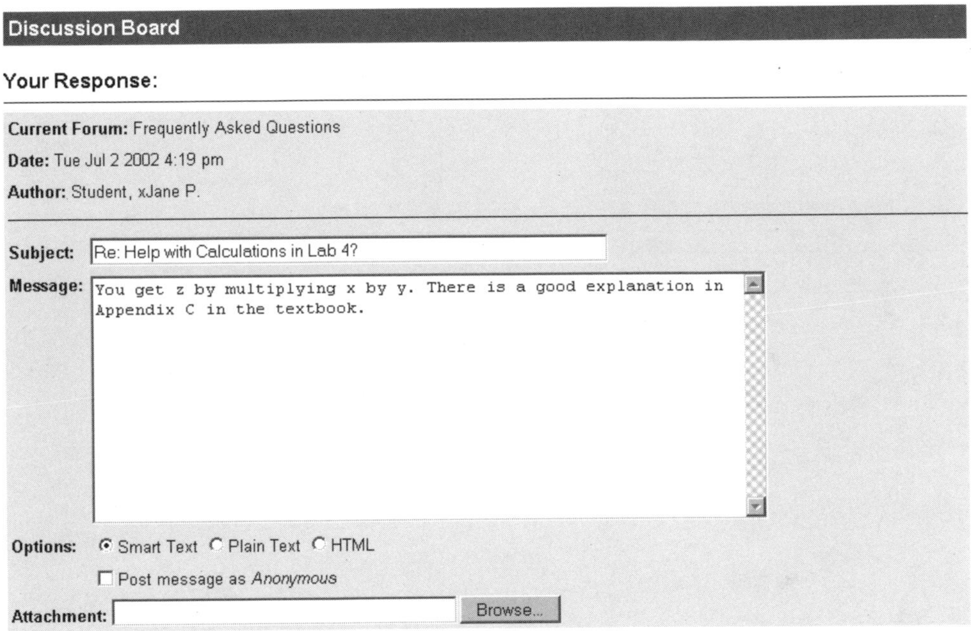

Fig. 3.26: A student answering the question of the student posting in Fig. 3.23. Property of Blackboard. Used with the permission of Blackboard.

dents to post messages anonymously. The "Post message as Anonymous" box, which is available only if you allow anonymous messages when you created the discussion (figure 3.18 shows a threaded discussion setup form that lets you allow the posting of anonymous messages), is checked in the message in figure 3.28, resulting in a message posted to the discussion outline without the posting student's name on it, as shown in figure 3.29. Students answering the question can do so either anonymously or with their names attached: an example of each is also shown in figure 3.29.

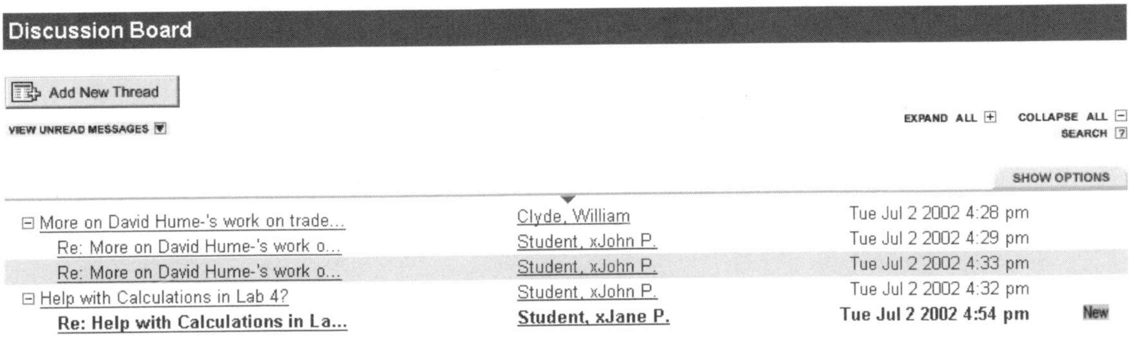

Fig. 3.27: The student reply from Fig. 3.26 added to the FAQs discussion. Property of Blackboard. Used with the permission of Blackboard.

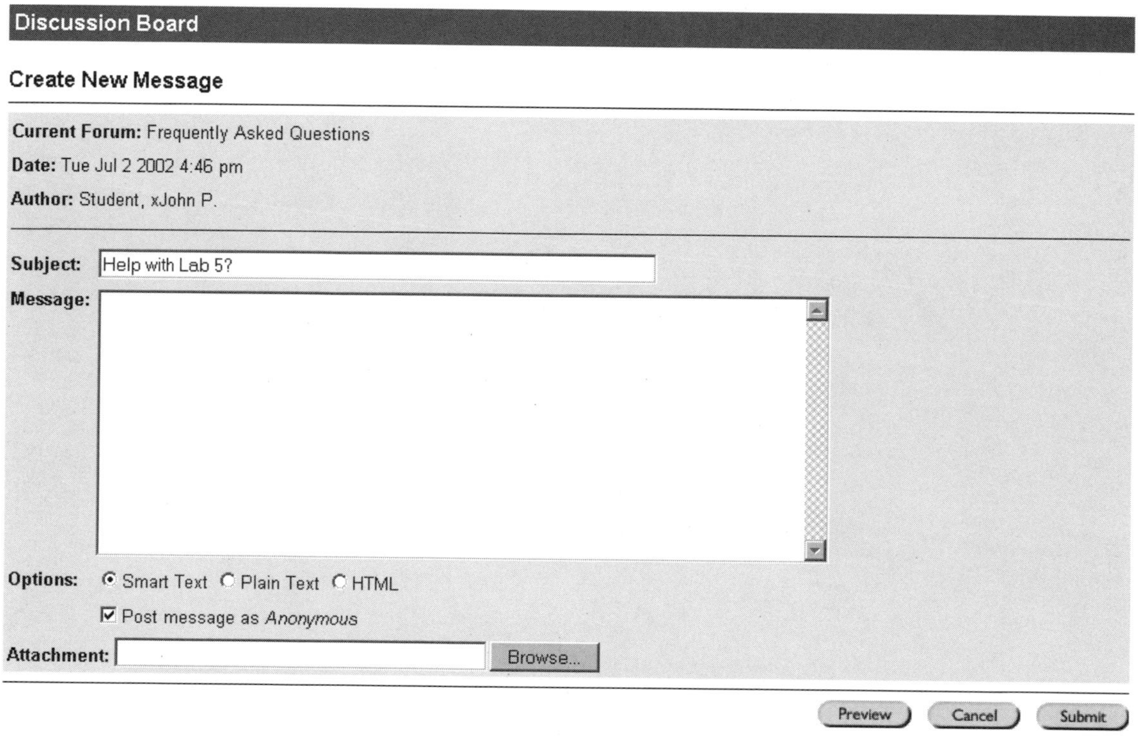

Discussion Board

Create New Message

Current Forum: Frequently Asked Questions
Date: Tue Jul 2 2002 4:46 pm
Author: Student, xJohn P.

Subject: [Help with Lab 5?]

Message:

Options: ⦿ Smart Text ○ Plain Text ○ HTML
☑ Post message as *Anonymous*

Attachment: [   ] [Browse...]

[Preview] [Cancel] [Submit]

Fig. 3.28: Student preparing to post a question to FAQs anonymously. Property of Blackboard. Used with the permission of Blackboard.

You must prepare your students for the freedom anonymous posting affords to ensure that it does not result in abusive messages being posted, but anonymity can be worth that risk if it results in a flowing, useful network of students helping students.

POTENTIAL PITFALLS

As in Scenarios 1 and 2, the main concerns with respect to using the technology discussed above are that all students have access to online computing and that they are competent in the use of Threaded Discussions. To the extent that you plan to allow your students to post anonymously, the risks discussed in Scenario 2 in Chapter 8 should be evaluated for your specific class.

SCENARIO 4: Fostering Peer Feedback

Teaching your students to seek and provide feedback on each other's work helps them develop self-assessment skills, gives them additional resources (each other) to help them refine their work, and reinforces the value of establishing a learning community in their careers. The issues involved in this scenario are dealt with in Chapter 8, Scenario 2.

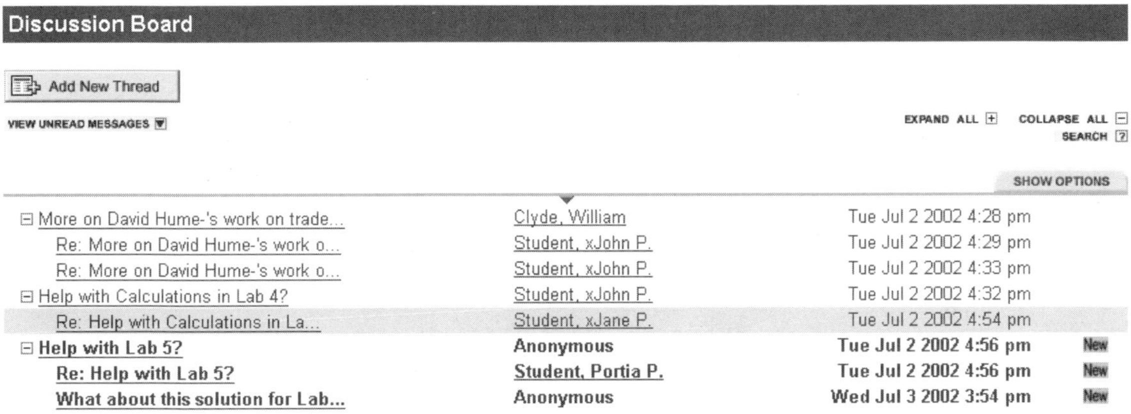

Fig. 3.29: A FAQs threaded discussion with an anonymously posted question, along with two student responses, one posted anonymously, one not. Property of Blackboard. Used with the permission of Blackboard.

SCENARIO 5: Assessing and Managing Team Performance

TRADITIONAL SOLUTIONS

As discussed at the beginning of this chapter, the main problem related to having students work in groups is that some students tend to dominate and others tend to lay back. While some of the strategies suggested in the scenarios above can help offset the roles of personalities and social norms in driving the disparities in member participation, there are other forces at work as well. Nearly every group will have both the "grade protector" (the A student who wants to do all the work to make sure the group gets an A) and the "free rider" (the student willing to take a C and confident that the group will achieve that grade without any work from him or her), resulting in uneven contributions by group members. The challenges to the instructor are to encourage all members to contribute equally if possible, and to account for any disparity in contributions when grades are given to group members. Traditional strategies for dealing with this problem are:

1. To make sure that teams identify their expectations of each other and the team before beginning work on the project (and to make sure that those expectations reflect fair distribution of work),
2. To monitor group activity throughout the project to ensure participation of all members, and
3. To give group members the chance to do teammate evaluations at the end of the project, which can be used to adjust grades.

The second of these can be difficult to accomplish if much of the work on the project is to be done out of class. If the third of these is done in class, or in any way that the ratings of one's teammates might be visible to those being rated, students may be loath to give candid evaluations. Fortunately, technology tools exist to solve both of these problems.

TECHNOLOGY ALTERNATIVES

The most important benefit that technology brings to the table for this scenario is access and accountability. These qualities result automatically when threaded discussions are used to facilitate and coordinate group projects.

Consider, for instance, the group thread used to facilitate work on a team project shown in figure 3.21. In that example team members post their contributions for the team project to the threaded discussion so that others can access, edit, and combine their work. Students see such threaded discussions as useful because they make the meetings required to pull together a group project more efficient. Students quickly become proficient at using the space to debate issues, build information, and edit the developing project, leaving only the most challenging things to do in face-to-face meetings, which can be difficult for groups to arrange when students have busy and diverse schedules.

In terms of assessment, the beauty of this solution is that it automatically provides a time- and date-stamped account of contributions of all group members. The quality, quantity, and timeliness of contributions are all visible to everyone online, and it's very easy for you, the instructor, to

- monitor the group dynamics during the project,
- prod participants as needed (either publicly, in the discussion, or privately, through an Email), and
- account for any disparity in contributions when grades are given to group members.

As such, this can help solve all of the problems associated with managing and assessing group work—and can help students by reducing the number of out-of-class meetings they need to schedule.

POTENTIAL PITFALLS

The main concern with respect to using threaded discussions is making sure that students know how to access and use them. Once students figure out the rules and strategies they will be able to apply that knowledge in all courses that use threaded discussions. Including training on their use in institutionwide technology instruction is efficient and takes the burden off of faculty. Such instruction is available from technology departments in most institutions. In any case, it is important to make sure that students are comfortable with this technology before asking them to use it to complete coursework.

CHAPTER 4   Helping Students Learn Through Experience

SCENARIO 1: Experiencing Visual Environments

You have been describing a visual element of your discipline (a painting, the human body, advertisements, a molecule, geography) to your students and wish they could really see it and explore it.

SCENARIO 2: Experiencing Strategy

You have been discussing the tactics and strategies employed by those being studied (Lee at Gettysburg, a foreign exchange trader, a biologist making a famous discovery, pioneers along the Oregon Trail). You wish your students could really appreciate those tactics and strategies—and even have a whack at improving upon them.

SCENARIO 3: Experiencing Calculations

Your discipline includes some basic calculations or problem-solving skills you have described to your students. You want your students to understand and be able to employ them.

SCENARIO 4: Experiencing Technology

Practitioners in your discipline increasingly use technology to do their jobs (making presentations, building spreadsheets, doing online research, collaborating with colleagues), and you want your students to become successful users of those technologies.

SCENARIO 5: Interacting with Experts and Practitioners

You would like to take your students on a field trip to interact with experts in your field but have neither the money nor the time for the trip.

Introduction: Some Background Information

In Experiential Learning . . . the learner is directly in touch with the realities being studied. . . . It involves direct encounter with the phenomenon being studied rather than merely thinking about the encounter or only considering the possibility of doing something with it.[1]

John Dewey is usually credited with establishing the importance of experience in formal education, asserting that "there is an intimate and necessary relation between the processes of actual experience and education."[2] Over the past twenty-five years research in this area has been building, and experience has become an ever-growing part of curricula in the forms of internships, service learning, and, most recently, computer-generated environments that allow students "virtual" experiences within disciplines being studied. Many strands of the recent research on the importance of experience in learning have been pulled together in a publication from the National Research Council, in which it is concluded that:

1. The functional organization of the brain and the mind depends on and benefits positively from experience.
2. Development is not merely a biologically driven unfolding process but also an active process that derives essential information from experience.[3]

As evidence of its importance builds, it seems clear that experience will play a growing role in education. The examples in this chapter show that technology can be a valuable tool in increasing the experiential components of learning.

A multitude of technology tools is available for helping students learn by "virtually" interacting with environments being studied. Increasingly, textbooks include video, CD, and online supplements that contain learning tools specifically targeted and linked to topics in the textbooks.

Another valuable source of such tools is the Multimedia Educational Resource for Learning and Online Teaching (MERLOT) found at www.merlot.org. As of September 2004, MERLOT had links providing access to well over 11,000 technology-based learning tools targeting topics in virtually all disciplines across the university, as indicated in table 4.1. All tools posted in MERLOT are peer reviewed and rated, and assignments using these tools (for instance, a lab procedure using a posted tool for virtual dissection of a frog) are often hyperlinked to them. Faculty in search of technology supplements can browse through these tools by subject or by subcategory, and can organize the tools listed in order of their ratings, titles, authors, dates posted, or item types (simulator, tutorial, drill and practice, collection, etc.).

With thousands of these tools available through MERLOT and as textbook supplements, it would be impossible to fairly represent their variety here. The examples that fol-

Table 4.1. Technology-based learning tools posted in MERLOT

Subject	Number of tools linked (as of September 2004)	Subcategories
Arts	286	general, fine arts, music
Business	2021	accounting, business law, e-commerce, economics, finance, general, information systems, international business, management, marketing
Education	1443	general, library and information studies, teacher education, teaching online in higher education
Humanities	1675	general, history, language and literature, philosophy, religion, world languages
Mathematics	716	general and liberal arts math, algebra and number theory, analysis, calculus, developmental math, discrete math, differential equations, dynamical systems, foundations of math, geometry and topology, mathematical modeling, numerical analysis, pre-calculus, probability and statistics
Science and technology	4454	general science, agriculture, astronomy, biology, chemistry, computer science, engineering, geology, health science, information technology, physics
Social sciences	789	general, anthropology, geography, law, political science, psychology, sociology, sports and games, statistics

low are meant to give an idea of what virtual visual environments might look like and how they might be used—and to whet your appetite. One other note: while all of the **URLs** referred to below were accessible at the time this was printed, any of them might become inaccessible by the time this is read.

SCENARIO 1: Experiencing Visual Environments

TRADITIONAL SOLUTIONS

Traditional methods of allowing students to experience visual environments include internships, field trips, in-class demonstrations, samples to be held, labs, and pictures. All of these are valuable in helping students perceive visual environments, allowing them to explore, study, and orient themselves within environments ranging from the facade of a building to the components within a computer, from the surface of a painting to the internal organs of an animal. Of these traditional methods, the least "interactive" is pictures—a printed or projected image usually offers the student little chance for manipulation and exploration. But pictures may be easily taken home for further study and consideration. Internships and field trips are probably the best ways to experience a visual environment, but due to budget and time constraints, relatively few environments can actually be experienced in these ways. The combination of interactivity and easy accessibility is hard to find but valuable if students are to truly familiarize themselves with a wide range of visual environments.

TECHNOLOGY ALTERNATIVES

As mentioned above, a wide range of technology tools is available for helping students learn by "virtually" interacting with environments being studied. One such environment commonly used in courses involving human anatomy is A.D.A.M., by A.D.A.M. Software, Inc. The several different versions of A.D.A.M. are targeted at courses in biology, physiology, and physical therapy, focusing on various regions, systems, and functions of the body. The most basic version, A.D.A.M. Interactive Anatomy, allows students to visually explore the entire body, virtually "picking up" bones, organs, muscles, etc. A student wishing to explore the skull, for instance (as in figure 4.1), can use the up, down, left, right, and diagonal rotate arrows at left to look at the skull from any angle. Students wishing to find or zoom in on specific components of the body part being studied can use the drop-down box to find the name of that specific component so that A.D.A.M. will zoom in and highlight that component (canines, in the example).

An example of a geographical aid that can help students visualize an idea or event (the escape of slaves from the South in this case) is shown in figure 4.2. This Web site has additional features, discussed below in Scenario 2, but simply allowing students to see the paths of escaping slaves—complete with notations of major cities, rivers, state boundaries, and location on the national map—allows students to better appreciate the challenges those slaves faced.

Teachers of art or art history commonly show slides of artworks or concepts being discussed. Classrooms in which art is taught often have two slide projectors and two screens to allow instructors and students to see works of art side by side to be compared and contrasted. While projection is an effective way to allow students to view work, it is not very flexible, as slides must be created well in advance and last-minute changes are not possible, and it is not generally available to students for further study once class is over.

> **Right-Clicking**—depressing the right mouse button, usually when the cursor is over a specific onscreen object; right-clicking is done only when the user wants to display features or options (which appear in a drop-down box) related to an onscreen object
> **Left-Clicking**—depressing the left mouse button, usually when the cursor is over a specific onscreen object; unless otherwise indicated, clicking means left-clicking

Technology offers an easy-to-use alternative in the form of digital (or electronic) versions of works of art that can be shown with a **Video Projector**, Emailed to students, and posted within course Web pages (see Chapter 2 on distributing materials to students). A digital version of Edward Hopper's *Lighthouse Hill* (figure 4.3), for instance, can be copied by **Right-Clicking** on the image of the painting on the Web page and then **Left-Clicking** "Copy" in the box of choices that appears. (See the Appendix for the discussion of the Digital Millennium Copyright Act of 1998 to make sure you are aware of the copyright issues regarding digital or electronic materials.)

A copy of this image can then be pasted into a word-processing document or presentation slideshow (as shown in figure 4.4) by right-clicking on some blank space on the slide or page on which you want the image to appear (upper left in figure 4.4a), and choosing "Paste" from the box of choices that appears (upper right in figure 4.4b). Move the image by clicking on it and dragging it to where you want it (with the left button of the mouse held down the whole time you are dragging). Resize by clicking on one of the small white circles in the corners and dragging. Relevant information can be typed below the image (at lower left in figure 4.4c), and the same procedure can be followed again with a different image for comparing and contrasting (figure 4.4d). This process can be used with electronic images from any discipline, from artifacts to astronomy; images can be pulled together in minutes if available (and thousands are, at MERLOT and other sites), and can easily be distributed to students for further study after class. It is even possible to assign students to create slideshows or documents of their own, or to create their own studies of artists, ideas, themes, etc.

Some concepts involve movement or a process that proceeds in a particular order or along a particular path. To visualize such a process, students need access to a tool that incorporates the dynamics involved through a video clip or an animation. One example of such an animation can be found through MERLOT and is shown in figure 4.5. It allows

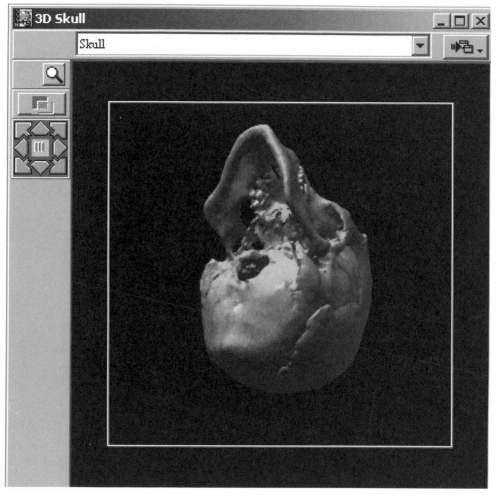

a

Fig. 4.1a–b: Exploring the human skull using A.D.A.M. Interactive Anatomy. Images provided by
A.D.A.M. Courtesy of A.D.A.M.

students not only to see the components involved in a biological process but also to watch
the process develop again and again (in the box at left titled "Animation"). This type of
tool can be used both as an in-class visual aid and as an out-of-class study tool for
students.

Another technology tool, this one with both interactive animated visual environments
for students to explore and video clips to demonstrate processes, is "Virtual Clinical Excursions, Version 1" a supplement for "Medical Surgical Nursing, 6/E," by Lewis et al.,
available through Elsevier. Upon starting the program, the student is presented with a
simulated clinical floor to negotiate, as shown in figure 4.6. The student sees both where

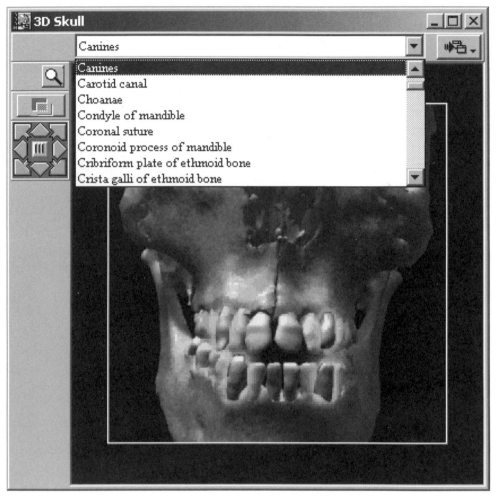

b

he or she is on the floor plan (at upper right), and a view of the floor as if he or she were standing on it (at left). The student turns or looks up or down by moving the cursor left, right, up or down, and moves around the floor by clicking in the direction he or she wants to go. This kind of interactive environment software can be found in simulators in many disciplines, ranging from science labs to securities trading floors to architectural designs. Whatever the discipline, such an interactive environment allows students to explore and have a better idea what to expect when they are confronted with the real environment.

Another component of the "Virtual Clinical Excursions" software is presented to students upon entering one of the rooms in the clinic: they are able to watch videos demonstrating how some basic tests and procedures are done. In the example in figure 4.7, blood pressure has been chosen from the vital signs at bottom left, resulting in the

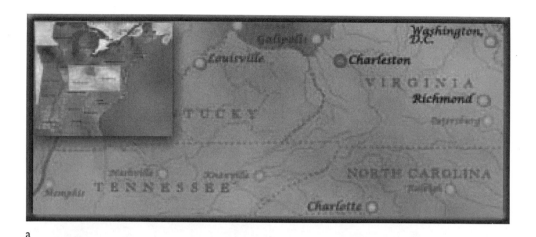

a

b

Fig. 4.2a–b: Visualizing the flight of slaves in the United States. Source: http://academic.bowdoin.edu/flightoffreedom/intro.shtml. Courtesy of Bowdoin College Department of Information Technology.

showing of a short video on how to take blood pressures, along with the animation at right showing how the pressure gauge would move as the test is being given in the video. Again, this kind of context-appropriate presentation of video clips, with associated animations for clarification, is available in a growing number of disciplines and can be very helpful to students trying to understand a visual environment or process.

POTENTIAL PITFALLS

The main concerns in trying to use tools like those above are

1. Sorting through the many tools that are available to identify those that best meet your needs,

2. Ensuring that the tools will run smoothly in the environments in which you and your students will be using them, and

3. Providing students with any training that will be required for them to successfully use the tools.

Most institutions have IT staff dedicated to helping faculty with at least the first two of these concerns. Staffers should be able to work with you to search for tools that might be relevant to the topics in your course and then help you explore how those tools that look promising might be used. Once tools have been chosen and access to them arranged, IT staff should also be able to ensure that they run smoothly and reliably in your computer labs and other environments in which the tools will be used. Little student training is necessary with most of these tools, but it must be planned and provided where it is needed. Where such support is available (and it is at the vast majority of institutions), your main responsibility is to plan ahead and give IT plenty of lead time to help you search for, evaluate, procure, and install these tools to ensure that your students will have a positive learning experience. It is usually best to begin this process a few months before the start of the semester, unless you feel you have the technical expertise and interest to do most of it yourself. In any case, planning is vital.

Fig. 4.3: Using Web resources to enhance the study of art: Hopper's *Lighthouse Hill* at the Dallas Museum of Art. Source: http://dmaws.dallasmuseumofart.org.

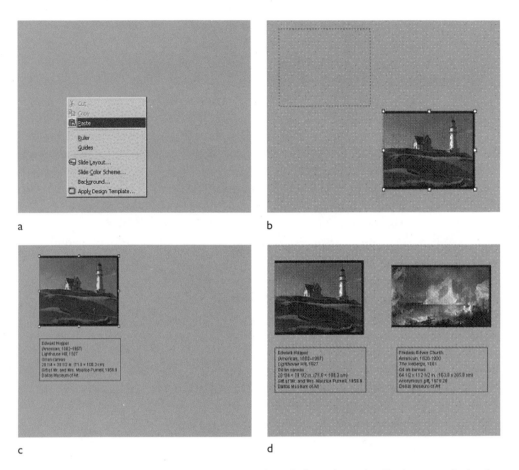

Fig. 4.4a–d: Building a course resource in PowerPoint to help students visualize images and related information. Source: http://www.dm-art.org. Microsoft PowerPoint™ screenshot reprinted by permission from the trademark holder, Microsoft Corporation.

SCENARIO 2: Experiencing Strategy

TRADITIONAL SOLUTIONS

Traditional methods for allowing students to experience strategy formation and execution include internships, role playing, labs, cases, and problem-solving projects. All of these are valuable activities in the right context, allowing students to consider, propose, and implement strategies for dealing with a situation or problem. Unfortunately, not all contexts lend themselves to such activities. Some, for instance, require more setup than is realistically possible, while others require constant immediate feedback (which is impossible for you to give each student) to get the feel of strategy implementation.

San Diego State University College of Sciences

<u>Biology 590</u> - Human Physiology

Actin Myosin Crossbridge 3D Animation*

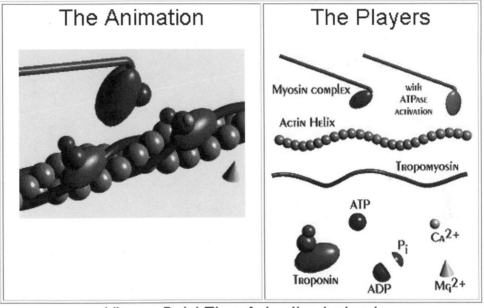

View a QuickTime Animation instead

Based in part on
Color Atlas of Physiology, Agamemnon Despopoulos, Stefan Silbernagl
Thieme Medical Publishers, Inc. , 1991, New York

Fig. 4.5: An online animation that helps students visualize a scientific process. Source:
http://www.sci.sdsu.edu/movies/actin_myosin.html. Developed by Jeff Sale, Roger Sabbadini, San
Diego State University.

TECHNOLOGY ALTERNATIVES

A growing multitude of technology tools is available for allowing students to experience
the creation and use of strategy in a wide range of fields. Most textbooks offer technology
supplements directly tied to concepts in the book, and, as discussed above, MERLOT is
a vital and growing source of such tools available online. The examples discussed below
in no way capture the variety of the "strategy simulators" that are available. They are

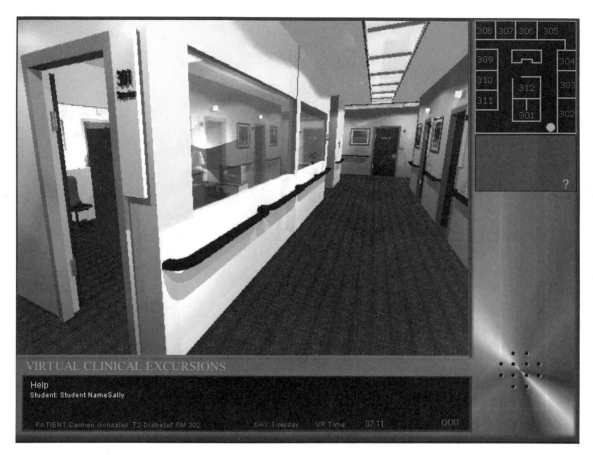

Fig. 4.6: "Virtual Clinical Excursions" helps students visualize a clinical setting. Reprinted from "Virtual Clinical Excursions, Version 1" (a supplement for "Medical Surgical Nursing, 6/E"), Lewis et al., copyright © 2001 Mosby, with permission from Elsevier.

meant only to give you some idea of that variety—and to encourage you to look for those in your discipline.

Business disciplines enjoy a range of simulators, allowing students to experience anything from trading stocks to running a start-up company. One such business management simulator is "Mike's Bikes—Advanced," created by SmartSims. "Mike's Bikes—Advanced" can be played as single-player (against the computer) or as multi-player (against other players online). The software requires students to make decisions in marketing, operations, finance, and new product development for their companies by clicking on the each of the four tabs at lower left on the "Decisions" screen (figure 4.8a). Each of these four areas has subcategories in which decisions must be made ("Products," "Distribution," and "Branding" are the subcategories for the "Market" tab, which is showing in figure 4.8a). Once decisions are made, the simulator "rolls forward" a year to allow the

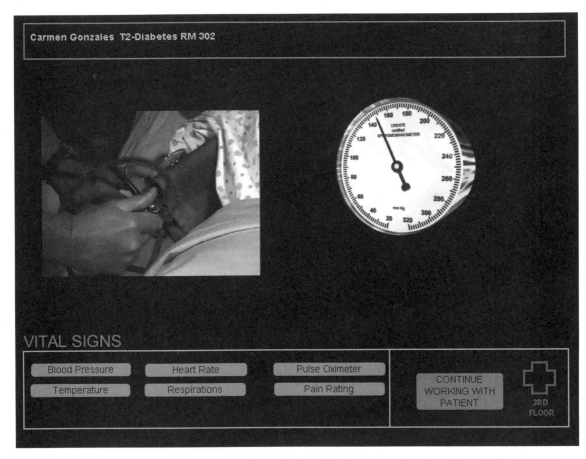

Fig. 4.7: "Virtual Clinical Excursions" helps students visualize clinical processes. Reprinted from "Virtual Clinical Excursions, Version 1" (a supplement for "Medical Surgical Nursing, 6/E"), Lewis et al., copyright © 2001 Mosby, with permission from Elsevier.

consequences of those decisions to take effect. Students are presented with a wide range of data (some of which is summarized in figure 4.8b), realistic reports (financial statements, production reports, marketing surveys, etc.), and graphs (like the one in figure 4.8b). Tutorials are available throughout the process to clarify concepts and issues as they are encountered. It is even possible to "roll back" the simulator to revise decisions that did not give the hoped for results. Clearly this sort of simulator (and there are many such business management simulators to choose from) gives students the opportunity to experience the complexity of formulating, implementing, and assessing business strategies to an extent that would be virtually impossible any other way.

Students of introductory psychology are usually exposed to the ideas of B. F. Skinner and operant conditioning, but rarely do they get the chance to experiment with those

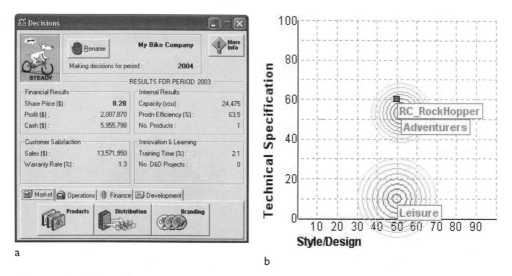

a

b

Fig. 4.8a–b: "Mike's Bikes—Advanced" online business simulator allows students to experience business decision making. Software shown: "Mike's Bikes—Advanced" by SmartSims.

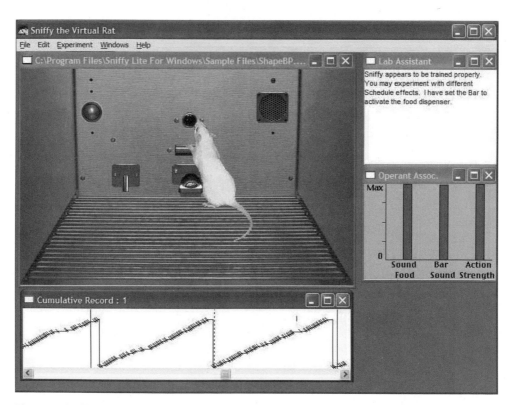

Fig. 4.9: "Sniffy, the Virtual Rat" allows students to experiment with the ideas of conditioning. Software shown: "Sniffy, the Virtual Rat Lite," Version 2.0 (with CD-ROM), 2nd ed. by ALLOWAY/ WILSON/GRAHAM. Copyright © 2005. Reprinted with permission of Wadsworth, a Division of Thomson Learning: www.thomasonrights.com (fax: 800-730-2215).

ideas. "Sniffy, the Virtual Rat," available through Thomson Learning (and shown in figure 4.9) presents students with a virtual Skinner Box with which they can experience discovery of those ideas. The accompanying booklet discusses several classical and operant conditioning phenomena and leads students through labs (as does the software—at lower right in figure 4.9), allowing students to condition Sniffy. As preparation for use of a real conditioning environment or as a virtual lab experience when a real lab experience is not possible, virtual labs like this can be valuable learning tools.

Another virtual lab, "Chemland," written by William J. Vining, allows students to explore a range of properties of matter, reactions (one of which is shown in figure 4.10), and other concepts and principles of chemistry without any of the dangers or costs of actually setting up and doing a real lab. Again, a tool such as this can be used to prepare students for a real lab, or to allow students many more (virtual) lab experiences than they would ever experience otherwise.

Historical simulators represent an interactive history lesson as much as the chance to experience strategy formation and execution. Whether it's fighting Napoleon at Waterloo, preparing for and traveling the Oregon Trail, or finding a route out of the South for a runaway slave, such simulators help students "become" participants in the events they are studying, absorbing and internalizing them as they explore and implement strategies

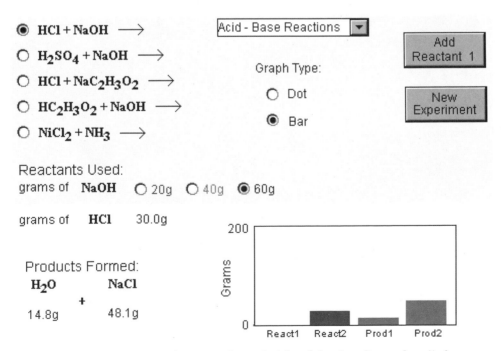

Fig. 4.10: "Chemland" allows students to explore principles of chemistry. Source: http://colossus.chem.umass.edu/bvining/free.htm

for solving the problems involved. In "Flight to Freedom" (shown in figure 4.11) by Patrick Rael of Bowdoin College, students must maintain the health, money, and freedom (in the area at top left in figure 4.11) of one of several famous runaway slaves (Frederick Douglass, Harriet Jacobs, Anthony Burns, etc.) while making decisions (bottom right in figure 4.11) that will lead him or her to the North and freedom. Events resulting from each decision are displayed in the middle gray area, along with references supporting the historical validity of events such as these. Help in visualizing the geography involved is provided through maps at lower left. Historical simulators such as this can help history come alive for students in new and exciting ways.

Health care and medical simulators like "Virtual Clinical Excursions" can allow students to master the logic and strategies associated with a given treatment or situation before ever seeing a patient. In the situation shown in figure 4.12, for instance, the student is required to decide which vital signs, physical exams, health history information, and

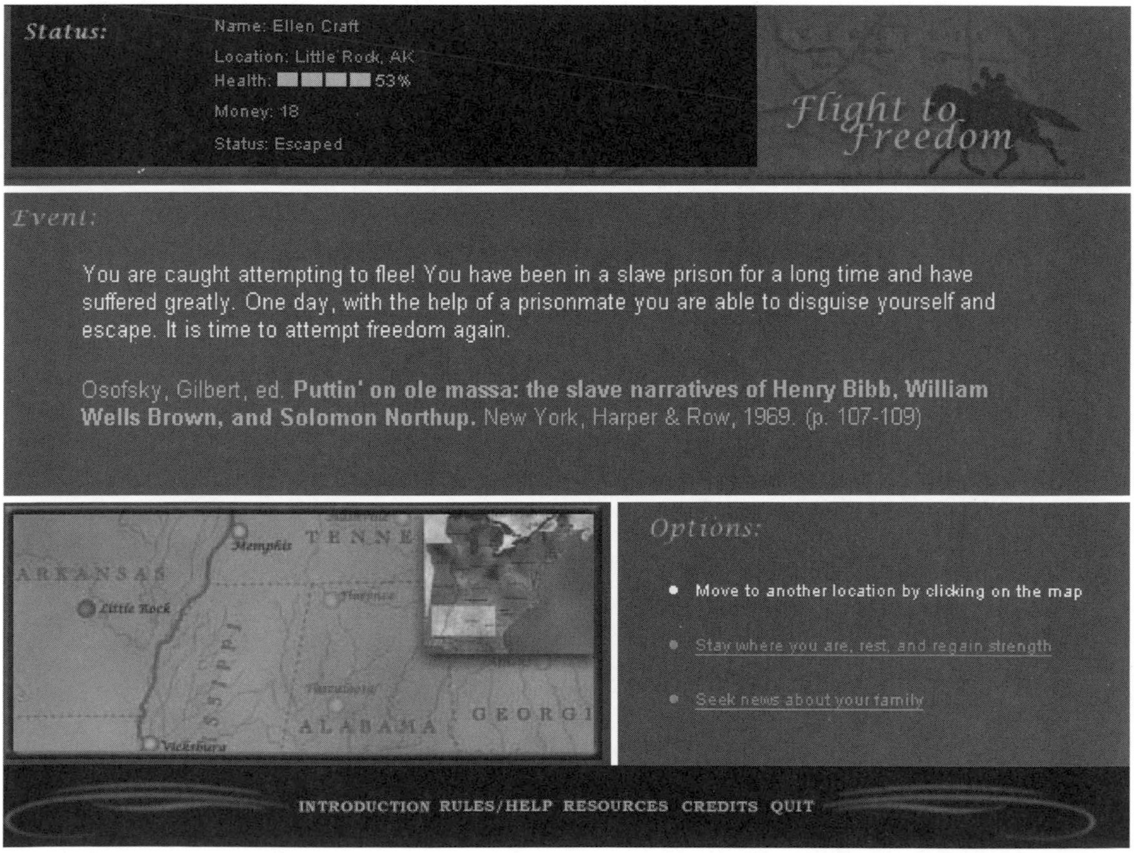

Fig. 4.11: "Flight to Freedom" allows students to plan and execute the escape of several famous runaway slaves. Source: http://academic.bowdoin.edu/flighttofreedom/intro.shtml. Courtesy of Bowdoin College Department of Information Technology.

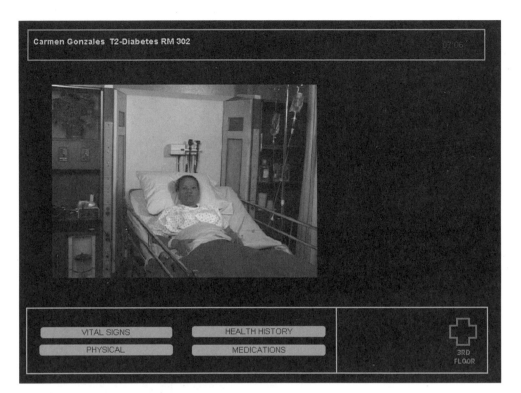

Fig. 4.12: "Virtual Clinical Excursions" allows students to explore clinical decision making. Reprinted from "Virtual Clinical Excursions, Version 1" (a supplement for "Medical Surgical Nursing, 6/E"), Lewis et al., copyright © 2001 Mosby, with permission from Elsevier.

medications are appropriate for the patient with type 2 diabetes. Such simulators can help those training in health care to learn strategies for everything from diagnosis to triage to treatment, increasing the effectiveness and reducing the cost of their training.

POTENTIAL PITFALLS

The potential pitfalls associated with using strategy simulators are the same as those discussed in Scenario 1. These tools can be easy to access and use, but you still need to give yourself and any IT staff supporting you enough time to find, implement, and test any such tools you will use.

SCENARIO 3: Experiencing Calculations

TRADITIONAL SOLUTIONS

Students have always been given the chance to experience calculations and computational problem-solving by doing practice problems and story problems. Such activities are critical in helping students develop competence and confidence. But students can sometimes focus so specifically on the details of the calculation that they lose track of where it fits into the "big picture": they are so busy studying the individual tree that they miss the forest—or don't even realize there is one. A well-constructed set of homework problems can require students to build the "forest" of calculations and then conclude by reflecting on that forest. But it can be useful for students to be able to explore and reflect on general relationships between key variables and the big picture before they begin mastering the actual calculations so that they understand the context of those calculations from the beginning.

TECHNOLOGY ALTERNATIVES

A growing number of easy-to-use technology tools are available which allow students to explore mathematical relationships and discover basic principles before even doing any calculations of their own. As was true in Scenarios 1 and 2, the examples below in no way capture the diversity of such tools available and are meant only to give a better idea what such tools might look like.

For students of geometry, for instance, a range of easy-to-use tools is available for gaining an intuitive understanding of geometric relationships. In the example shown in figure 4.13 the student is presented with a geometric drawing like that in figure 4.13a and prompted by the text below the drawing to do some exploring. In the example, students can "grab" any of the three vertices (A, B, or C) by moving the cursor to one of them and holding down the left button of the mouse. That vertex can then be "dragged" by moving the cursor to the desired new location for that vertex (while still holding down the left button of the mouse). The vertex C has been moved in the **Screenshot** shown in figure 4.13b. Such activities in no way replace good old-fashioned homework problems. They simply make the working of those problems more interesting and more effective learning experiences because students understand what they expect the answers to be and what their implications are.

Students grappling with the behavior of complex equations or systems of equations may benefit by experimenting with a tool like that shown in figure 4.14, created by Bart Stewart and Jeff Libby at the U.S. Military Academy. Students using this tool (beginning with a screen like that in figure 4.14a) can explore harmonic motion by changing any of the coefficients in the differential equation at top left to see how the eigenvalues, general solution, time series plot (all at left), and phase portrait (at right) are affected (shown in figure 4.14b). This site even offers a tutorial showing how to create such tools in Excel, meaning you and/or your students might be able to expand the number of offerings of this type of tool available.

In fact, the ability to easily add simple spreadsheets to PowerPoint presentations gives anyone who can

Screenshot—an image of what is on a computer screen; a screenshot can be captured on the clipboard (to be pasted elsewhere) by pressing the Prnt Scrn (Print Screen) key on the top row of most computer keyboards

Incircle

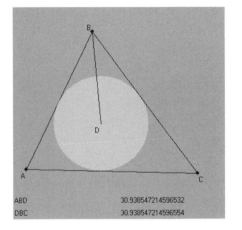

The circle is defined to be tangent to the lines AB, BC and AC.

What do you observe about the angles ABD and DBC as you move the triangle's vertices around?

a

Incircle

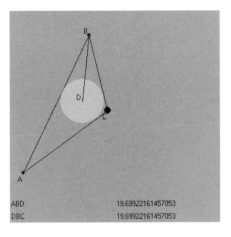

The circle is defined to be tangent to the lines AB, BC and AC.

What do you observe about the angles ABD and DBC as you move the triangle's vertices around?

b

Fig. 4.13a–b: Students can visually explore mathematical relationships using online tools. Source: Saltire Software: www.saltire.com.

write a spreadsheet the ability to create a tool that lets students explore and understand the context of calculations. The process for copying a spreadsheet into a slideshow is much the same as that for copying artwork into a slideshow, as shown in Scenario 1. (The section of the spreadsheet to be copied is highlighted, copied, pasted into the slideshow, and then positioned and resized as needed.) This process allows the slideshow creator to insert a "calculation lab" into a slide with some directions on its use, as shown in figure 4.15. The inserted section of spreadsheet (at right in figure 4.15) is fully functional, allowing students to explore how changing inputs (the yield in this case) will affect any outputs (the bond's value in this case). Students still need to master the calculation by practicing it, but having such a calculation lab allows them to gain an appreciation of the relationships involved—and means they can make up their own practice problems, checking their answers against those generated by the spreadsheet.

POTENTIAL PITFALLS

The concerns related to using tools such as those shown above are the same as those discussed in Scenarios 1 and 2: you need to make sure you give yourself and any IT support staff you rely on the time needed to find, implement, understand, and work the bugs out of any tool you decide to use, and you need to make sure that your students are able to use it.

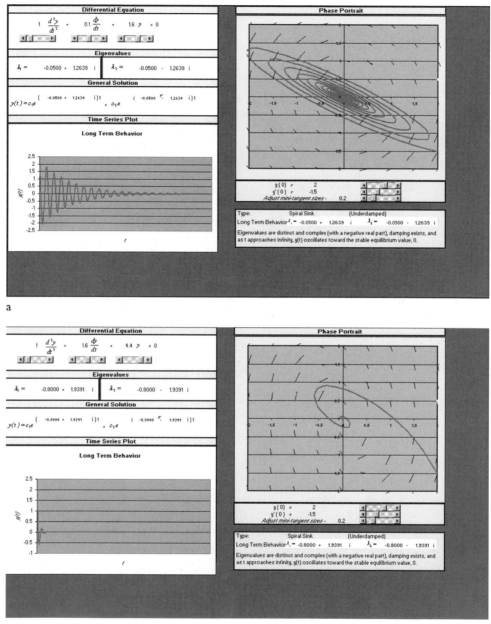

a

b

Fig. 4.14a–b: Students can explore the behavior of complex systems of equations using online tools—or even learn how to build such tools themselves. Source: Bart D. Stewart, United States Military Academy, http://www.dean.usma.edu/math/people/stewart/interactive_tools.htm.

Explore the impact of Yield Changes

- Plug in various interest rates as the yield to study the impact of yield on the Bond's value.

- Compare each answer you get with the spreadsheet to that you get with your calculator—**you will need to master this calculation on the calculator** to pass the Mastery Quiz.

- Describe the relationship between the Yield and the Bond's Value:

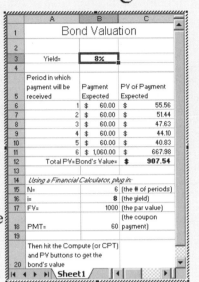

Fig. 4.15: A PowerPoint presentation with an Excel spreadsheet embedded can allow students to explore relationships and master calculations. Microsoft PowerPoint™ and Microsoft Excel™ screenshot reprinted by permission from the trademark holder, Microsoft Corporation.

SCENARIO 4: Experiencing Technology

TRADITIONAL SOLUTIONS

Whether or not we are comfortable with it, it is obvious to all of us that technology is increasingly important in our daily professional and personal lives. Recognizing this, educators are gradually introducing technology-related competencies into the objectives of their curricula. The traditional method for allowing students to experience technology is to offer courses that are basically technology training courses: "Introduction to Computer Science," "Internet Studies," etc. While such courses may be important to help students reach basic levels of technology competency, they present a problem: they treat technology as a separate issue instead of as something relevant to and used in each discipline, as we know technology increasingly is. "Writing Across the Curriculum" is a plan for expanding the building, assessment, and perceived relevance of writing skills from freshman English into the rest of the curriculum. If students are to experience technology and understand its increasing importance in most of the disciplines we teach, they need to see technology in the context of those disciplines, being used by practitioners of those disciplines.

TECHNOLOGY ALTERNATIVES

In fact, this entire book is about ways in which technology might be meaningfully integrated into curricula across a wide range of disciplines. Whether students are learning to communicate electronically (as in Chapter 1), collaborate online (as in Chapter 2), gain experience and training using technology tools (as in this chapter), use technology resources to assist them on research projects (as in Chapter 7), or use online assessment techniques (as in Chapter 8), they will be using, and learning to appreciate, technology in the context of their work, better preparing them for life outside the university.

POTENTIAL PITFALLS

Because they involve the ideas in every chapter of this book, the technology alternatives suggested here for helping students experience technology are exposed to all of the potential pitfalls described elsewhere. Beyond that, the integration of relevant use and experience of technology throughout the curriculum requires an institutional commitment and plan to support that integration: writing does not get integrated across the curriculum without being thoughtfully supported, and neither does technology. Laying out a plan for institutional support of technology integration is beyond the scope of this book, but such plans must include:

1. Creating forums in which faculty are informed of exciting opportunities and strategies for using technology to enhance learning,
2. Providing practical and useful training, hardware, software, and other resources to help faculty exploit those opportunities and strategies,
3. Supporting faculty efforts to integrate technology so well that "wheel spinning," frustration, and lost class/learning time are rigorously minimized, and
4. Valuing faculty projects using technology to enhance learning when it comes to promotion and tenure.

SCENARIO 5: Interacting with Experts and Practitioners

TRADITIONAL SOLUTIONS

Giving your students the chance to interact with experts and practitioners in your discipline can be a wonderful way to add credibility and relevance to what they are learning in class. The war stories that such experts can share allow students to vicariously experience the discipline, and the diverse perspectives of these experts can help students better understand the thought processes used by its practitioners.

Traditional methods for allowing students to interact with experts include inviting them into class as guest lecturers and visiting them on class field trips. Field trips are particularly valuable, allowing students to experience visual environments as well as interact with practitioners in a discipline. Unfortunately, field trips are not always practical. Policy, time, and budget constraints often present barriers large enough to prevent such outings, and field trips are therefore not common in higher education. Guest lecturers are generally easier to deal with in terms of these institutional constraints, but potential guests will have constraints of their own that add to the complexity and reduce the likelihood of actually getting such a guest into your class. The net result of all of this is that students are not given the opportunity to interact with experts as much as might benefit them.

TECHNOLOGY ALTERNATIVES

Technology offers a variety of ways to allow your students to interact with experts and practitioners, ranging from conference calls to Chat sessions to video conferences (the latter being beyond the scope of the tools discussed in this book).

Perhaps the simplest of these is the conference call, in which your students can talk by speakerphone with one or more guests—all without you and your students traveling from the classroom or the guests traveling from their offices. Such conversations can be supplemented with slideshows and other visual materials if they are sent ahead, though the interactivity of these visual elements is limited—guests will not be able to add or edit materials to help clarify points.

A slightly more sophisticated and flexible technology solution is presented by Chat, which was also discussed Scenario 4 of Chapter 1 and in Scenario 1 of Chapter 3. Chat sessions allow many participants to interact online from many different locations no matter where they are in the world. As shown in Scenario 4 of Chapter 1, some Chat software (that provided with Blackboard, for instance), allows participants to use a whiteboard to create diagrams and drawings throughout the Chat session. Even Chat sessions that are limited to text (like the example in figure 4.16) provide benefits over telephone conference calls, in that

- Participants can be anywhere in the world that they can get online—there is no practical limit to the number of "lines" coming in to the Chat session (as there is with the number of phone lines coming in to most conference calls), meaning that such sessions can easily take place outside of class time (perhaps at a time most convenient for the guest) and students can participate from wherever they are at that time, and
- A written record of the discussion is automatically created, which can easily be saved and studied by any participant interested in doing so.

In the Chat session shown in figure 4.16, a writing instructor (William Clyde) has arranged to have his Author Friend and a Publishing Executive interact with his students (Isaac, Sue, and Portia—but there could be many more) to help them understand what it really takes to get written work published. Such sessions often start with opening remarks

```
Isaac Student has joined.
Sue Student has joined.
Portia Student has joined.
Publishing Executive has joined.
Author Friend has joined.
William Clyde : Greetings everyone and thanks for coming
William Clyde : I'd like to thank our two guests, Publishing Executive and Author Friend for
joining our conversation on strategies for getting written work published. I've asked each of them
to write a short paragraph with opening remarks on the subject to get the conversation started.
William Clyde : So unless someone has a preliminary question, why don't we start with Author
Friend?
Author Friend : Thank you. And thank you for this chance to work with some developing
writers. I believe that the most important things for you to think about as a writer are....
William Clyde : Thanks Author. Before we move to questions, why don't we hear from
Publishing Executive?
Publishing Executive : Thank you Dr. Clyde....
William Clyde : And now, why don't we open the discussion to student questions?
Isaac Student : Mr. Friend, can you describe what your first contact with publishers was like?
How many manuscripts did you have to send out before you received a reply?




Well, that was 23 years ago, but...
```

Fig. 4.16: A chat session can allow your students to interact with an expert or practitioner in your field. Microsoft Windows Messenger™ screenshot reprinted by permission from the trademark holder, Microsoft Corporation.

by the guests, which may be written in advance by the guests and copied into the Chat or may be sent ahead in a document or presentation that can be studied by students before the Chat even begins. Any participant can contribute to the Chat at any time (though some Chat software gives the moderator the ability to limit when contributions can be made by some or all participants) by typing (or copying) in his or her comments in the space at the bottom ("Well, that was 23 years ago, but . . . " is being written by Author Friend in response to Isaac Student's questions) and hitting Enter to submit those comments (comments are not visible to others until their author submits them to the Chat). Such a session can be relatively easy to arrange, require little time or resource commitment from anyone involved, and yet allow students to gain many benefits from interacting with experts and practitioners anywhere in the world.

POTENTIAL PITFALLS

While Chat is a widely used and robust tool, it is always wise to make sure in advance that all parties can gain access to the Chat and that you know what to expect from it. The best way to do this is to do dry runs with all participants before the actual event. A few minutes in a computer lab (with IT staff present if you need help) will allow you and your students to confirm that you can all meet and communicate in the Chat environment—and give any training required to students who have trouble. If students will be elsewhere (on their own computers at home or at work, for instance) for the actual event, it is wise to follow up the in-lab test with a dress rehearsal in which students access the Chat briefly from the computers they plan to use for the real Chat. Such tests/training need be done with your students only before the first such guest Chat in a semester, but they are critical in ensuring that all students benefit from these events. Brief tests confirming that the guests can access the Chat are also important.

CHAPTER 5 Clarifying Linkages Within Your Course

SCENARIO 1: Linking the Mission Statement and Objectives

You have written a great mission statement for your course and have measurable objectives for each week. You are concerned that, once the first page of your syllabus is turned, your students will lose sight of the mission and the relevance that goes with it.

SCENARIO 2: Linking Activities and Assessments to Objectives

You have carefully created activities to help your students achieve and demonstrate competence related to each of the course objectives. Once they start in on the assignments, however, it seems as though your students view the assignments as a list of things to get done and do not relate them to the objectives and mission for the course.

SCENARIO 3: Linking Activities to One Another

You have a series of assignments that build on one another, and you really want your students to do them in order to get the most out of them.

SCENARIO 4: Linking Activities and Objectives to the Real World

You know that your students are more highly motivated when they see that course activities are what people in the field actually do. Even if course activities are grounded in the real world, it is critical that your students see that link.

SCENARIO 5: Linking Activities and Objectives to Policies and Resources

A wide range of university policies and resources are relevant to the students in your class—it's just a matter of getting access to them in front of your students at the right times and places.

Introduction

Students are often so used to missing the forest for the trees—moving from one activity or concept to another without seeing how they relate to each other or fit into the big picture—that their knee-jerk reaction when confronted with new material is not to ask, "Where does this fit into what I already know?" or "What am I learning from this?" but "Will this be on the test?" A variety of technology tools are helpful in clarifying these

> **Strategic Planning Model**—a plan for creating, implementing, assessing, and revising the strategy of an organization; components usually include a mission statement, measurable objectives that support that mission (that, if accomplished, will mean the mission has been accomplished), and action plans (actions needed to accomplish the objectives)

linkages, none more than **Hypertext**. The ability to allow students to **Hyperlink** to more detail (a definition, a picture, an assignment, a Web site, a quiz), but always to revert back to the big picture, is invaluable in helping students begin asking the right questions and constructing their knowledge.

SCENARIO 1: Linking the Mission Statement and Objectives

TRADITIONAL SOLUTIONS

It is increasingly common for instructors to build and present their courses using the framework of the **Strategic Planning Model**. Instructors using this model begin by defining the mission of the course with a brief statement indicating why the course exists and what knowledge and competencies students will build by taking it. A sample mission statement is presented below.

> The mission of this course is to help students become familiar with the variety and diversity of securities that exist in the United States and throughout the world: the forms they take, how they are valued, how they are interrelated, and how and why they are used. Markets and instruments considered will include foreign exchange, equity, fixed income, and derivatives markets. Various course activities will allow students to develop research, computer, problem-solving, writing, and presentation skills.

Supporting the course mission are specific, measurable course objectives, such as:

1. Master the definitions and appreciate the importance of basic market terminology
2. Develop a pool of resources for gathering market information
3. Understand and appreciate the variety of market and economic indicators used by market participants
4. Understand and be able to contrast and apply the various concepts of market efficiency

5. Master the basic terminology of currency markets
6. Understand the variety of factors that help determine currency exchange rates

With the creation of the course mission and objectives, an instructor has defined the "forest" her students will be exploring. The "trees"—the specific activities that will help students understand, appreciate, and perhaps even be able to live in that forest—are discussed in the next section of this chapter. But before students will be able to understand how the course activities derive relevance from the course objectives and mission, they need an appreciation of the relevance of the mission and how the objectives support it.

The content of the mission and objectives are, of course, critical in helping students appreciate their relevance. But even well-thought-out and well-written missions and objectives need to be presented prominently and often if students are to realize and remember their importance. Faculty employing the strategic planning model often present the mission and objectives at the top of the syllabus, making them among the first things discussed on the first day of class. To the extent that a list of activities is handed out each week, the course mission, along with the week's objectives, can be included in the handout, reminding students that there is a "forest"—and where they are in it. Class discussion can also reinforce the course structure if it is continually put in the context of the mission and objectives.

TECHNOLOGY ALTERNATIVES

Technology, in the form of hyperlinks in electronic documents, offers a powerful yet simple way of keeping the course mission and objectives linked and in front of students throughout the course.

Beginning with a syllabus, like that in figure 5.1, the course mission can be presented prominently and linked to the course objectives. Clicking on the hyperlinked "Objectives in support of this Mission" takes students to another document listing the objectives of the course, shown in figure 5.2 (objectives may also be listed on the syllabus, but many feel that this can make the syllabus too long). From the "Objectives of the Course" students can return to the syllabus (by clicking on "Mission of this Course"), go to a week-by-week outline of the course (like that in figure 5.3—also available from the syllabus) by clicking on the hyperlinked "weekly Web pages," or go to the Web page for the week in which a given objective is addressed by clicking on the hyperlinked "Week 1," "Week 2," etc. (see figure 5.2).

From the week-by-week outline of the course shown in figure 5.3 students can get to the objectives and assignments for any week by clicking on the topic line for that week.

Upon arriving at the Web page for the week (as shown in figure 5.4) the student is immediately presented with the objectives for the week, along with the opportunity to refer back to the mission of the course via the hyperlink.

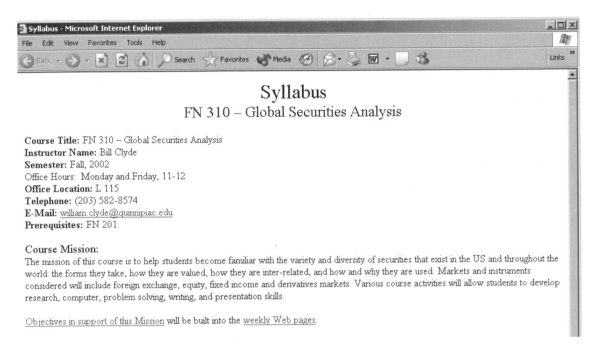

Fig. 5.1: Course mission and links to the course objectives in the syllabus. Microsoft Internet Explorer™ screenshot reprinted by permission from the trademark holder, Microsoft Corporation.

Fig. 5.2: Web document listing course objectives and providing links to the weeks in which those objectives are covered. Microsoft Internet Explorer™ screenshot reprinted by permission from the trademark holder, Microsoft Corporation.

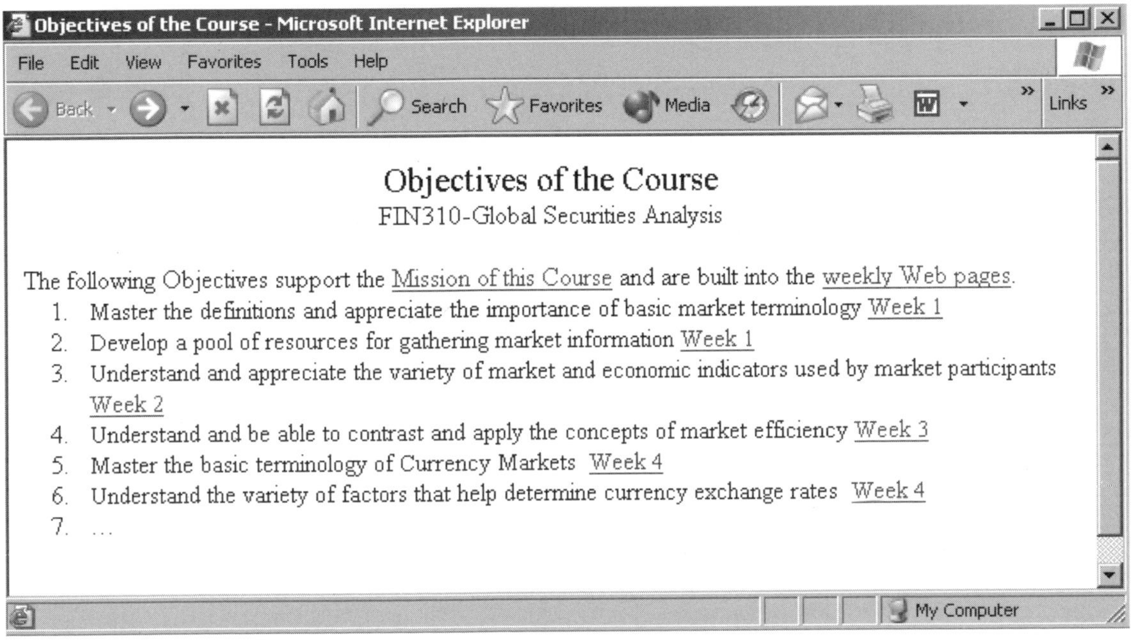

Dead Link—a hyperlink for which the associated Web page does not exist or is not available; the user will get an error message instead of being taken to the intended Web page
Misdirected Link—a hyperlink to the wrong target material or pages
Target—the Web page or resource to which a hyperlink takes the reader

Creating these links between the mission and objectives is simple—Web pages with hyperlinks can easily be created in Word and in many other software tools. The process of creating such pages in Word is laid out in Scenario 2 of this chapter.

POTENTIAL PITFALLS

The most important concern when creating hyperlinks is ensuring that all links actually take the reader where you want them to go. **Dead Links** and **Misdirected Links** cause readers confusion and frustration and will not reinforce the strategic plan of the course. You must be careful to get the links right in the first place and to update them if you should change the locations of any of the **Target** pages.

Aside from ensuring that your links are good, your main concern should be organizing your links in ways that give your students access to information you want them to have when and where you want them to have it. Randomly distributed hyperlinks to your course mission and objectives will not be seen as useful, and your students will quickly learn to disregard them. By carefully considering the best points at which to reinforce the mission and objectives by providing access to them—and whether to do so by printing them on the page or hyperlinking to them—you can optimize your students' appreciation of the relevance of the course.

SCENARIO 2: Linking Activities and Assessments to Objectives

TRADITIONAL SOLUTIONS

With the mission and objectives in place, the next step is to help students see the relationships between course activities and course objectives. This second set of links is vital if students are to see the relevance of course activities—the mission and objectives are just talk unless students clearly and constantly perceive how course activities are related to them.

Faculty wishing to help their students understand the links between course objectives and course activities might hand out a list of objectives for the week, indicating the activities for the week that are associated with each of those objectives. Table 5.1 shows five objectives to be met in week five of a course, and four activities for the week (ACT 5.1.1, ACT 5.1.2, ACT 5.1.3, and ACT 5.1.4) in support of the first objective (OBJ 5.1). The list of activities would continue to include those for the other four objectives. With assessments (quizzes, tests, and/or other evaluated activities) built in, these activities should help the student both develop and demonstrate the competencies required by the objectives. This form of presentation can help students perceive the links between activ-

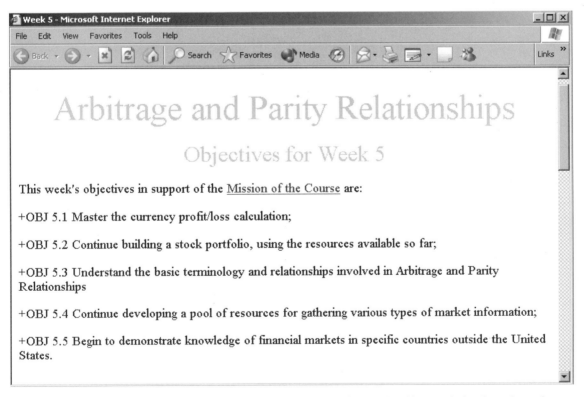

Fig. 5.3: Week-by-week course outline with links to the objectives and activities for each week. Microsoft Internet Explorer™ screenshot reprinted by permission from the trademark holder, Microsoft Corporation.

Fig. 5.4: Web page for the week. Microsoft Internet Explorer™ screenshot reprinted by permission from the trademark holder, Microsoft Corporation.

Table 5.1. A handout describing course objectives and activities for a given week

---

Arbitrage and Parity Relationships

Objectives for Week 5

OBJ 5.1 Master the currency profit/loss calculation

OBJ 5.2 Continue building a stock portfolio, using the resources available so far

OBJ 5.3 Understand the basic terminology and relationships involved in Arbitrage and Parity Relationships

OBJ 5.4 Continue developing a pool of resources for gathering various types of market information

OBJ 5.5 Begin to demonstrate knowledge of financial markets in specific countries outside the United States

Activites

OBJ 5.1 Activities

Activity 5.1.1 Study the "Notes for Calculating Profit/Loss in Currency Transactions" presentation in the attached file (0.5 hours)

Activity 5.1.2 Master the calculation by working problems on the attached "Drill Sheet for Currency Profit/Loss Mastery Quiz" (0.5 hours)

Activity 5.1.3 Pass the Currency Profit/Loss Mastery Quiz (0.25 hours)

Activity 5.1.4 Complete and submit Lab 2 (1.5 hours)

---

ities and objectives so long as students keep referring to this list of objectives and associated activities for the week. If students lose the list, or set it aside and focus on the activities (that is, if their personal objectives become simply to complete the activities instead of to meet the course objectives), the link between course objectives and course activities may be lost.

TECHNOLOGY ALTERNATIVES

Technology, in the form of hyperlinks, allows faculty to constantly remind students of the relationship between course objectives and course activities, thereby reinforcing the relevance of the latter. By presenting the information in table 5.1 in a Web page (like that shown in figure 5.5), with the hyperlinks from the objectives and activities for the week page to each activity, faculty can force students to return to the list of objectives to get to each new activity. If the activities for the week can be found only through the links on this

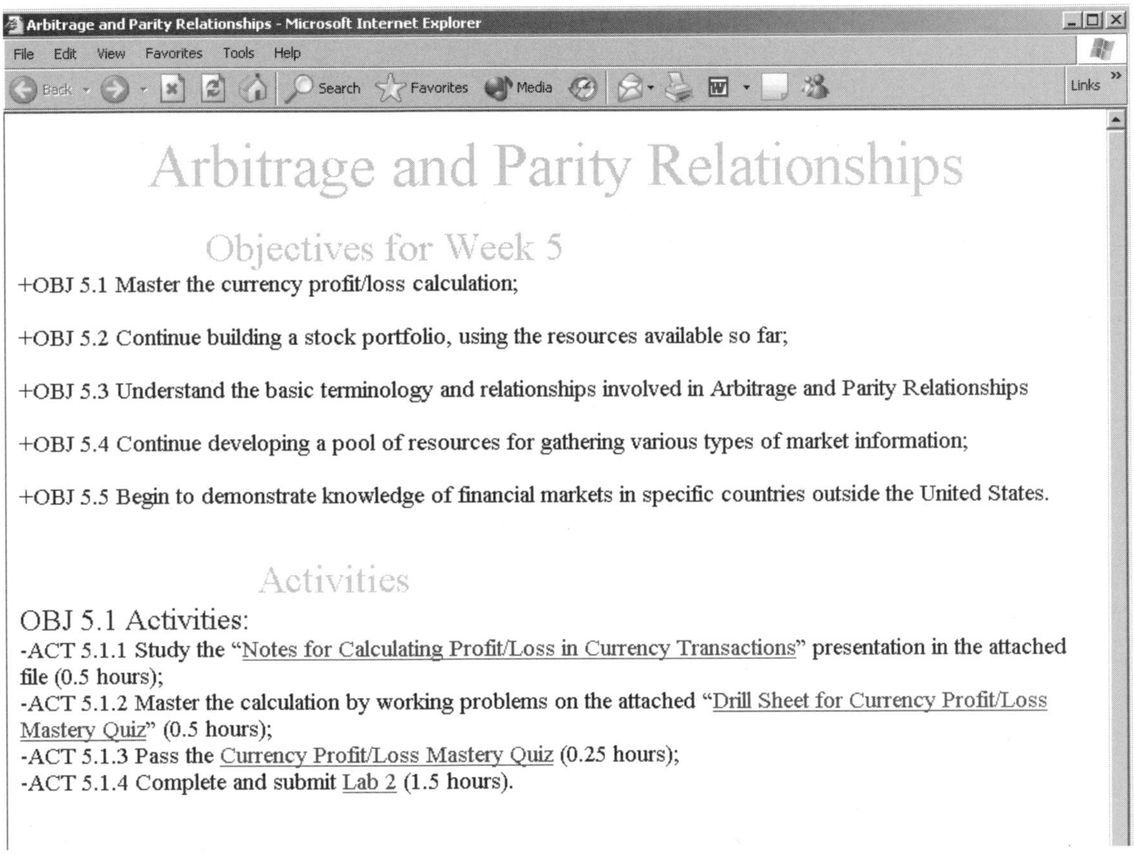

Fig. 5.5: Web page laying out objectives and activities for a given week, complete with hyperlinks to the resources needed for each activity. Microsoft Internet Explorer™ screenshot reprinted by permission from the trademark holder, Microsoft Corporation.

page, students must repeatedly select their activities from this framework. This mechanism simply yet powerfully reinforces the relevance of those activities in terms of course objectives.

By clicking on the hyperlinked "Notes for Calculating Profit/Loss in Currency Transactions," students are taken to this first activity, shown in figure 5.6, so that they can work on it.

After completing this activity students return to the page listing objectives and activities for the week (see figure 5.5), from which they click on the hyperlinked "Drill Sheet for Currency Profit/Loss Mastery Quiz" (figure 5.7).

After developing competence related to the objective (by working problems from the drill sheet), students return to the objectives and activities page yet again to find the link

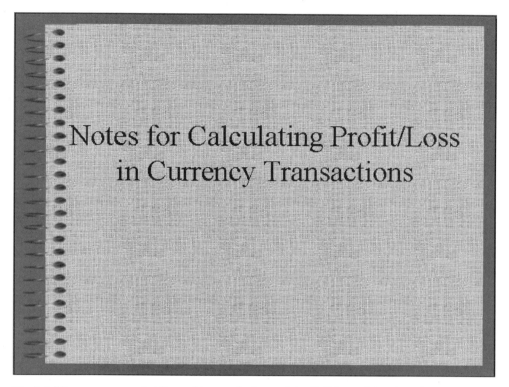

Fig. 5.6: The resource needed for working on the first activity (ACT 5.1.1) listed on the Web page shown in Fig. 5.5. Microsoft PowerPoint™ screenshot reprinted by permission from the trademark holder, Microsoft Corporation.

Drill Sheet for Currency Profit-Loss Mastery Quiz

Calculating Profits								
Given a long position of	And expectations that the Exchange Rate will move from		to	Your profits will be				Answer
$	900	JPY/$	110.00	115.32	$		$	41.51
$	100	JPY/$	115.00	112.67	$		$	-2.06
$	800	SFR/$	1.4000	1.3755	$		$	-14.24
$	420	SFR/$	1.3000	1.1888	$		$	-39.28
GBP	280	$/ GBP	1.5000	1.5555	GBP		GBP	9.99
GBP	970	$/ GBP	1.5000	1.6789	GBP		GBP	103.36
AUD	800	$/AUD	0.6000	0.6798	AUD		AUD	93.91
AUD	420	$/AUD	0.7000	0.8297	AUD		AUD	65.65
NZD	570	$/NZD	0.6000	0.4444	NZD		NZD	-199.57
NZD	830	$/NZD	0.5000	0.5632	NZD		NZD	93.13
...								

Fig. 5.7: The resource needed for working on the second activity (ACT 5.1.2) listed on the Web page shown in Fig. 5.5. Microsoft Excel™ screenshot reprinted by permission from the trademark holder, Microsoft Corporation.

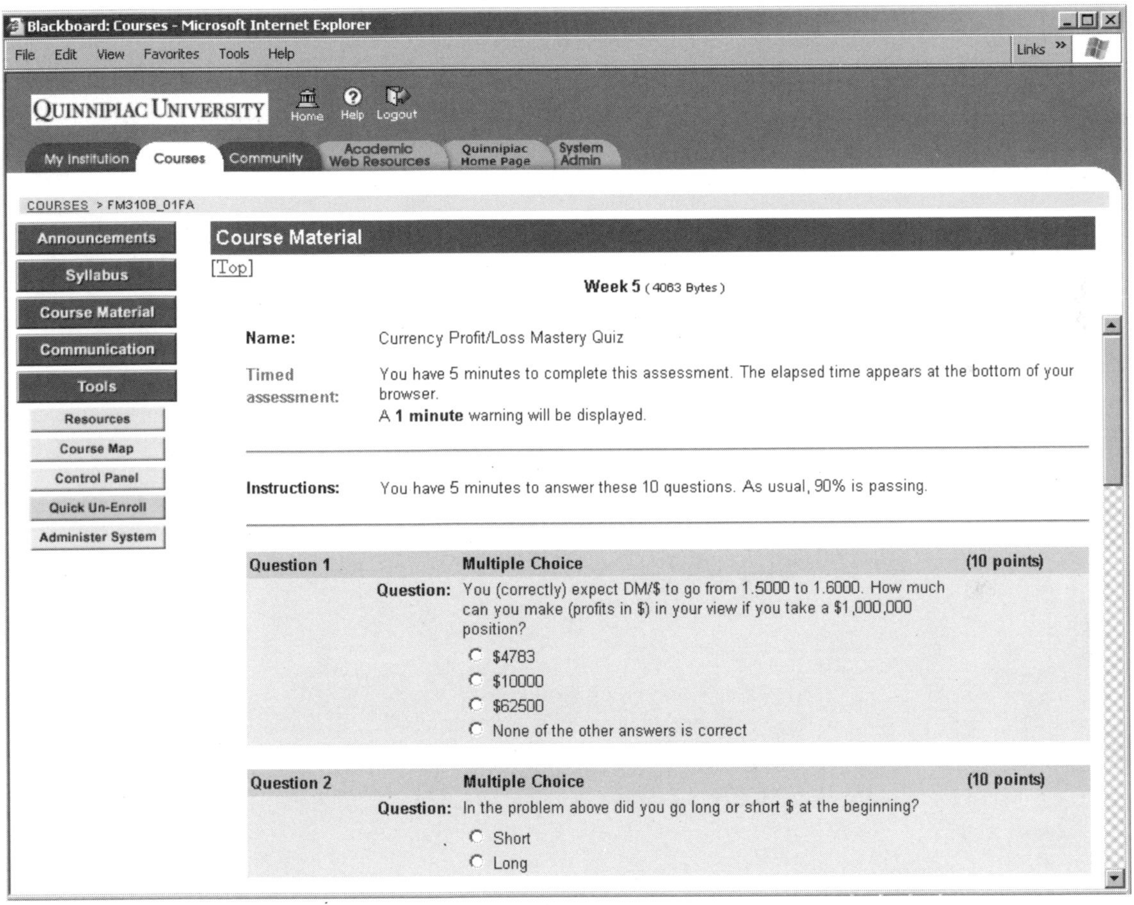

Fig. 5.8: The resource needed for working on the third activity (ACT 5.1.3) listed on the Web page shown in Fig. 5.5. Property of Blackboard. Used with the permission of Blackboard. Microsoft Internet Explorer™ screenshot reprinted by permission from the trademark holder, Microsoft Corporation.

to the "Currency Profit/Loss Mastery Quiz" (figure 5.8) to demonstrate their newfound competence at a basic level. (See Chapter 8 for ideas on how to build and use online assessments.)

Finally, after demonstrating basic competence with the objective through a simple, automatically graded online quiz, students return to the objectives and activities page to complete the activities in support of this objective by clicking on the link to "Lab 2." This activity (shown in figure 5.9) gives students the chance to further develop and demonstrate the abilities required by the objective in a more realistic or experiential setting of an online simulator (see Chapter 4 for ideas on how to integrate experiential activities into your course).

When students complete this last activity for the objective and return to the objectives and activities page, they will see that they have completed all of the activities for the

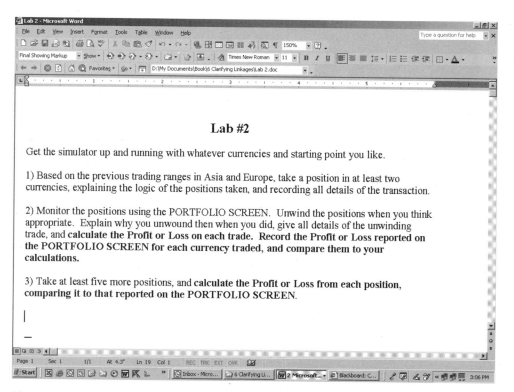

Fig. 5.9: The resource needed for working on the fourth activity (ACT 5.1.4) listed on the Web page shown in Fig. 5.5. Microsoft Word™ screenshot reprinted by permission from the trademark holder, Microsoft Corporation.

objective (each hyperlink changes color as it is accessed, allowing students to keep track of where they are in the week's activities). If you think your students need more reinforcement to see that the activities have helped them develop and demonstrate the competencies associated with the objective, you can either:

- Include one last activity for the objective that asks them to reflect on whether they believe they have met the objective, or
- Include a two-minute survey at the end of the week (it can be paper or online—see Chapter 8 for ideas and methods for using such surveys), asking students whether they believe they have completed each of the objectives for the week (ask, e.g., "To what extent do you feel you have mastered the currency profit/loss calculation?" for the Objective 5.1 in figure 5.5).

Creating Web Pages with Hyperlinks

Creating Web pages with hyperlinks is relatively easy and can be done using a wide range of software—including your word-processing program. What follows is a demonstration of how to transform the Word document shown in figure 5.10 (a basic word-processing

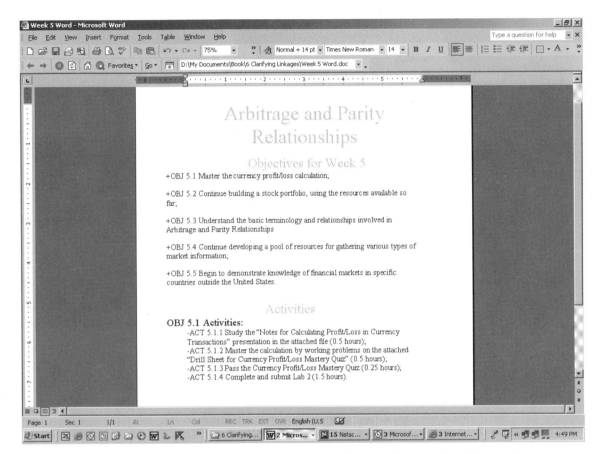

Fig. 5.10: Word-processing document before being converted to a Web page. Microsoft Word™ screenshot reprinted by permission from the trademark holder, Microsoft Corporation.

document with no hyperlinks) into the Web page shown in figure 5.5 (complete with hyperlinks to the appropriate Web pages). Details on how to post Web pages, documents, and other course materials to course Web pages within a course management system can be found in Chapter 2.

Before you can create a hyperlink in your document, you must know the **Web Address** (also known as the **URL** of the existing Web page to which you would like to link). The easiest way to find that Web address is to open your **Browser** and **Navigate** your way to the page to which you would like to hyperlink. Assuming the target page is that shown in figure 5.11, you find the needed Web address by **Right-Clicking** on the portion of the page you want your students to hyperlink to (the page may be made up of several **Frames**—in this case the buttons at left may be in

Web Address—the unique string of characters (usually beginning with www.) assigned to a Web page and used to access it from the Web

Navigate—to use hyperlinks to move from page to page in a network or on the Web

Frames—blocks or sections of a Web page that have been created and loaded separately to be combined into the complete Web page; frames may be thought of as mini—Web pages, as each frame will have its own Web address or URL

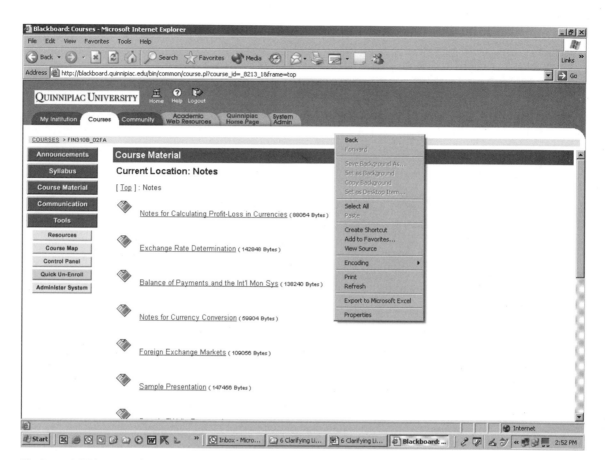

Fig. 5.11: A Web page to be targeted by a hyperlink. Property of Blackboard. Used with permission of Blackboard. Microsoft Internet Explorer™ screenshot reprinted by permission from the trademark holder, Microsoft Corporation.

one frame, the long rectangular area with Quinnipiac University written in it may be in another frame, and the area below the darker, thinner rectangular area with the words "Course Material" may be in yet a third frame—and you need to make sure you find the Web address that includes the frame you want your students to see), and then **Left-Clicking** on "Properties" (the bottom choice in the gray box in the middle of figure 5.11) to produce yet another **Pop-Up Box**, as shown in figure 5.12.

The Web address in the middle of the gray pop-up box in figure 5.12 must be **Highlighted** —be sure to start at the top of the address and drag down to just below the bottom of the address to ensure that the entire address is being seen (there may be more than the two visible lines of address). Once this is done the Web address can be copied by right-clicking on that highlighted address, resulting in yet another pop-up box, as shown in figure

> **Highlighted**—when an onscreen item has been visibly chosen (changed in color), usually so that some operation such as copying can be applied; items are highlighted by clicking on them, or, in the case of more than one item, by clicking on one of the items and then dragging the cursor over all of the items to be highlighted

5.13. Left-clicking on Copy in this pop-up box will place a copy of that Web address on your **Clipboard** so that you can paste it anywhere you want it.

To create the desired hyperlink in the Word document, you simply:

> **Clipboard**—part of a computer's memory dedicated to holding data (text, images, files, etc.) that have been copied or cut from one application (e.g., text from a word-processing document) so that they can be pasted into another

1. Highlight the text on which you want to create a hyperlink (as shown in figure 5.14),
2. Right-click on that highlighted text to produce the pop-up box shown in figure 5.15,
3. Left-click on Hyperlink in that pop-up box, resulting in another pop-up box (shown in figure 5.16),
4. Paste the Web address of the target page (the address copied to the clip-

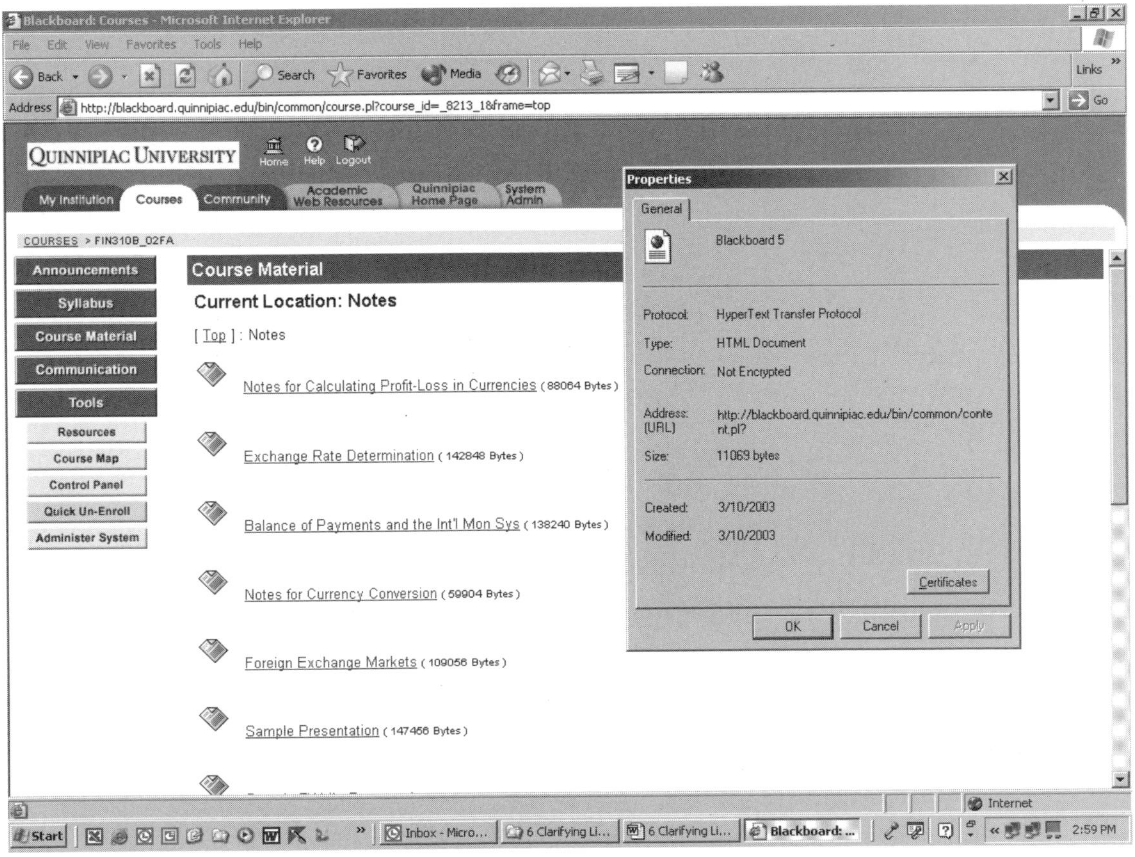

Fig. 5.12: Finding the URL for a Web page to be targeted by a hyperlink. Property of Blackboard. Used with the permission of Blackboard. Microsoft Internet Explorer™ screenshot reprinted by permission from the trademark holder, Microsoft Corporation.

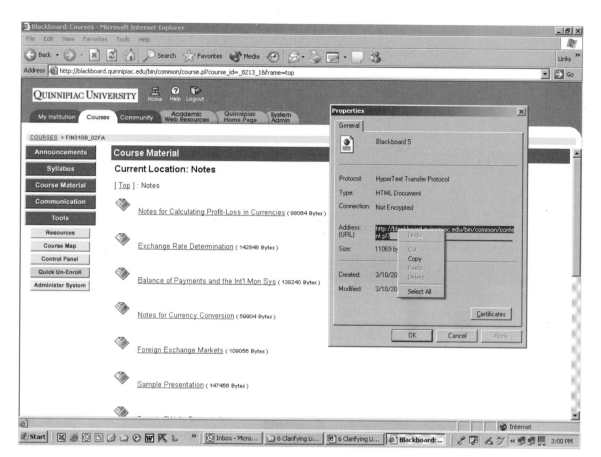

Fig. 5.13: Capturing the URL for a Web page to be targeted by a hyperlink. Property of Blackboard. Used with the permission of Blackboard. Microsoft Internet Explorer™ screenshot reprinted by permission from the trademark holder, Microsoft Corporation.

board in figure 5.13) into the white space labeled "Address" (near the bottom of the pop-up box shown in figure 5.16), and

5. Left-click on the OK button.

The result of this process (which can be done in seconds with just a little experience) is the now visible hyperlink—"Notes for Calculating Profit/Loss in Currency Transactions" is now underlined—in the Word document, as shown in figure 5.17.

Repeating this process for the other activities produces hyperlinks for each of the activities, as shown in figure 5.18.

To save this document as a Web page to be posted within the course pages of a course management system (again, details on how to actually do this posting can be found in Chapter 2), you:

1. Left-click on File, resulting in the **Drop-Down Box** shown in the upper left of figure 5.19,

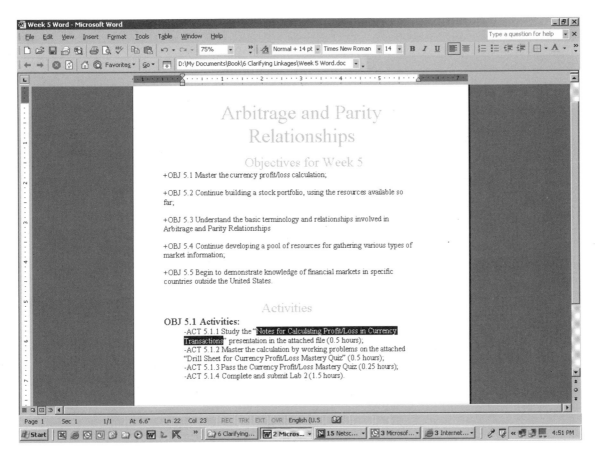

Fig. 5.14: Identifying the text to be converted into hypertext. Microsoft Word™ screenshot reprinted by permission from the trademark holder, Microsoft Corporation.

> 2. Left-click on Save As in the drop-down box, resulting in the pop-up box shown in figure 5.20,
> 3. Choose Web Page in the "Save as type" drop-down in that pop-up box, as shown in figure 5.20, and
> 4. Left-click on OK.

This process results in the creation of a Web page that looks little changed from the word-processing document (see figure 5.21) but is now viewable in a browser (like Internet Explorer or Netscape Navigator), as shown in figure 5.22. This Web page is ready to be posted to the Web for your students' use.

POTENTIAL PITFALLS

As in Scenario 1, it is important that your links be correct—that they take your students to the right pages. By checking each of the links once the page has been posted you can catch any errors, averting student frustration and late assignments.

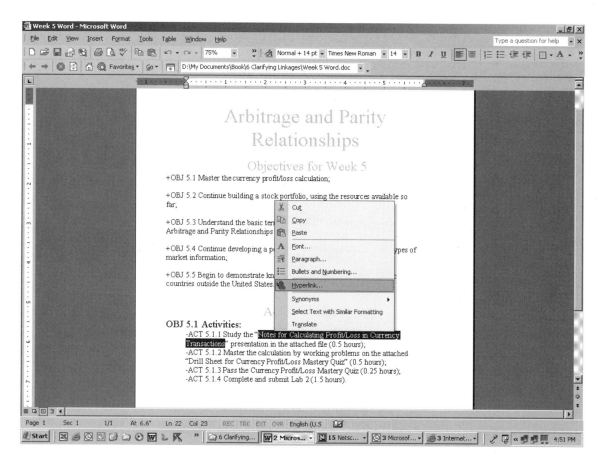

Fig. 5.15: Creating a hyperlink. Microsoft Word™ screenshot reprinted by permission from the trademark holder, Microsoft Corporation.

SCENARIO 3: Linking Activities to One Another

TRADITIONAL SOLUTIONS

Given the importance of linking activities to course objectives, you may not want your students to be able to get to the week's activities in any way other than one that links objectives and activities. Still, there may be times when you want to emphasize the sequence of activities and the links between them (in addition to or instead of to the objectives they support). In such cases you may even force students to follow the sequence by limiting their access to the second assignment until the first is done, and so on—though this degree of control is probably uncommon. Doing this with traditional tools may be as simple as providing a handout of the week's activities, with language emphasizing the importance of the sequence, or as forceful as withholding later assignments until earlier assignments are submitted. The former may not be effective at getting students to understand

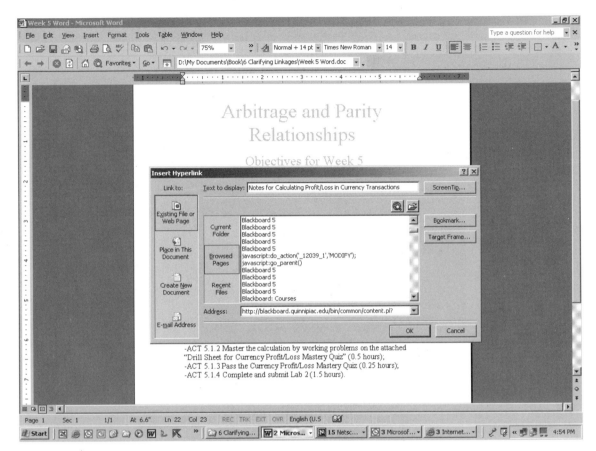

Fig. 5.16: Defining the URL to be targeted by the hyperlink. Microsoft Word™ screenshot reprinted by permission from the trademark holder, Microsoft Corporation.

and follow the sequencing—especially once they lose the handout—and the latter may be administratively cumbersome and demanding on you.

TECHNOLOGY ALTERNATIVES

Technology allows you to emphasize and even force sequencing whenever it is important. In addition to, or instead of, allowing your students access to the week's activities through a Web page like that shown in figure 5.22, you may end each activity with a link to the next activity. For instance, on the last slide of the PowerPoint presentation (shown in figure 5.23) for activity ACT 5.1.1 (from figure 5.22), you can give your students a link to the resource for the next activity (ACT 5.1.2 in figure 5.22), a document containing the Drill Sheet for Currency Profit/Loss Mastery Quiz. At the bottom of that drill sheet, you can then provide a link to the resource for the next activity in the sequence (as shown in figure 5.23), in this case an online quiz. These links lead the students through

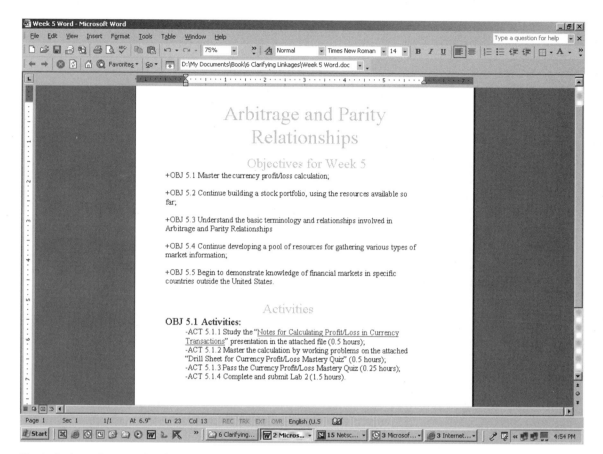

Fig. 5.17: A word-processing document after a hyperlink has been added. Microsoft Word™ screenshot reprinted by permission from the trademark holder, Microsoft Corporation.

the activities in the prescribed order, making it easy for them to follow your preferred sequence.

Should you need to be more forceful in encouraging your students to follow the proper sequence, it is easy to password protect any or all resources needed for the activities, so that students cannot get to them without knowing the passwords (Word, Excel, PowerPoint, and Acrobat all offer this feature). You can then provide students the password once you know they've completed all previous activities or, better still, define the password as something that is an outcome of the required previous activity. If, for instance, you want to make sure that your students have completed the PowerPoint presentation (the last page of which is shown in figure 5.23) before going on to the drill sheet shown in figure 5.24, you could end the presentation with a question or problem, the answer to which is the password for getting into the drill sheet. Upon trying to access the drill sheet, your students would be presented with a pop-up box like that shown in figure 5.25. Assuming they had completed the previous assignment and therefore knew the password, they would type it in, click on OK, and be given access to the drill sheet.

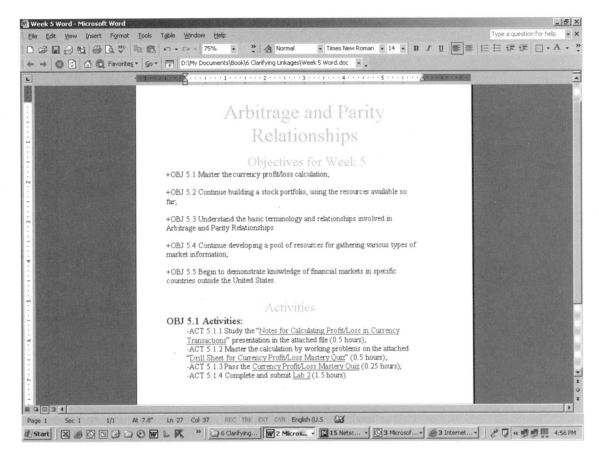

Fig. 5.18: A word-processing document after a few hyperlinks have been added. Microsoft Word™ screenshot reprinted by permission from the trademark holder, Microsoft Corporation.

POTENTIAL PITFALLS

As in the earlier scenarios in the chapter, the most important concern is being careful that the links and passwords are correct. Checking each of these once they are posted takes only a few seconds and will avoid student frustration—and your having to spend time answering questions and fixing mistakes.

SCENARIO 4: Linking Activities and Objectives to the Real World

TRADITIONAL SOLUTIONS

A critical component of student engagement in the learning process is the understanding that the concepts being taught and the activities being assigned are grounded in reality and therefore are and will be relevant to them. Faculty may try to establish this relevance in many ways, with field trips, outside speakers, stories or materials from the outside

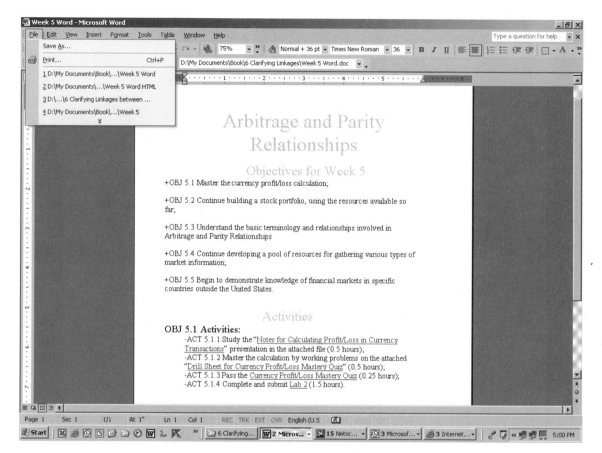

Fig. 5.19: A word-processing document about to be converted to a Web page. Microsoft Word™ screenshot reprinted by permission from the trademark holder, Microsoft Corporation.

world. All of these are important and valuable, but time and budget constraints may limit the number of field trips and outside speakers you can offer your students.

TECHNOLOGY ALTERNATIVES

Technology offers many tools to help students perceive the relevance of course concepts and activities. To the extent that students see them as realistic, many of the experiential activities discussed in Chapter 4 can make powerful contributions to that perception—indeed, that is one of their great strengths. Using a simulator to see how course calculations fit into currency trading or to visualize a medical facility or process, using a Chat session to interact with experts and practitioners in your field, or any of the other experiential activities discussed in Chapter 4 can help students see the value of course concepts and activities in the world and therefore in their lives.

Links from course Web pages to resources on the Web can also play an important role in helping students see the relevance of course concepts and activities. Current re-

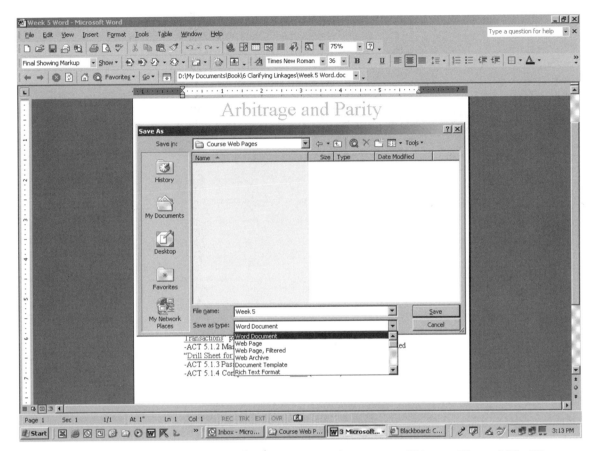

Fig. 5.20: Choosing the file type for converting a word-processing document to a Web page. Microsoft Word™ screen-shot reprinted by permission from the trademark holder, Microsoft Corporation.

search, newspaper articles and commentaries, recent statistics, government reports, annual corporate reports, and a range of other resources online are easy to access and integrate and can give students a clear understanding that class activities are the kinds of things that professionals in the field really do.

POTENTIAL PITFALLS

The concerns related to the experiential activities described in Chapter 4 are discussed there. The two main concerns in linking to Web resources in your course Web pages are:

1. That the links are good and have not changed, and
2. That the material you are linking your students to is authoritative and accurate.

The first of these concerns is similar to that discussed above with an added twist: Web pages that you do not control (to museums, governmental organizations, research

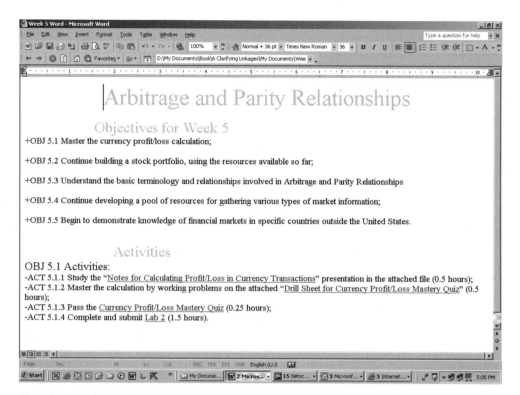

Fig. 5.21: A Web page that has been created from a word-processing document and as viewed in a word processor. Microsoft Word™ screenshot reprinted by permission from the trademark holder, Microsoft Corporation.

institutes, corporations—every link to the outside world) can change, be moved, or be removed at any time without your knowing it. Web page owners understand the importance of stability, so links—especially those to authoritative sources—do not change often, but it is something you should be aware of.

The second of these concerns relates to the fact that anyone can post anything to the Web—there is no one ensuring the authenticity and accuracy of posted material, and there is plenty of incorrect information out there. Doing your own source review is critical. Scenario 1 of Chapter 7 deals with resources for Web page source review.

SCENARIO 5: Linking Activities and Objectives to Policies and Resources

TRADITIONAL SOLUTIONS

Faculty commonly refer students to university policy on academic integrity, attendance, technology use, and other matters related to a course, hoping to make students aware of university and instructor expectations and to head off problems before they get started.

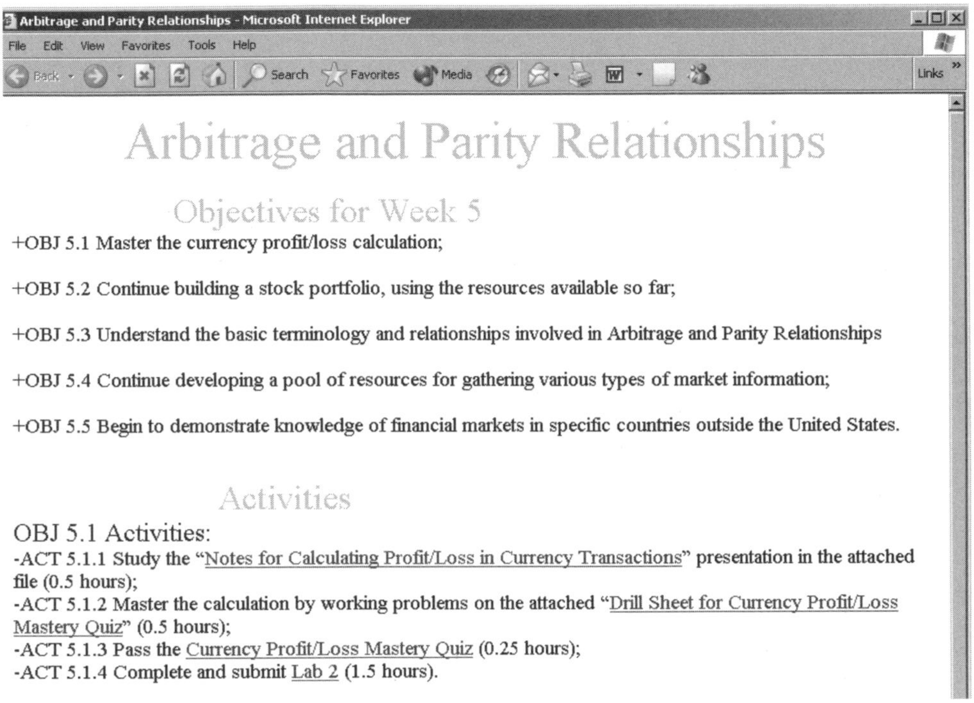

Arbitrage and Parity Relationships - Microsoft Internet Explorer
File Edit View Favorites Tools Help
Back Search Favorites Media
Links
Arbitrage and Parity Relationships
Objectives for Week 5
+OBJ 5.1 Master the currency profit/loss calculation;
+OBJ 5.2 Continue building a stock portfolio, using the resources available so far;
+OBJ 5.3 Understand the basic terminology and relationships involved in Arbitrage and Parity Relationships
+OBJ 5.4 Continue developing a pool of resources for gathering various types of market information;
+OBJ 5.5 Begin to demonstrate knowledge of financial markets in specific countries outside the United States.
Activities
OBJ 5.1 Activities:
-ACT 5.1.1 Study the "Notes for Calculating Profit/Loss in Currency Transactions" presentation in the attached file (0.5 hours);
-ACT 5.1.2 Master the calculation by working problems on the attached "Drill Sheet for Currency Profit/Loss Mastery Quiz" (0.5 hours);
-ACT 5.1.3 Pass the Currency Profit/Loss Mastery Quiz (0.25 hours);
-ACT 5.1.4 Complete and submit Lab 2 (1.5 hours).

Fig. 5.22: A Web page that has been created from a word-processing document and as viewed in a browser. Microsoft Internet Explorer™ screenshot reprinted by permission from the trademark holder, Microsoft Corporation.

Some final tips…
Always focus on the currency the XR is the price of ($ for European terms quotes and F.C. for American terms quotes) and decide whether to go long or short that currency based on whether the XR is going up or down.
Once that's done, always go ahead and write down what you are doing (going long or short) with the other currency (it's the opposite of what you're doing with the first currency
You have to begin the trading calculation with the currency you have an amount for—whether it's the first currency or the second.
NOW ON TO THE Drill Sheet for Currency Profit-Loss Mastery Quiz !

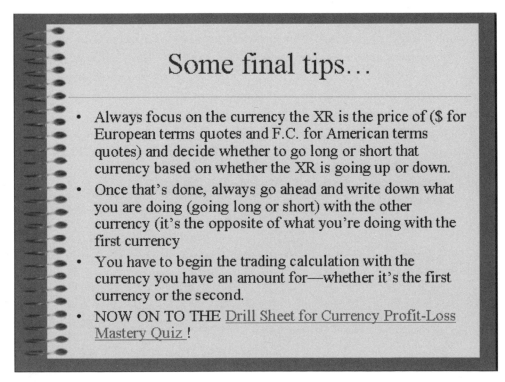

Fig. 5.23: A PowerPoint presentation with a hyperlink to the next activity to be done by the student. Microsoft PowerPoint™ screenshot reprinted by permission from the trademark holder, Microsoft Corporation.

Drill Sheet for Currency Profit-Loss Mastery Quiz

Calculating Profits							
Given a long position of	And expectations that the Exchange Rate will move from		to	Your profits will be			Answer
$	900	JPY/$	110.00	115.32	$	$	41.51
$	100	JPY/$	115.00	112.67	$	$	-2.06
$	800	SFR/$	1.4000	1.3755	$	$	-14.24
$	420	SFR/$	1.3000	1.1888	$	$	-39.28
GBP	280	$/ GBP	1.5000	1.5555	GBP	GBP	9.99
GBP	970	$/ GBP	1.5000	1.6789	GBP	GBP	103.36
AUD	800	$/AUD	0.6000	0.6798	AUD	AUD	93.91
AUD	420	$/AUD	0.7000	0.8297	AUD	AUD	65.65
NZD	570	$/NZD	0.6000	0.4444	NZD	NZD	-199.57
NZD	830	$/NZD	0.5000	0.5632	NZD	NZD	93.13
...							

Once you feel you have mastered the Currency Profit-Loss calculation, you should take the Currency Profit-Loss Mastery Quiz.

Fig. 5.24: A word-processing document with a hyperlink to the next activity to be done by the student. Microsoft Word™ screenshot reprinted by permission from the trademark holder, Microsoft Corporation.

An instructor teaching an intensive writing course, for instance, might wish to ensure that all students are aware of the university policy regarding plagiarism—and even what plagiarism is. It is not uncommon for an instructor in such a course to copy all or part of the relevant university policy into the course syllabus—or at least direct students to the pages in the student handbook in which the policy can be found.

Likewise, faculty may actively direct students to university resources, be they unusual library holdings, a learning center, or technology training sessions. These direc-

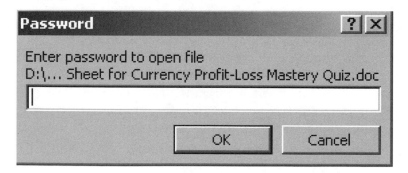

Fig. 5.25: A pop-up box allowing a student to enter a password and gain access to an assignment or activity. Microsoft Word™ screenshot reprinted by permission from the trademark holder, Microsoft Corporation.

tions may range from a paragraph in the syllabus to a class trip or to a visit from someone representing a resource, but the goal in all cases is to make students aware of, and give them access to, university-supplied resources that can help them be successful.

Whether or not you decide to make copies of university policies and resources or use class time to discuss them, you will need to make those references readily available to your students. Providing constant reinforcement and access can be effective in terms of better adherence to policy and better use of university resources, but it can be costly in terms of paper and class time used.

TECHNOLOGY ALTERNATIVES

Technology, in the form of hyperlinks, can help you introduce university policies and resources to your students, *and* help you put those policies and resources in front of your students whenever you want them to be there. Figure 5.26 shows an excerpt from a course syllabus in which the expectations of the students and the instructor are clearly laid out. One component of that statement of expectations includes reference and access (via the hyperlink) to the university's academic integrity policy. To help create a strong impression, the student is required to complete an expectations agreement (again, accessed via the hyperlink), which is simply an online quiz repeating each of the expectations as true or false questions.

Later in the semester, when students are about to hand in a major assignment, they will be reminded of the policy through the Web pages shown in figure 5.27 (again via hyperlink). This kind of just-in-time placement of reference and access can help students remember—and know that you remember—that relevant policies exist and will be enforced.

References and access to any relevant university resources can be made in syllabi and throughout course Web pages, as in figures 5.26–5.28, and they can be collected together in an announcement area (see Scenarios 1 and 2 of Chapter 1) or as course materials (see Scenarios 2 and 3 of Chapter 2).

POTENTIAL PITFALLS

As always, the most important concern when using these technology tools is making sure that your links are good and that you understand the policies and resources they link to.

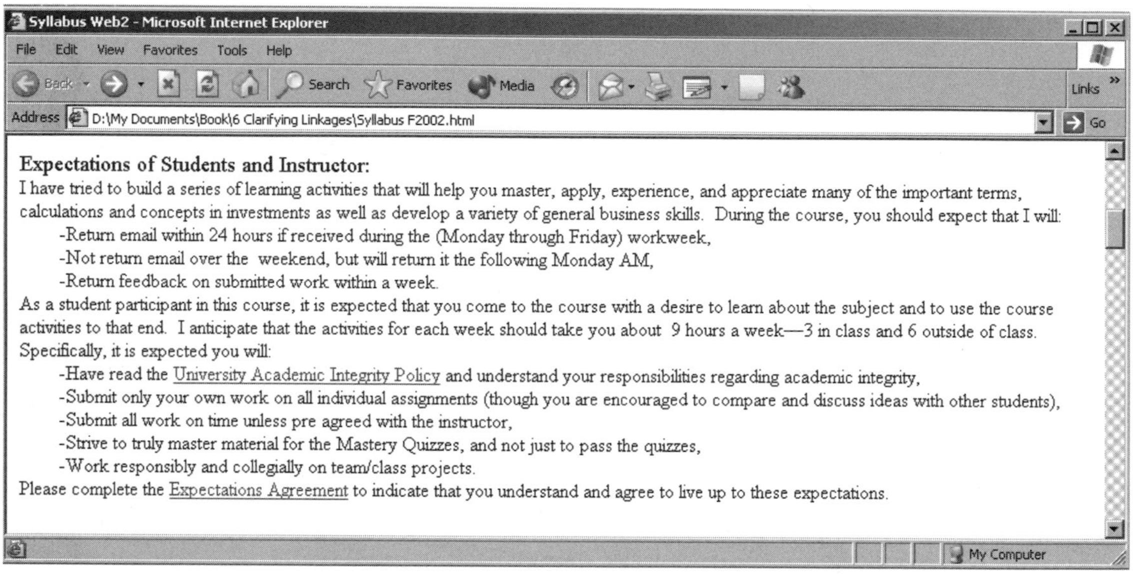

Syllabus Web2 - Microsoft Internet Explorer

File Edit View Favorites Tools Help

Address D:\My Documents\Book\6 Clarifying Linkages\Syllabus F2002.html

Expectations of Students and Instructor:

I have tried to build a series of learning activities that will help you master, apply, experience, and appreciate many of the important terms, calculations and concepts in investments as well as develop a variety of general business skills. During the course, you should expect that I will:

-Return email within 24 hours if received during the (Monday through Friday) workweek,
-Not return email over the weekend, but will return it the following Monday AM,
-Return feedback on submitted work within a week.

As a student participant in this course, it is expected that you come to the course with a desire to learn about the subject and to use the course activities to that end. I anticipate that the activities for each week should take you about 9 hours a week—3 in class and 6 outside of class. Specifically, it is expected you will:

-Have read the University Academic Integrity Policy and understand your responsibilities regarding academic integrity,
-Submit only your own work on all individual assignments (though you are encouraged to compare and discuss ideas with other students),
-Submit all work on time unless pre agreed with the instructor,
-Strive to truly master material for the Mastery Quizzes, and not just to pass the quizzes,
-Work responsibly and collegially on team/class projects.

Please complete the Expectations Agreement to indicate that you understand and agree to live up to these expectations.

My Computer

Fig. 5.26: Reference and access to the university academic integrity policy in the course syllabus. Microsoft Internet Explorer™ screenshot reprinted by permission from the trademark holder, Microsoft Corporation.

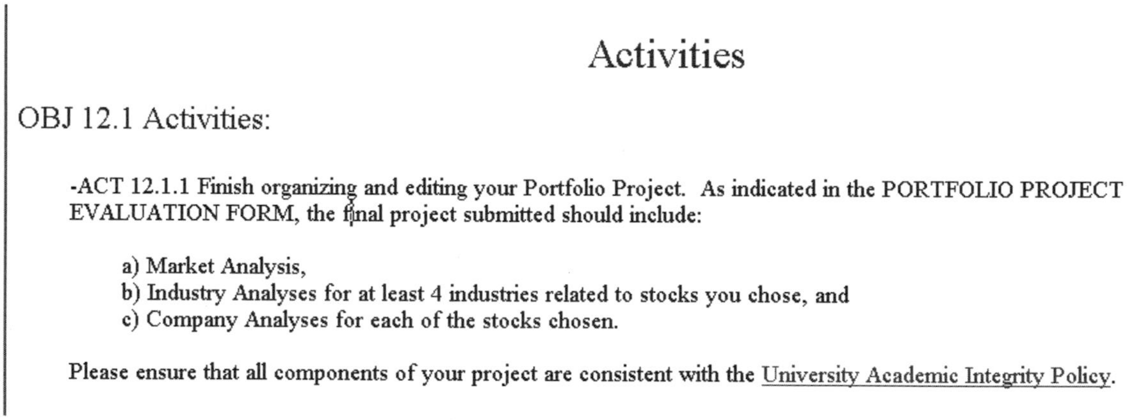

Activities

OBJ 12.1 Activities:

-ACT 12.1.1 Finish organizing and editing your Portfolio Project. As indicated in the PORTFOLIO PROJECT EVALUATION FORM, the final project submitted should include:

a) Market Analysis,
b) Industry Analyses for at least 4 industries related to stocks you chose, and
c) Company Analyses for each of the stocks chosen.

Please ensure that all components of your project are consistent with the University Academic Integrity Policy.

Fig. 5.27: Reinforcement of expectations related to the university academic integrity policy by associating reference and access to it with a course assignment

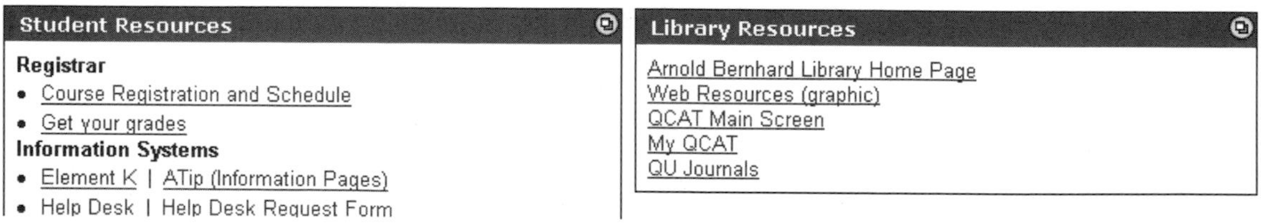

Student Resources

Registrar
- Course Registration and Schedule
- Get your grades

Information Systems
- Element K | ATip (Information Pages)
- Help Desk | Help Desk Request Form

Library Resources

Arnold Bernhard Library Home Page
Web Resources (graphic)
QCAT Main Screen
My QCAT
QU Journals

Fig. 5.28: Links to university resources can be collected together (as here) or sown throughout the course Web pages, as relevant. Property of Blackboard. Used with the permission of Blackboard.

CHAPTER 6 Improving Student Writing

SCENARIO 1: Increasing Writing Opportunities

You want your students to have more opportunity to write. Whether an essay, a summary of an article, a journal entry, or a short response, writing allows students to order and evaluate their ideas. The more your students practice writing, the more they practice thinking.

SCENARIO 2: Evaluating Writing Assignments

Your students would like more feedback than you've been able to fit into the margins of their papers—and they'd like to be able to read your handwriting.

SCENARIO 3: Collecting and Returning Writing Assignments

You often leave class with such a disheveled pile of papers that you are concerned you might have missed one. And then there are those submissions pushed under your door—did they make it into the right pile?

SCENARIO 4: Identifying Plagiarism

You have assigned a paper that requires research, and you are concerned about plagiarism.

SCENARIO 1: Increasing Writing Opportunities

TRADITIONAL SOLUTIONS

Most professors acknowledge that writing can be a powerful tool. Writing is a means by which students take responsibility for their thoughts. It forces the writer to move more slowly over new ideas, contextualizing information and testing assumptions in a way that is not done when he or she simply thinks through the information. So it would stand to reason that writing is an important link—in any discipline—for moving students toward better, deeper thinking.

Invariably, however, when we hear "more writing opportunities," we think "more time correcting and discussing student writing." Beneficial though it is, writing often loses ground to priorities like covering content. Our perception of contact time—needed to make writing a meaningful experience—often informs our decision to limit writing.

Professors know that students can smell busy work a mile away. Consequently, we think that student writing must be transactional—students invest effort in writing and earn a grade. Selling students on expressive writing—writing for the sake of thinking and not for a grade—is difficult to do. So we assign students work that we must review, grade, and discuss, thinking this to be the only way to secure a valid effort from our students. We assign work that we must take time to correct (adding to our time invested in the course outside of class time), and we discuss this work in class (taking away from time that might better be spent on new content).

Common practice has students bring to class a printed copy of their work to be read and discussed. Perhaps you would collect these essays, make copies for the entire class, and bring them to the next class meeting. Perhaps you would ask students to bring two copies to facilitate a peer review. Regardless of your method, you inevitably could be more efficient with this process. In addition, the time lag between a student's wrestling with the material or its articulation and its subsequent review in a structured environment decreases the learning opportunity. Technology can move our students closer to instruction and reflection "in the moment."

We usually see three points of contact for a student as he or she "learns." The student interacts with the professor leading the course, the student interacts with other students in the course, and the student interacts with the content of the course. Historically, each of these interactions has limitations. For example, interaction between the student and the professor occurs either in the classroom or during office hours. Nothing wrong with this so far, but often these contact times are removed from the learning opportunity. A student, given an assignment in class, attempts the assignment that evening and, during that attempt, has an insight, a question, or perhaps a problem. In most cases that student will either wait until the next class to ask for clarification or guidance, or perhaps seek out the professor during office hours, if possible. The processes of discovery, of construction, of learning are put on hold, which can drastically change the outcome. Some simple technology, readily available, can decrease this lag time, offering the opportunity for a potentially better draft in a more efficient manner. Certain applications of technology can address the less-than-efficient time between contacts, as well as provide management tools to collect and store this valuable interaction derived from the contacts.

TECHNOLOGY ALTERNATIVES

Using Email

After presenting new material, you want students to engage individually with it. So you assign a short writing assignment that they must bring to the next class meeting, during which you will discuss it. So far, the process does not really provide an alternative. Many of us do this without technology. However, this process takes time. If we mean to discuss the writing, we often must collect it, copy it, and then disseminate it to the whole class, all of which can take more than one class period. In a better instance, we should be acting while the questions and discussion are still fresh. Email, whether institutional or commercial, offers a variety of uses, from generating current examples of student work for teaching tools to allowing more contact time with and among students.

Immediate Reinforcement

Faculty can take advantage of their students' learning opportunities through some simple use of Email. Ask students, at the close of the class, to send you a paragraph that discusses the most important or perhaps the most confusing point made in class that day. The simple acts of review and summary help students engage with the concepts presented in class. In addition, you can build from these submissions to make the next class more relevant to the work the students have done on their own.

Generating Contextual Examples

Students can send you a copy of their work prior to the next class, enabling you to make enough copies to bring to class. If it is a short assignment, you can create one document by cutting and pasting from the various submissions you receive. Now you can bring enough copies for everyone to review without taking two or three class meetings to do so. There are several ways to bring current examples to support your next lecture or learning objective:

- Copy the entire essay/assignment
- Cut and paste portions of individual submissions

You can bring paper copies to class, or you can Email files back to your class (singly or via an Email **Distribution List**) so students can print them out and bring them to class.

Sending Examples

In addition, you can further enhance contact time and engagement by returning examples to your class and asking students for their review. Depending on your objective, you can reinforce material discussed in the previous class or frontload discussion for the coming class. Simply save the sample/example in the appropriate format (Word, Excel, Power-Point), and attach it to an Email that you send back to your students. You have the ability to send the same example to all you students through your distribution list, or you can send individual examples to individual students. They read a forwarded piece, review it, and are better prepared for the coming class.

More Feedback

Email also offers the student more chances for feedback on his or her own writing. Traditionally we assign a writing task that is due no earlier than the next class; often the student has more time than that. A student seeking input or review of his or her work would have to bring that writing to you for review and comments.

But by using Email, your student has better, more convenient access to you. The professor shares this convenience as well. For example, on Monday you assign a one-page response that will be due Wednesday. Traditionally, your students would bring their work to Wednesday's class, you would collect it, review it, and bring it to Friday's class to discuss and return. You may even copy a few examples to hand out and discuss in class. By the time the writing is returned, the ideas are cold, the process of writing and thinking disrupted.

Using Email, your students can send you an Email message, attaching the file containing their writing, as soon as they have finished it. You, at your convenience, open the message and the file. Then you can comment directly in the file before you, typing your comments and suggestions directly on the student's page (see Scenario 2). Having finished, you save the document (a simple click of the icon on the top of the screen) and send the file back to the student.

Early Submission

You can also build early submission into the process, whereby a student can submit work for your review prior to a deadline. This kind of review and feedback can direct students even as they work independently, ensuring a better experience for all. Develop a policy whereby students know the limitations of sending material for review. (Don't find yourself with eighteen assignments for your review two hours before class begins.) They will send writing via Email, and you can review, comment on (see the next scenario on evaluating student writing), and return it in time for your students to revise and submit before the due date. Email submission and response can keep your students closer to their learning opportunities. Instead of a four- to five-day turn-around, you could have the assignment reviewed and returned well before the next class meeting.

We already know that your comments, considered during the revision process, can make a significant impact on the students' writing. If a student can consider your comments that much sooner, closer to the act of composing the assignment, the material is more relevant, more useable. In addition, earlier review and revision also mean that more opportunities for writing can be incorporated into the writing assignment.

Collection and Archiving

Email also allows you to keep a record of your students' submissions. Depending on the application you use, you may also be able to maintain a record of your responses to them. These records can be helpful during conferencing and can help provide a history of a student's development. To collect and archive your students' submissions you may consider a series of folders, as discussed in Scenario 2. To find a record of your responses to your students, review the file options in your Email.

Using a Drop Box

If you are using a course management system, your students should have access to a **Drop Box** where they can leave files for you. (In Blackboard, it's called a Digital Drop Box.) It can be accessed through the Tools icon on the student's course page, as seen in figure 6.1. Students, after logging in to their course page, can use this option to leave assignments for your collection and review. This option can be used much the same way you use Email.

After clicking on the Digital Drop Box icon, students will use the next screen, seen in figure 6.2, to post the file.

Creating a title can be very important for both faculty and student. The order of the files is based on the time they are submitted. Once students begin turning in several assignments whose due dates overlap, you will realize the importance of titling a file. Clear directions to students regarding the title format lessen the frustration of searching for a specific file later on. You might consider the assignment name—Essay 1—and certainly a further qualifier if you expect more than one Essay 1, perhaps "Essay 1 drf1."

Students can locate the correct file by clicking on the Browse button. This function allows them to search their own computer's memory for the correct file. Once they select the correct file, they can follow the submission process laid out for them. Once the file has been submitted to the Drop Box, you can access the file by clicking on the link (figure 6.3).

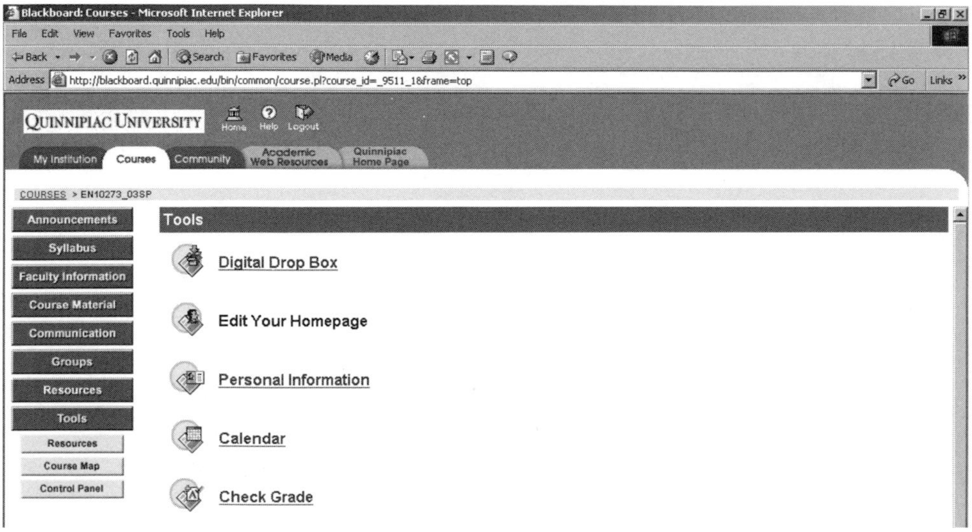

Fig. 6.1: A view of the Tools page in Blackboard. Property of Blackboard. Used with the permission of Blackboard. Microsoft Internet Explorer™ screenshot reprinted by permission from the trademark holder, Microsoft Corporation.

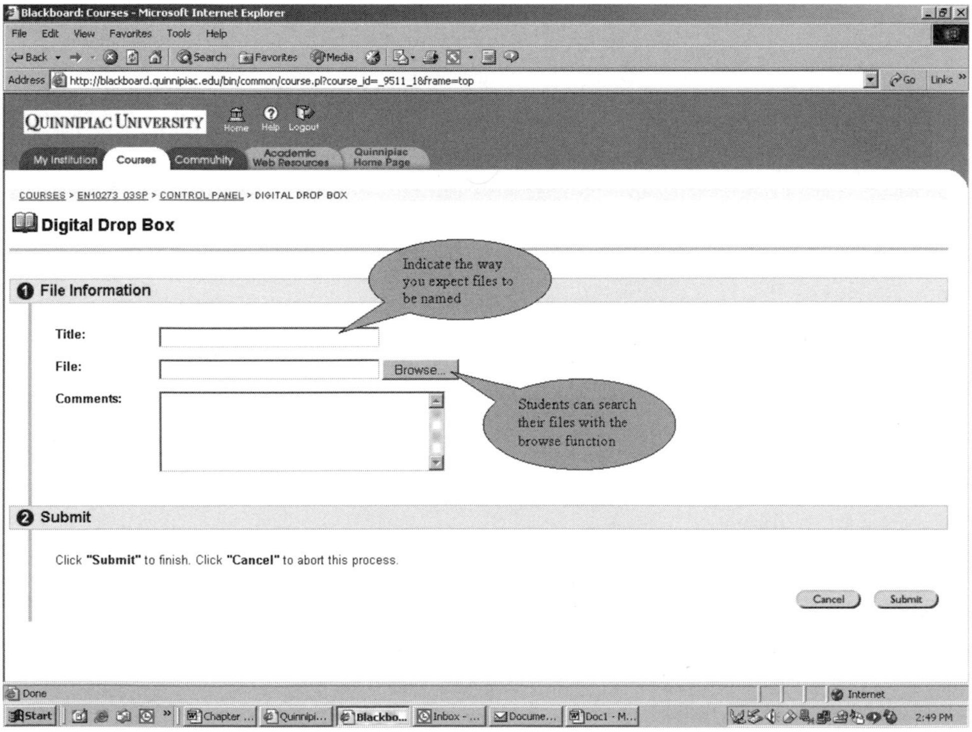

Fig. 6.2: Placing a file in the Drop Box. Property of Blackboard. Used with the permission of Blackboard. Microsoft Internet Explorer™ screenshot reprinted by permission from the trademark holder, Microsoft Corporation.

Fig. 6.3: Accessing the file in the Drop Box. Property of Blackboard. Used with the permission of Blackboard. Microsoft Internet Explorer™ screenshot reprinted by permission from the trademark holder, Microsoft Corporation.

When using a submission folder, one difference to consider is the manner in which you save the files. With institutional Email you can create a series of folders named and organized to suit your needs. In these folders you save the various Email messages with the files attached or the text embedded in the message, as discussed in Scenario 2.

With a submission folder provided by a course management system, students send the file and not an Email. Consequently, if you intend to save a student's submission you will need to save the file in the appropriate software program, not to your Email folder. For example, if your students are sending you an essay written in Microsoft Word, you will have to create a series of folders in your Word application in which to save these submissions. If you want to save the student's work to your own folder, select the Save As function under the File button on the toolbar, and then select the folder from the browse screen (figures 6.4 and 6.5).

Ease of access should be considered when creating and organizing these folders. You may find it useful to create a folder for each assignment, given the number of students in that class, as seen in figure 6.6. In addition, you may consider creating a folder series for each section you teach.

Writing in Class

Technology really has affected the ability of faculty to manipulate in-class writing. Students can more easily compose, edit, and share their work than they may have using traditional methods. Historically, classes began to be scheduled in computer labs to provide each student with computer access during class time. Faculty leading these classes would cruise the room, assisting students as need arose. Students could save their work to a disc or perhaps to space provided to them on the university's server. This method succeeded

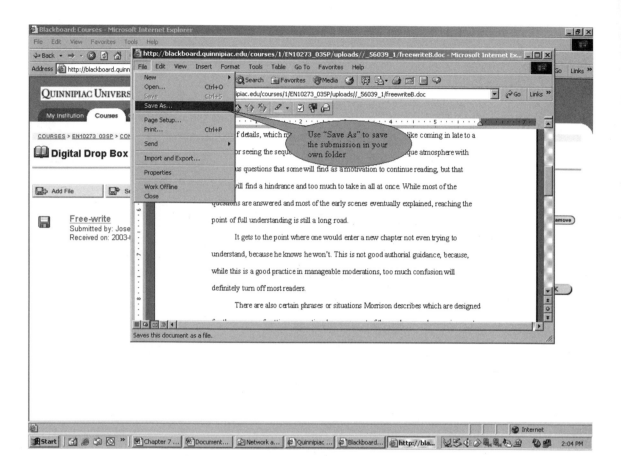

Fig. 6.4: Finding the Save As function in Microsoft Word. Property of Blackboard. Used with the permission of Blackboard. Microsoft Internet Explorer™ screenshot reprinted by permission from the trademark holder, Microsoft Corporation.

because direction and support could be offered at the best time, closest to the learning opportunity. The pitfall, of course, was that students continued to work in relative isolation. The next step has been to include mobile computer carts, a wireless station laden with enough laptop computers for the whole class. The technology presented here allows students to network in class, sending copies of their work to their peers and to their instructors in real time, creating opportunity for discussion in class, whether that discussion is out loud or online. Now, as perhaps the next step, many universities are adopting a policy that mandates laptop computers for all entering students and includes developing a wireless environment, allowing linked access across campus.

Again, the opportunity exists to adopt as little or as much as you might like. The degree to which you may use this technology, however, is informed by how you are supported in the classroom.

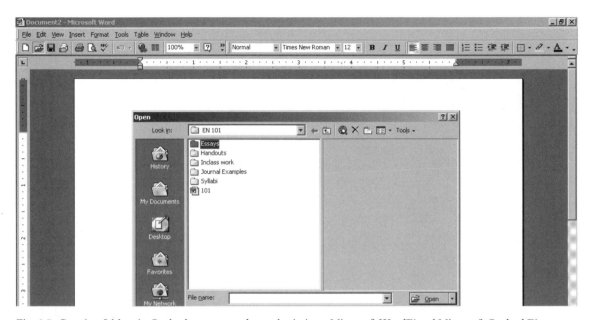

Fig. 6.5: Creating folders in Outlook to save student submissions. Microsoft Word™ and Microsoft Outlook™ screen-shot reprinted by permission from the trademark holder, Microsoft Corporation.

Revising and Comparing Drafts

In the early stages of using technology as a part of writing in class, you should consider spending some time modeling the processes you expect your students to perform. As your students become more comfortable with the technology and with your expectations, you can have them do more out of class. Your ability to provide support in the beginning of this process is very important. Students will embrace the process better if they can raise their hands and ask you a question. An easy way to start is by asking them to bring a draft of their assignment to class.

Students can access a copy of their work in several ways. They may bring it with them on a disc. If the campus is networked, they can access it from their server space. If they can get to the Internet, they can retrieve a copy they sent to themselves by Email. If you are using a course management system, they can begin a thread in the discussion board with the file attached.

Once they access the file, you can begin. You may consider asking students to review the coherence or organization of their essay. A simple way to begin is by using the copy and paste functions. Ask students to open a new file and name it according to its relationship to the file containing the draft. Then ask them to minimize both screens so that they can easily navigate between them. Ask them to identify the thesis in the introduction, copy it, and paste it to the new file. Returning to the original draft, ask them to identify

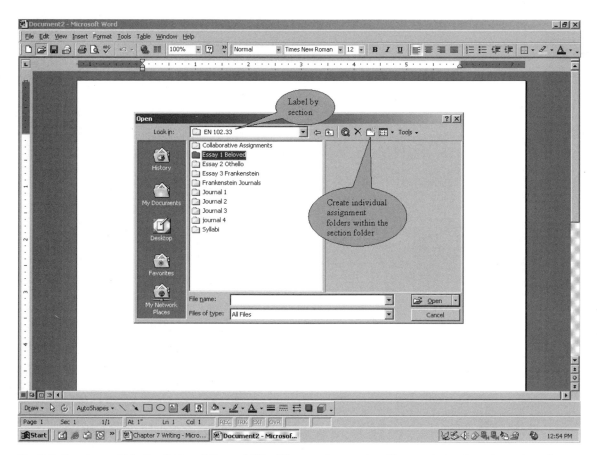

Fig. 6.6: Creating and labeling folders. Microsoft Word™ screenshot reprinted by permission from the trademark holder, Microsoft Corporation.

the topic sentences, copy each and paste them, in order, into the new document. Then ask them to repeat the process with the restated thesis from the conclusion. Having finished, ask them to read what they have copied to the new document for coherence. Seeing the organizational aspects of the essay in isolation provides a new perspective for these writers.

Another possibility for review is the use of the **Find** function. This function allows you to look through the open document for a specific word. To access this function pull down the Edit menu and highlight Find as seen in figure 6.7. You might consider asking students to look for all occurrences of the word "is" in their essay and decide if their choice of verbs is appropriate or if they should look for another verb to better convey their intent. The Find function will identify each occurrence of the word in the document, as seen in figure 6.8.

Find—a feature of word-processing and other applications in which the user types in a string of letters and/or numbers (a word, phrase, number, etc.) that can be found in each occurrence within the file (e.g., a document) to which the search is being applied

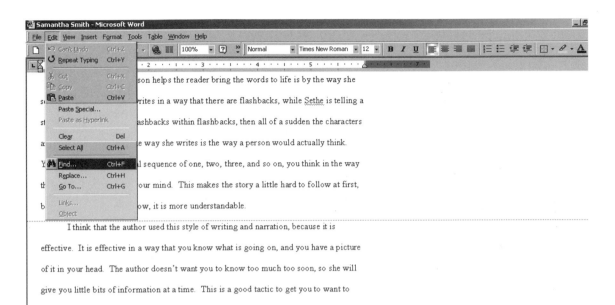

Fig. 6.7: Accessing the Find function in Microsoft Word. Microsoft Word™ screenshot reprinted by permission from the trademark holder, Microsoft Corporation.

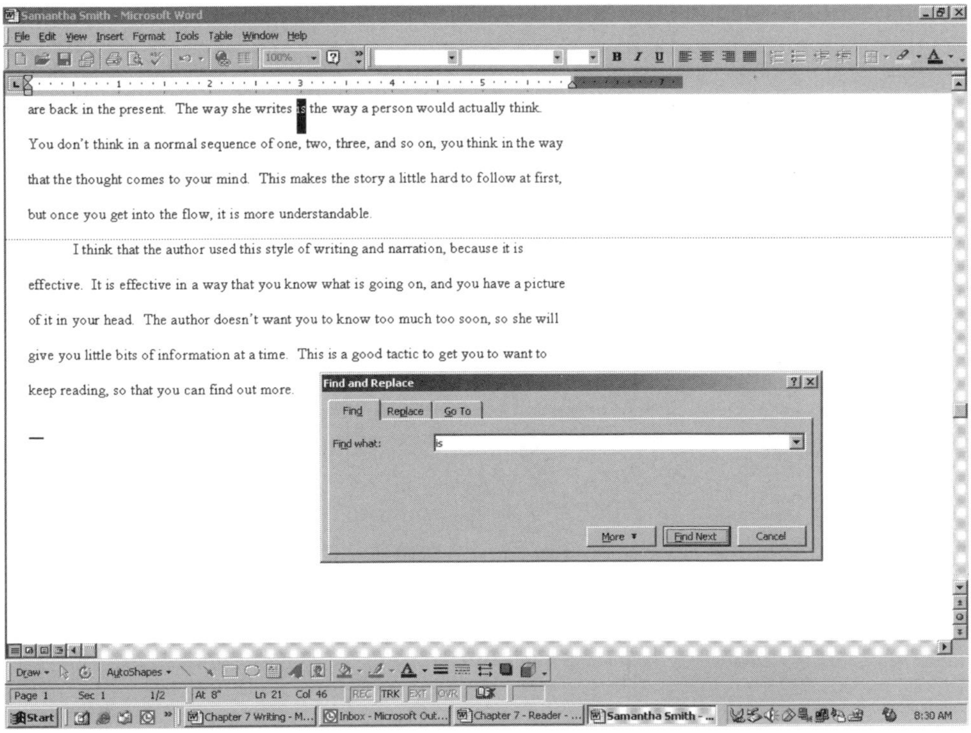

Fig. 6.8: Using the Find function. Microsoft Word™ screenshot reprinted by permission from the trademark holder, Microsoft Corporation.

Projection

The use of an LCD projector allows you to project what you see on the screen of your computer onto a screen or wall. Combined with the Emailing of files, this device can help you revise the way you deal with handouts and in-class instruction. These projectors are versatile, being small and relatively user-friendly. Used with your own laptop they help you model composing, revising, and editing in a way that creates a powerful message. Students can watch your thinking process as seen through the words you type on your own screen.

A good use of this technology incorporates current student submissions. As you read through your students' work, you get an idea of what you should be reinforcing in class. If you have been asking your students to submit electronic copies of their work, you can review what you have, looking for writing that will support your next class. You can project examples from the previous assignment for the entire class to view, modeling the skills and strategies you expect them to employ as they review their own work. You might consider using the tools discussed in Scenario 2 of this chapter to focus their attention on specific aspects of the example.

Another advantage to this process is your ability to send your example to your students' Email accounts. Having made your points and perhaps having left a trail of notes and highlighting for them to follow, you can Email the document, either as an attachment or as a message, as seen in figure 6.9. Click on the File button and then highlight Send To. Either of the first two choices will allow you to send the example. This process will be easiest if you have already created your distribution list, which you can access after you have chosen the Send function.

Peer-Reviewed Assignments

Many instructors acknowledge that peer review is a good method for accomplishing several things. (See Chapter 3 for more ideas on promoting collaboration among your students, and Scenario 2 of Chapter 8 for more on peer assessment.) Students, applying skills and information garnered from lectures and exercises, develop these skills as they evaluate someone else's work. Students also can get an idea of what their peers are doing, perhaps giving inspiration or confidence to the reviewer. Well-structured peer review is also a good way to place more of the responsibility of learning on students.

Done the wrong way, peer review can be cumbersome. Collecting papers in one class, copying them between class, and returning at the next class with yet more copies of papers to hand out can cure many people of using peer review. Add to that the class period needed to conduct the review, and faculty may not find it useful. Peer review, when structured well, can continue to help students. Peer review, using technology, can decrease faculty workload and free up class time as well.

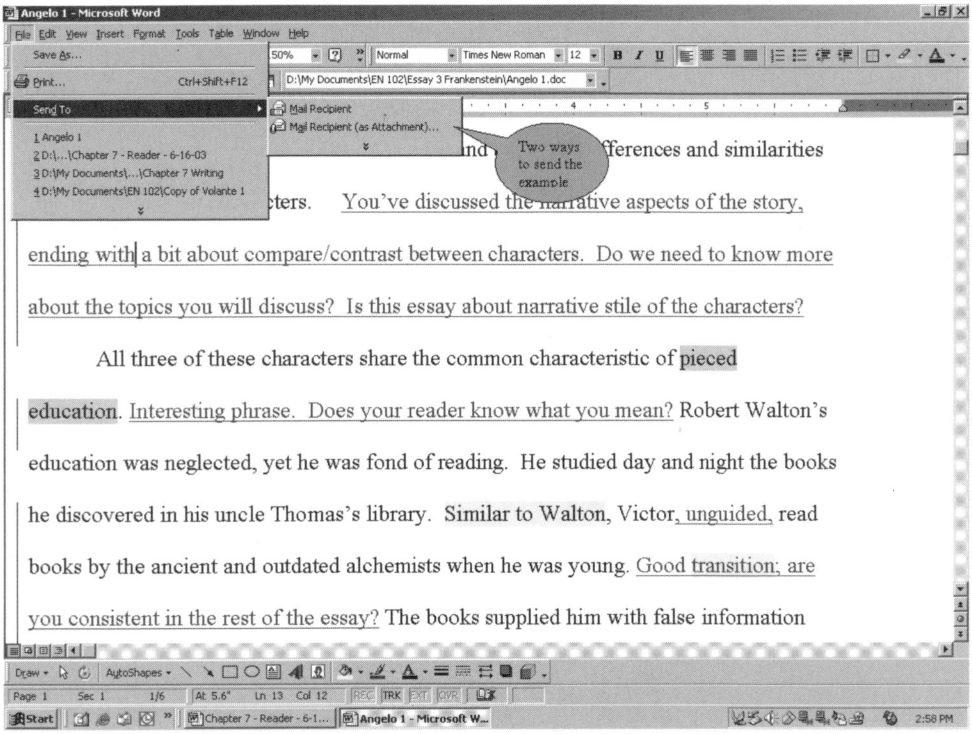

Fig. 6.9: Finding the Send options in Microsoft Word. Microsoft Word™ screenshot reprinted by permission from the trademark holder, Microsoft Corporation.

Giving students a clear idea of expectations is necessary for this process to have validity. You may choose to conduct one review in class, addressing process questions as they occur. This sets a benchmark for students not used to evaluating the work of others and using the tools you have been discussing in class. A checklist of issues or a list of questions is helpful.

Using Email for Peer Review

Once your students know your expectations, ask that the review be completed online. Students can do this work on their own time, which will open up more time in class. You can also ask that when the reviewer returns the review to the writer, you be **Cc'd** so that you have a copy for your records. This allows you to make sure that the student reviewers are performing to expectations. A reviewer not addressing the issues you need examined, or addressing them in the wrong manner, provides an excellent teaching opportunity.

Getting the copies to the students no longer requires a trip to the copy machine. A simple method for distributing essays is to assign students to groups (three

Cc'd—when a person besides the primary recipient of an Email message is also sent the message, that secondary person is said to be "copied" on the Email correspondence (based on the idea of the carbon copy)

Thread—a posting identifying a primary component or aspect of a subject being discussed in a threaded discussion, along with all replies and subsequent postings related to that original posting

is a good number), making sure that students know who is in their group. Ask that the writer send his or her paper to each of the other group members. This can be done by attaching the file to an Email message or by making a copy of the text of the paper and then pasting it into the message portion of the Email, as shown in figure 6.9. A longer assignment lends itself to attachment, while a shorter assignment is easily incorporated into the text of the Email. To diminish potential frustration, ask the reviewer to place his or her remarks within the text of the sample, and then to return that sample to the writer. If you intend to use the functions mentioned in Scenario 2 you may consider investing some class time to show students how these functions are used. A little class time spent modeling these evaluation functions can improve the peer-review process and can mitigate questions that arise from your evaluations of the students' papers.

Using a Discussion Thread for Peer Review

Many course management systems, like Blackboard and WebCT, offer discussion boards. A discussion board allows students to post messages to a specific place that can be accessed by other students in the class. This discussion board can be developed to serve a variety of objectives, such as providing a place to post questions about class or responses to a question posed in class. Students can follow the discussion **Thread**, posting comments about the comments, answering the previous question from their own perspective, or posing new questions as information is shared and processed. In addition, each posting is recorded in order, so that viewers can follow the history of the conversation.

The responses are organized by indentation. The tab indicates the response's rela-

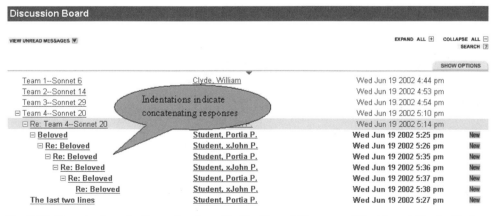

Fig. 6.10: Organization of a discussion thread in Blackboard. Property of Blackboard. Used with the permission of Blackboard.

tionship to those above it. A running commentary, a series of responses one after another, may look like a descending staircase. Students here are responding to the previous response and not to the original thread. Responses to the same thread, however, are indented the same distance, in relationship to that thread. Examples can be seen in figure 6.10. More detailed information regarding threaded discussions can be found in Scenario 1 of Chapter 1.

Using the discussion thread as a writing tool has a variety of benefits. It provides a history of the conversation. Students can review these threads for insight into issues they are resolving. They can ask questions of their peers, and they can review samples that others post. Faculty can review the work contributed to these threads, looking for insight from various responses. Reviewing the material posted by students can inform the direction of subsequent classes. The recurrence of a particular question may merit attention during class, or even the redevelopment of an assignment.

POTENTIAL PITFALLS

The biggest challenge here is good organization. Take the time to organize your Email folders. Nothing is more frustrating than scrolling through folder after folder looking for the file you know you have seen. Taking the time to develop a good system will pay off in the end. Even though you can ask your student to resend the message, looking for the errant Email and attached file can be frustrating. Label your discussion threads clearly. You should also consider modeling the process for your students prior to assigning responses.

Consider posting your own replies to threads. Students will take more away from the experience if they know you are following and participating. A bit of guidance or praise can provide motivation. If you are using Email, consider sending examples of good responses to the entire class.

Make sure you respond to reviews in a timely fashion. If you decide to offer students the opportunity to submit material for review before the deadline, you must monitor your Email. A student who submits material early can become disheartened by the lack of a timely response. Your response to this process will dictate the degree to which students do or do not validate it.

Better access can be a double-edged sword. While you have better access to your students, they have better access to you. Be aware that your workload could actually increase, depending on how often you review your students' work and to what depth you review it. You may consider incorporating some expressive (rather than transactional) writing into your assignments. The students will still derive the benefit of writing, but you will have less prose to grade. You should also consider assigning more self- and peer evaluation. Take the time to help students understand your expectations and model some means to achieve them early in the semester.

Invest in your own training time and then practice. Just as you have taken time to learn some aspects of the software you use, take the time to make an appointment with your media services or audiovisual staff to learn how to use the projector. A little time spent with staff and then a bit more practicing on your own is worth the effort. Once you know the right icons to push, use of this technology is quite easy. Consider also keeping your skills sharp. Review the technology you want to use before you walk into class.

SCENARIO 2: Evaluating Writing Assignments

TRADITIONAL SOLUTIONS

The writing assignment . . . a task often viewed with similar angst by student and faculty alike, much of it caused by the evaluation process. Students emphasize the product over the process, often waiting until the night before to do the assignment. What most of them want is not just a grade but detailed feedback—though it's hard for them to be excited when they receive papers back with red writing all over them. Faculty dread the pile they will be collecting when the assignment is due, only to break out the red pen and sequester themselves for the duration.

TECHNOLOGY ALTERNATIVES

Using the Change Tracking Function

Change Tracking allows you to make comments directly in the text of the student's writing. You can make suggestions or clarifications within the text itself, guiding the student response in the appropriate direction. Your comments will appear in a different color type. There are two ways to access the Tracking function:

1. Pull down the Tools menu, highlight Track Changes, and a pop-up will offer you some choices. Within the pop-up, Options will offer you format changes regarding colors of the texts. Red is helpful for deleted text and blue for inserted text (your comments).
2. If you have already set your options, you can double-click TRK at the bottom of the page (second row from the bottom). TRK looks darker than the other options when it is engaged.

See figures 6.11, 6.12, and 6.13.

USING THE HIGHLIGHT FUNCTION

To draw attention to specific information in a sentence or a paragraph, you might consider using the Highlight function.

This function and the tracking function allow you to focus the student's attention

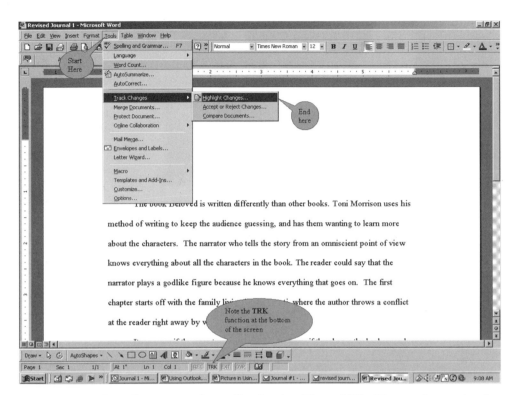

Fig. 6.11: Using the toolbar to set up the tracking function. Microsoft Word™ screenshot reprinted by permission from the trademark holder, Microsoft Corporation.

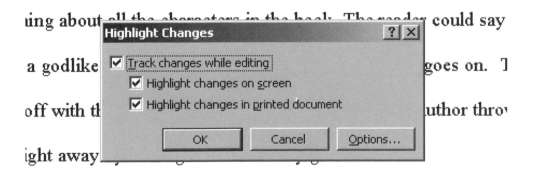

Fig. 6.12: Setting up the Tracking display. Microsoft Word™ screenshot reprinted by permission from the trademark holder, Microsoft Corporation.

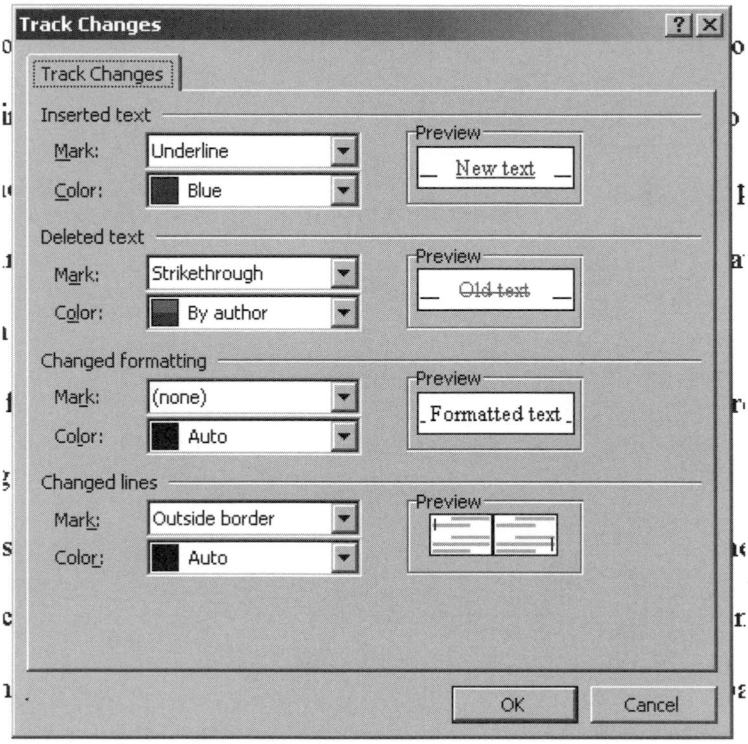

Fig. 6.13: Setting up the colors for Tracking. Microsoft Word™ screenshot reprinted by permission from the trademark holder, Microsoft Corporation.

Fig. 6.14: Finding the Highlight function in Microsoft Word. Microsoft Word™ screenshot reprinted by permission from the trademark holder, Microsoft Corporation.

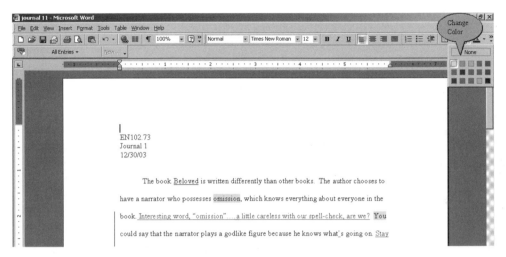

Fig. 6.15: Changing the Highlight color. Microsoft Word™ screenshot reprinted by permission from the trademark holder, Microsoft Corporation.

and to use few descriptors in the inserted text (figure 6.14). Highlighting diminishes ambiguity, building a better bridge between your comments and the student's text.

You can change the color of the highlight function by clicking on the arrow to its right. I usually begin with yellow, and I add colors as needed. An example can be seen in figure 6.15.

USING THE COMMENT FUNCTION

When there is much to say about a student's writing, you can use the **Comment** or annotation function (figure 6.16). This allows you to make significant comments within the context of the student's writing. While very useful, the Comment function requires more time to place your comments and more time for the student to assimilate the information.

There are two ways to insert comments:

1. The first is rather easy but requires an extra click. Remember to place your cursor where you want to insert the comment. You can also highlight (left-click and drag) as much text as you like, which allows you to highlight the prose you are discussing in the comment. Having placed the cursor or highlighting, pull down Insert and select Comment, as shown in figure 6.17.

2. The second method requires you to add some icons to your Toolbar. Some initial effort is required, but I find having the icon on the toolbar reduces the number of clicks overall. Pull down the View menu, then highlight Toolbars to get to Reviewing. Figure 6.18 shows how to access this toolbar.

> **Comment**—a feature (also called Annotation) available on most word processors that allows the reader of a document to insert suggestions or comments as a bubble or margin note that does not disrupt the flow of the original document

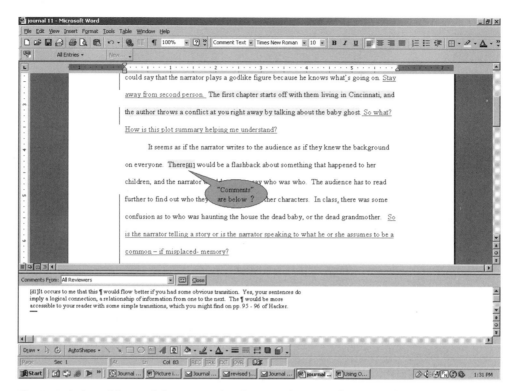

Fig. 6.16: A view of the word document using the Insert Comment function. Microsoft Word™ screenshot reprinted by permission from the trademark holder, Microsoft Corporation.

One click on Reviewing will add another line of icons to your toolbar. This toolbar offers many new gadgets, but the icon that inserts comments is the most useful for the purpose of this scenario. Once you have added this set of icons to your screen, it will take fewer clicks to insert comments.

Having added these icons, you now can place your cursor at the appropriate place in the document and click. This action indicates the placement of the comment (the place

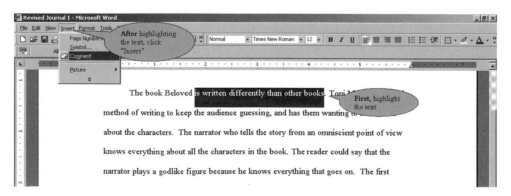

Fig. 6.17 Using the Comment function from the Insert menu in Microsoft Word. Microsoft Word™ screenshot reprinted by permission from the trademark holder, Microsoft Corporation.

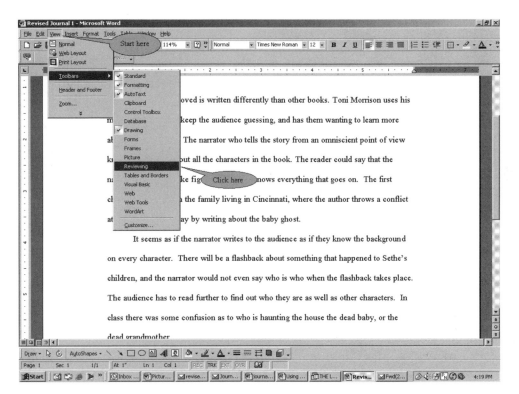

Fig. 6.18: Adding the Reviewing toolbar to your screen. Microsoft Word™ screenshot reprinted by permission from the trademark holder, Microsoft Corporation.

should be marked by a blinking vertical line). Having set the place to insert the comment, you can select the Insert Comment icon, one of the icons you have just added to your toolbar. This icon is shown in figure 6.19.

An added feature of this toolbar configuration is that you can choose the format for returning the evaluated text to the student. You can embed the text in an Email message using the Email icon, or you can send the file as an attachment to the Email message; these options are seen in figure 6.20.

POTENTIAL PITFALLS

Remember to save the document. If you don't save the document prior to sending it, you will lose all the work you did. This is especially important if you want to keep a copy of your comments for your own records. A simple click on the Save icon will save you a great deal of frustration.

Students will appreciate structure. Consider using specific colors for specific responses. If you are highlighting a grammatical error, perhaps red will send the right message. If you are calling a student's attention to a good word choice, consider another color, perhaps green.

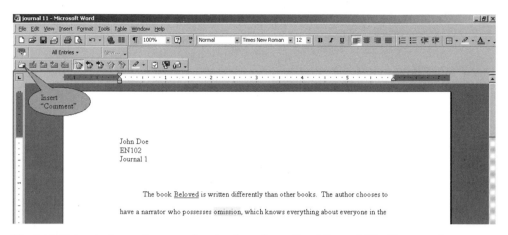

Fig. 6.19: Using the Insert Comment function from the toolbar. Microsoft Word™ screenshot reprinted by permission from the trademark holder, Microsoft Corporation.

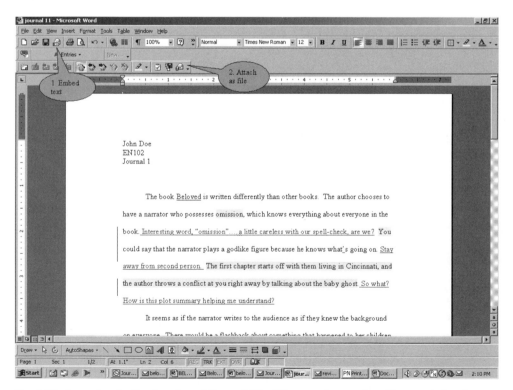

Fig. 6.20: Accessing the Send options. Microsoft Word™ screenshot reprinted by permission from the trademark holder, Microsoft Corporation.

If you are using the Insert Comment function, consider using a different color for your highlighting. Using the same color for highlighting that is used to highlight the comment can create confusion.

SCENARIO 3: Collecting and Returning Writing Assignments

The issues associated with collecting and accounting for student assignments are treated in Scenarios 4 and 5 of Chapter 1.

SCENARIO 4: Identifying Plagiarism

A good deal of our concern about plagiarism is informed by our sense of how easy it is to surf the Web, find information, and then cut and paste the text into a Word document. Couple this with the student who is used to downloading "shareware," MP3 music files, and video files, without a clear understanding of or respect for issues of intellectual property and ownership, and we tend to be a bit concerned.

TRADITIONAL SOLUTIONS

We ask that copies of the resources be turned in with the final draft. We ask that students submit annotated bibliographies. Then we sit down and begin our comparisons. Or do we? It may be that we look at resources only when we sense a change in coherence, in diction, in the level of thought that the paper presents. Do we really check all our students' sources, or do we check only when we perceive a problem?

In reality, we can search as easily as our students can. We also have the advantage because we know a bit more about the content and can define the criteria for the sources they will use. With the Web, we also can get an idea of the material out there with a few clicks of the mouse.

TECHNOLOGY ALTERNATIVES

Perform a Web search

The more you read your students' writing, the more you come to know their styles. If you assign writing often and early, you will no doubt notice a phrase or perhaps even a word that seems out of place for a particular student. If this occurs, two options present themselves when using the Web as a resource.

Consider searching the Web using the word or phrase that caught your attention. Often a search using a phrase set in quotation marks can yield results. You should experiment with the various engines available. Google has often proved to be a good first response for researching potential plagiarism issues. Simply access the browser's site—http://www.google.com/—and type in a phrase from the suspect material. Some surfing

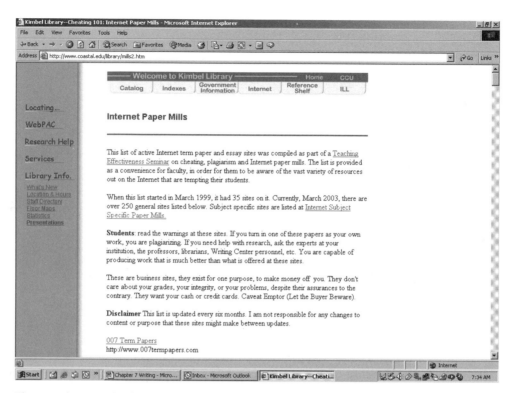

Fig. 6.21: An example of a page listing paper mills. Used with permission of Margaret Fain, Kimbel Library, Coastal Carolina University. Microsoft Internet Explorer™ screenshot reprinted by permission from the trademark holder, Microsoft Corporation.

may be necessary, but most students have not developed an understanding of Boolean logic, making our jobs a bit easier.

Consider also searching the Web from the student's perspective. Try a few key words of the assignment in various combinations with other information pertinent to the assignment. This information may include author or poet's name, the kind of criticism being researched, or a relevant historical word. For example, "Morrison and narrative" or "Morrison and point of view" incorporate the name of the primary text's author and key words of the assignment.

Paper Mills

Of concern to faculty may be a service offered to Web browsers. Thinly veiled as resources for "research," these Web sites offer commentary on various literary works, such as discussion of plot development or thematic content, and character analysis. Then, for a subscription fee, users can have access to essays that are intended to help with research, essays that can be quickly downloaded. Perform a quick search of your own with the key words "paper mill" or "essay." You will see that many lists have been compiled and posted by educators who want to make others aware of these sites. Such a site can be seen in figure 6.21.

By way of sensitizing your students to the perils of using a paper mill, you may consider telling them you are aware of these sites, and perhaps even post the URLs. Once you have made students aware that you know of the sites, they may be less tempted to use the material in an inappropriate manner. You may go further by taking the time to debunk the sites and the "free" material they contain. In most cases, careful consideration of your assignment can result in a topic specific to your class's progress. A topic developed through linked assignments or from the dialogue created among your students is usually more idiosyncratic than the topics explicated in these generic essays from paper mills.

Web-Based Services

You might also consider using one of the several plagiarism detection software packages. These services generally are grouped into two types, each of which requires you to submit a copy of the essay. One type will search the Web for word strings similar to those found in the file you submitted. The other will compare the text of the essay with the essays it has in its essay pool. Some sites are beginning to offer both resources. Interestingly, a question of copyright has arisen in using a service that offers its own database as a resource. Many services of this type will add the material that you are sending for comparison to their database, thus increasing their resource. The question arising is one of ownership. Some argue that the material belongs to the student, which could impact copyright. Others argue that the student waives his or her "ownership" in responding to an assignment. The issue is still being defined in practice and in law. Hoping to explain this issue, most plagiarism services have information posted to their Web sites that discusses ownership issues.

These sites are becoming increasingly more complex. In addition to plagiarism detection, some of these sites offer other services that are not unlike some of the tools offered by course management systems. These include peer review and portfolio options. You may consider reviewing some of these sites if your institution does not offer a course management system. For a partial listing of the sites, refer to the Appendix. Many of these services offer Web-based trials. You can use the service for a limited period or for a limited number of searches to see if it meets your needs.

POTENTIAL PITFALLS

Reviewing the material generated by your Web searches may be quite time consuming. One feature that may help is the Find function, located in the Edit menu. The Find function helps you skim documents, looking for specific words or phrases.

Some paper mills require subscription for access to essays. These essays are not accessible to nonsubscribers and consequently may not show up in a Web search you might perform.

The Web-based programs, while often exhaustive, look for matches—words, phrases, sentences. They do not distinguish among different ways in which the student may have used the repeated information. Consequently, even though a student may have cited the information correctly, the service will still identify it. Take the time to compare the report with the student's original submission.

CHAPTER 7 Developing Student Research Skills

SCENARIO 1: "I Can't Find Any/Enough Information"

After researching the topic you've assigned, your students claim they can't find enough information.

SCENARIO 2: Poor Source Review

Even before your students claimed to be Web-savvy, the sources they chose to use were too pedestrian or, in some cases, not academically appropriate. Now that they are using the Web for searching, their choices seem to be getting worse.

SCENARIO 3: Encouraging Higher-Order Thinking

Your students are becoming better at responding with their own ideas, but you want them to develop the skills to evaluate the ideas of others.

SCENARIO 4: Reviewing Progress

You've assigned a topic for research, and you've asked that students check in with you to discuss sources. They can come to office hours or see you after class, but many of their questions arise at a time when they have no access to you.

SCENARIO 5: Helping Students Avoid Plagiarism

With the ease of cutting and pasting, and an environment that nurtured Napster, you are increasingly concerned about your students' understanding of plagiarism.

SCENARIO 1: "I Can't Find Any/Enough Information"

TRADITIONAL SOLUTIONS

Many of the traditional solutions employed to address poor source review are applicable to this scenario as well. Reviewing student work, both in and out of class, helps students understand the instructor's expectations. Discussing a student's working bibliography with the student can help the student understand how to build research on past work, ferreting out key words and connections. Selecting a bibliography or two for class discussion can help mired students see new opportunities or even validate their confidence.

Another solution has been to devote more class time to discussing research. As students' responses become more frustrating, instructors will spend more time addressing the issue in class. Spending this kind of time is appropriate—to a degree. Too much repetition and not enough active experimentation can take its toll on the syllabus schedule.

Helping students to use library resources, such as the reference librarian, is another response to the student having trouble. A short visit with a reference librarian can encourage a student's sense of discovery and inquiry.

TECHNOLOGY ALTERNATIVES

Library Databases

Larger portions of libraries' acquisition budgets are being used to buy access to electronic resources. These resources are usually academically appropriate, being composed of credible research and authors. The challenge is to navigate them.

Databases are arranged in a variety of ways. Most often, the organizing feature is made clear when you begin, as shown in figure 7.1.

Student access to these databases is usually quite easy. If they can get to the Web they can usually access these resources. Increasingly, universities are protecting their resources. Students must log on to their university account to be recognized and allowed access.

You may choose to ask a reference librarian to lead your class through some exercises designed to help them navigate the databases. You should also consider reviewing these resources yourself prior to assigning research. The librarian can help with this also, listening to what you need and then directing you to appropriate sources.

Change Search Engines

Students often are not as proficient with technology as we may assume them to be. They may be able to search the Web, but they probably have not evaluated the various search engines available to them.

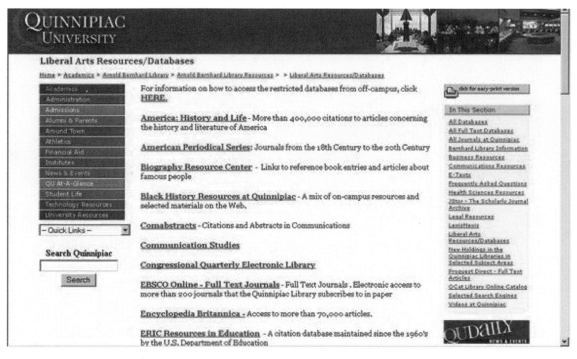

Fig. 7.1: Databases arranged by school or college at Quinnipiac University. Source: www.quinnipiac.edu/x6375.xml. Courtesy of Quinnipiac University.

Check with your institution's library for a list or a review of Web engines (figure 7.2). Depending on your assessment of your students' skills, you may choose to send this document to them or you may choose to simply mention it in class.

You should consider a class discussion of search engines and the variety they can produce. In addition, a short discussion of the differences is also helpful. One important difference is the default word in the search box. While most of the engines' logic is **Boolean**, different engines supply different connecting words that indicate further instructions to the engine. For example, a student typing "Morrison Narrative" into Alta-Vista is asking the engine to search for "Morrison" OR "Narrative". However, the student inputting the same two words into Google is asking for "Morrison" AND "Narrative". These searches may yield different results. Your students may also be able to include some of these search terms into their own searches. Different terms can yield different results.

You should also consider reviewing the search options in the engines you most frequently use. Figure 7.3 shows a page from AltaVista that gives examples and ex-

> **Boolean**—a logical method applied to online searches for information in which the search connects key words with operators such as AND if both key words must be present in the search results, OR if either word being present is sufficient, NOT if a key word should not be present in the search results, etc.

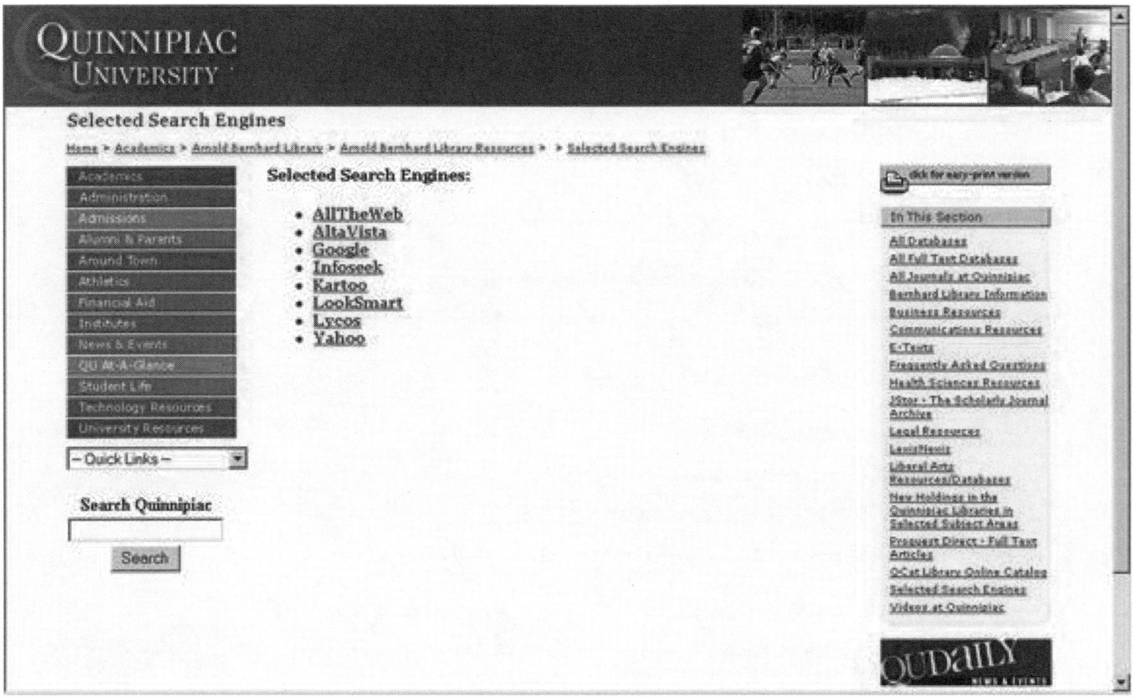

Fig. 7.2: A list of search engine links from Quinnipiac University. Source: www.quinnipiac.edu/x6379.xml. Courtesy of Quinnipiac University.

plains their functions. These pages may provide some insight to pass on to your students. For the student having trouble finding material, encourage experimenting with connecting words like "or," "and," and "not" to see if the engine returns different information.

You can research the Web for reviews of the search engines. An example of one page providing this kind of information can be seen in figure 7.4.

Descriptors from Previous Searches

We have all learned the trick of pillaging the bibliography of relevant research to find even more relevant research. This process can be applied to Web searches as well. Every time a search is performed, various bits of information pop up. Students often focus on the result of the search—the link—and pay little or no attention to the synopsis or sample of the link as it appears in the search results page. For the student having trouble generating resources, these results can be mined for more key words to be used in varying combinations. While the words used in the search are often highlighted in the sample, other words within the sample can provide new search ideas.

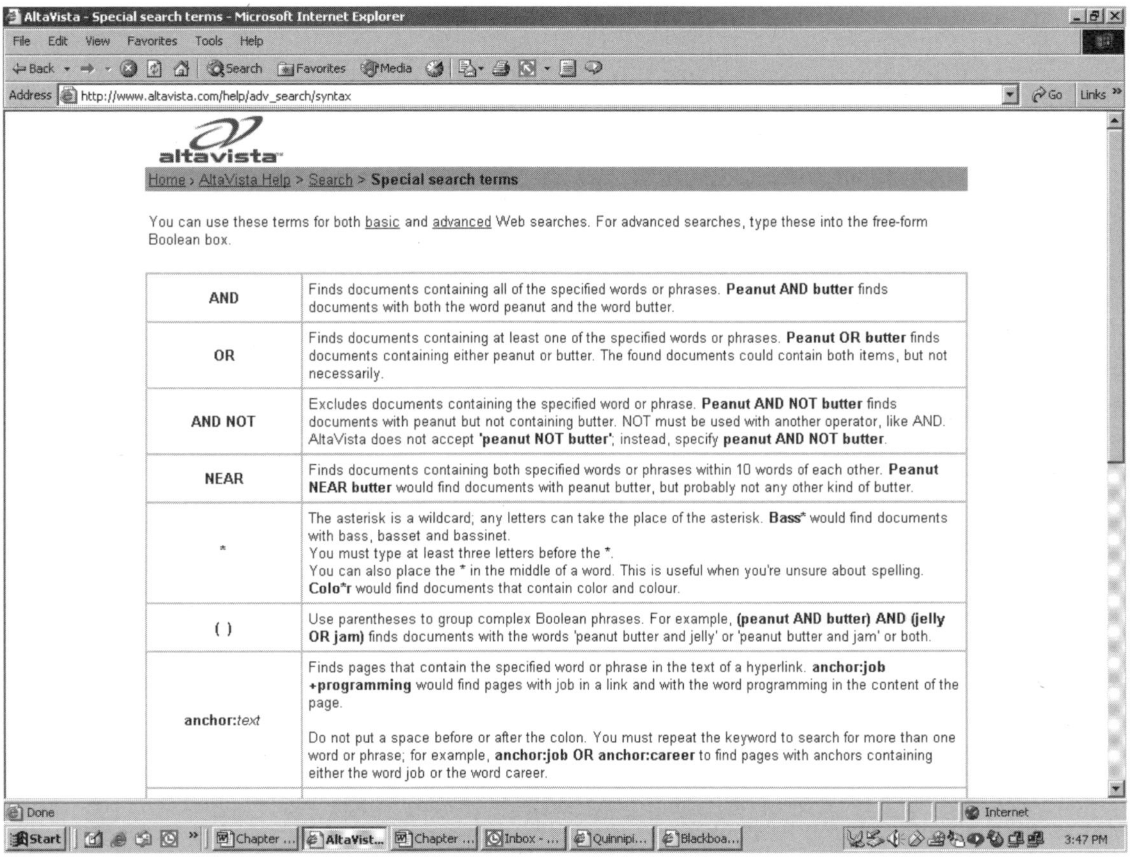

Fig. 7.3: An example of search terms from AltaVista. Reproduced with the kind permission of AltaVista Internet Solutions, LTD. Microsoft Internet Explorer™ screenshot reprinted by permission from the trademark holder, Microsoft Corporation.

Some engines also provide the user with other key words to try. AltaVista, for example, provides other key words even before offering the search results, as seen in figure 7.5.

The search results pages of some databases can also provide more key words for the struggling student. Some offer an abstract that summarizes the sources. Others go as far as offering a list of descriptors that were used to identify the source. Figure 7.6 shows the results of a search done in the ERIC database that offers an abstract as well as both major and minor descriptors. Students can often find more key words to employ in their searches for research material by reviewing these sources.

POTENTIAL PITFALLS

Search mechanisms and their organization differ greatly among these databases. You should consider investing some time experimenting with different search engines. Your

KANSAS CITY PUBLIC LIBRARY

search

○ Site Only ○ Catalog Only

Home | Catalog | Subject Guides | Local History | Kids | About the Library

Home > Guides > Search Engines   Change Font Size

The Search Engines Guide   return to guide

Search Engine Feature Comparison Chart

LINKS

Database
EBSCOHost
FirstSearch
ProQuest

Website
AskJeeves
Google
HotBot
Search Engine Showdown
Search Engine Watch
Yahoo!

Basics	Yahoo!	Google	Ask Jeeves
Size	Very Large...	Over 4 billion pages	Over 1.5 billion pages
Full Text	Searches first 500KB of page	Searches first 101KB of page	Not sure
Default Search	AND	AND	AND
Boolean	+, -, AND, OR, NOT, AND NOT, ()	+, -, OR	+, -, AND, OR
Phrase Search	Quotation marks	Quotation marks	Quotation marks
Truncation	No	~ will find synonyms, plurals, singulars, etc (ie., kansas ~library)	No
Case Sensitive	No	No	No
Wildcard	Yes, with stop words in phrase search (ie., "kansas city it library")	Yes, with asterisk in phrase search (ie., "kansas city * library")	No
Limiters	Limit by date, language, format, domain, filetype, country, adult content	Limit by site, language, date, domain, file format, and numeric range	Limit by location of words or phrases, language, domain, site, region, date
Field and Specialized Searches			
HTML Title (one word)	intitle:	intitle:	On advanced search page

Fig. 7.4: Search engine feature comparison chart by Kansas City Public Library

knowledge of the variations will allow better-informed suggestions for your students and improve your own search capabilities.

Be aware of students' reactions to your suggestions. The student who claims to have been underwhelmed may quickly become overwhelmed with these new sources. You may consider showing your class an example or two of using the various resources.

You should consider reminding your students to keep notes of their searches, their keyword use, or anything that they have tried during their research. They may find something of value but move along before printing it out or jotting down the citation.

SCENARIO 2: Poor Source Review

TRADITIONAL SOLUTIONS

Instructors' response to poor source review is usually some degree of scaffolding—modeling the skills and the process. Often, instructors take the time to develop a list of characteristics exhibited by appropriate sources. Perhaps instructors will even distribute

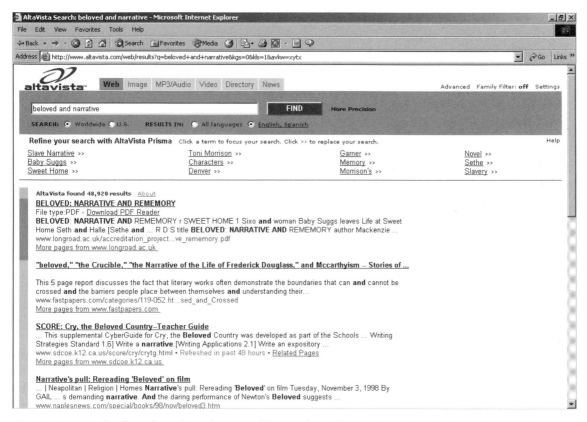

Fig. 7.5: An example of search results and suggested key words in AltaVista. Reproduced with the kind permission of AltaVista Internet Solutions, LTD. Microsoft Internet Explorer™ screenshot reprinted by permission from the trademark holder, Microsoft Corporation.

a list of sources themselves for the first assignment and hope that exposure to these sources will inform the student's next search. Class time is given over to discussing sources and their characteristics. Individual appointments during office hours to reinforce the process or to review the fruits of the search often follow this discussion. Each of these responses takes time. Some students will need the material examined in class to be repeated in an individual or small-group setting. Office hours can be spent on this.

Another way to address this need is seeking out the librarian, who will often take charge of the whole class and lead students through practice searches for appropriate material. A benefit to this process is that students can meet a new resource, one they may be more likely to approach when needing help with research. The usual cost of this benefit is class time lost to library instruction.

One more response is to assign an annotated bibliography. Early and consistent review of this assignment gives instructors a bit more feedback on students' research processes. The instructor can review the sources as well as the students' understanding.

In terms of reaching the learning objective, each of these responses has merit in its

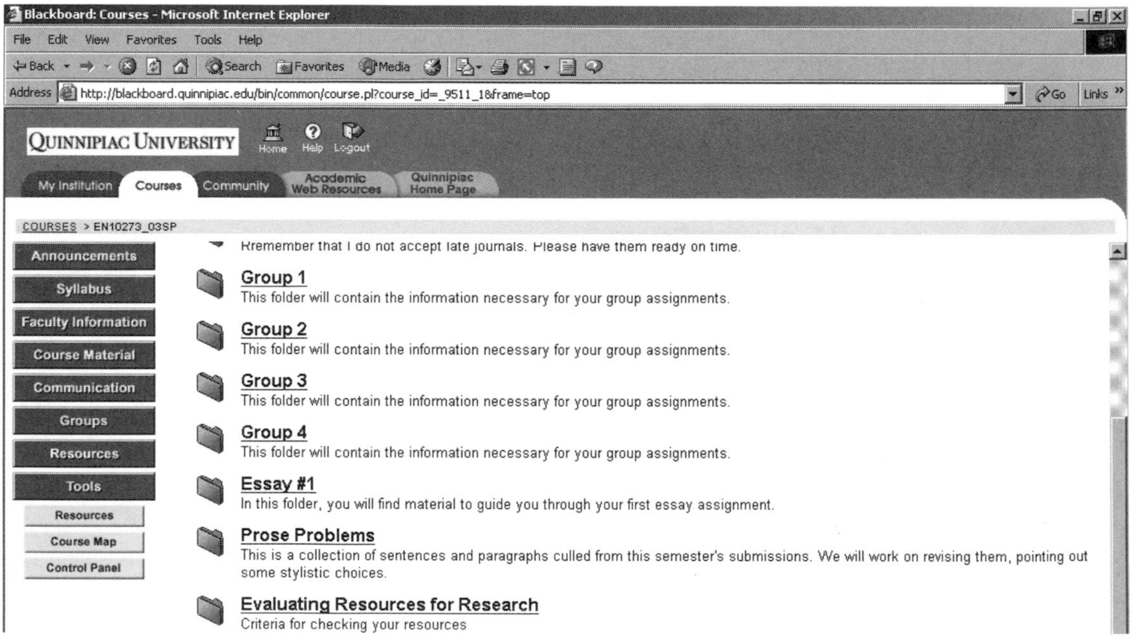

Fig. 7.8: Posting resources on evaluation criteria to your course Web pages. Property of Blackboard. Used with the permission of Blackboard. Microsoft Internet Explorer™ screenshot reprinted by permission from the trademark holder, Microsoft Corporation.

Assign an Annotated Bibliography

Having students annotate their bibliographies helps them in many ways. It encourages them to build the habit of recording the information they will need for citations, it gives them a record of their exploration, and, through the summarizing involved, it helps them to develop higher-order thinking much earlier in the research process. Compelling them to save their work to a file in Word and then send it to you or to other students can provide other benefits as well.

You may consider an early, more focused approach that will help students work through this process. Develop an assignment in which you give the students the articles they need to annotate. In the document you create for the assignment, embed links to articles you have already found. While you may initially lose the advantages associated with a constructivist perspective of learning, you will have the added advantage of focusing your students on appropriate material. Students can be further directed to submit their annotated bibliographies via Email. In this way, you have a copy—in essence, a record— of their development as higher-level thinkers. In addition, you can use their responses as teaching tools, identifying strong samples and weak samples or simply showing differing responses to the same article. Each of these tasks is made easier through your ability to cut, paste, and send copies of your students' work.

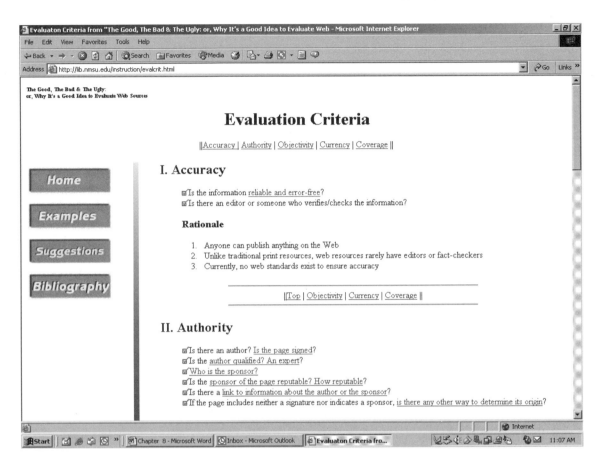

Fig. 7.9: Example of a checklist site at New Mexico State University Library. Created by Susan E. Beck, New Mexico State University. Microsoft Internet Explorer™ screenshot reprinted by permission from the trademark holder, Microsoft Corporation.

Format and Post a Template for Evaluation

Using the criteria you have developed or researched, you can create a template for your students' use. This can be as simple as a checklist that students use as an outline, as shown in figure 7.9.

A checklist like this can also be incorporated into an annotated bibliography assignment. Ask students to address specific criteria in their annotation. Eventually, using these criteria will become a habit if you show the value of the process and if you incorporate it into your assignments consistently.

POTENTIAL PITFALLS

Keep it simple. Like much of the wired world, information can overwhelm a student quickly. Resist the temptation to provide too much detail or too many criteria.

Keep the criteria as objective as possible. Questions to which students can answer yes or no are usually more useful than are questions with less definitive answers.

Beware the fallacy "Post it and they will come." Take the time to model the use of evaluation criteria.

If you link material to your documents, make sure that the links are still active and correct. As Web sites are developed and upgraded, URLs change or are discarded. You lose credibility when your students arrive at an error message rather than the site you promised.

Make sure that students understand your expectations for source review. Also, make sure that you have walked them through finding and applying your criteria.

Make sure that your resource pages are well organized. Assess the way you organize for yourself and for others, and make navigation as easy and as useful as possible. Make it a goal to get to the information with as few clicks as possible.

SCENARIO 3: Encouraging Higher-Order Thinking

We recognize that students grappling with new material are quick to make connections among various pieces of foundational information, but they are less apt to see the bigger picture or develop critical insights. Likewise, it's far easier to criticize someone else's work than it is to turn our gaze upon our own work. Moving students toward critical thinking, meta-thinking, evaluation, self-cognition—whatever term you prefer—is always a challenge. Many of the technology alternatives in Chapter 3 speak directly to promoting higher-order thinking.

TRADITIONAL SOLUTIONS

The activities we use to promote higher-order thinking in research often have a restriction that precludes their best use. Also, a persistent idea that students must master content before they can move to evaluation—as in, for example, many entry-level science courses—decreases the opportunity for reflection and evaluation. Yet asking the right questions—not "what" but "why"—assumes that the student has enough grasp of the foundational knowledge to make a judgment about the knowledge.

So we ask that students provide annotated bibliographies with the idea they would benefit from the "evaluation" associated with this task. We ask that students use peer-reviewed sources in an attempt to make themselves critical consumers of knowledge. Sometimes we dedicate a class to modeling or discussing the criteria for source evaluation. Each of these tasks offers some aspects of higher-order thinking, but none offers the benefit of an individual's being challenged—by herself or by her peers—to work through the process of synthesis, analysis, or evaluation in a way that takes advantage of both public and private forums at the same time. Students need to be challenged in both forums if they are to develop as successful lifelong learners.

As the student researches a topic or, for that matter, narrows or expands a topic to research, she is already looking for connections among the sources (synthesis), selecting useful pieces of various sources (analysis), and creating order based on the usefulness of her findings (evaluation). In a real sense, this student is using higher-order thinking.

This student, however, is using these aspects of higher-order thinking as a means to an end, that end being the completed project. If you can develop an assignment that asks the student to review and comment (present) on the process she used to evaluate the various sources or explain how she ranked them for usefulness, you are shifting the student's attention toward meta-cognitive skills. Add to this some collaborative processes, and you can more easily and effectively help students to develop the higher-order thinking necessary for their success.

TECHNOLOGY SOLUTIONS

Email

Collaboration is an important tool for helping your students develop their thinking skills, and Email is useful in building collaboration. Divide students into groups and ask them to evaluate a Web site or journal article whose link you have posted to your syllabus or course page. Ask that they apply criteria you have discussed in class and that they develop a group response to share with the class. Make sure that students remember to include all group members in the address box or, if responding to an Email, use the Reply to All option, as seen in figure 7.10.

Fig. 7.10: Using the Reply to All option in Email. Microsoft Outlook™ screenshot reprinted by permission from the trademark holder, Microsoft Corporation.

You may consider identifying several different resources for a particular assignment and asking each group to send an evaluation, a summary, or an annotation to you for distribution to your class. After receiving the review you can easily copy it or attach it to an Email to your class distribution list.

Asking students to evaluate a source with the knowledge that their evaluation will be a tool for their peers changes how students engage with the assignment. Because the information will be shared with their peers, students will engage more readily and deeply in the process. In addition, each response is an example of modeling for other students.

Online Discussion

Online discussion applications—**Chat**, **Threaded Discussion**, **Instant Messenger**—allow for group discussion but also arrange the Email messages in the order in which they were received. Most will save the discussion threads and their attachments for later use as well. Aspects of these applications are discussed in Chapter 3.

Your degree of organization will vary from tool to tool. If your institution is not offering you a course management system that has a Chat feature or a discussion board, you may choose to use Instant Messenger or Windows Messenger despite their lack of archiving. If your institution does offer a course management system, you may choose the threaded discussion feature in it for the benefits of organization (see figure 3.6).

In addition, some course management systems allow you to place students into groups that have their own discussion board, independent from the class members not in the specific group. Students can access the group page of the course management system, as seen in figure 7.11.

Once the students click on their group link, they can have access to various tools that will be independent of the other groups. So you can offer each group its own discussion board, its own virtual classroom, and its own distribution list for group Email, as shown in figure 7.12.

PowerPoint

Asking students to present can be compelling motivation. Coupled with the pressure of putting one's work before critical peers are the possibilities of being able to contribute and to learn as well. Different cognitive processes accompany different aspects of a presentation. Assigning a PowerPoint presentation as a result of one's research is a good activity to bridge the cognitive processes associated with personal learning and those associated with communicating with an audience.

Implicit in the idea of creating a presentation is that the presenter must communicate with an audience other than himself. The word "presentation" conveys a different sense of responsibility than does the word "Email." Communicating successfully requires that

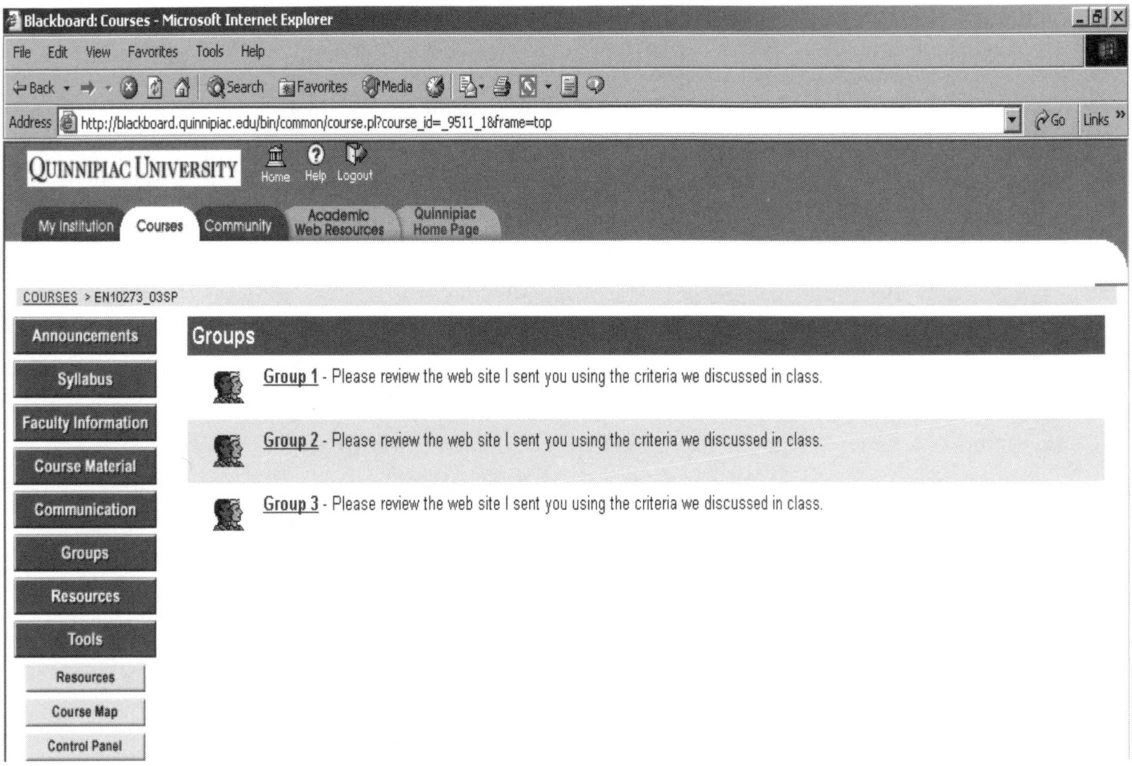

Fig. 7.11: A view of the group page in Blackboard. Property of Blackboard. Used with the permission of Blackboard. Microsoft Internet Explorer™ screenshot reprinted by permission from the trademark holder, Microsoft Corporation.

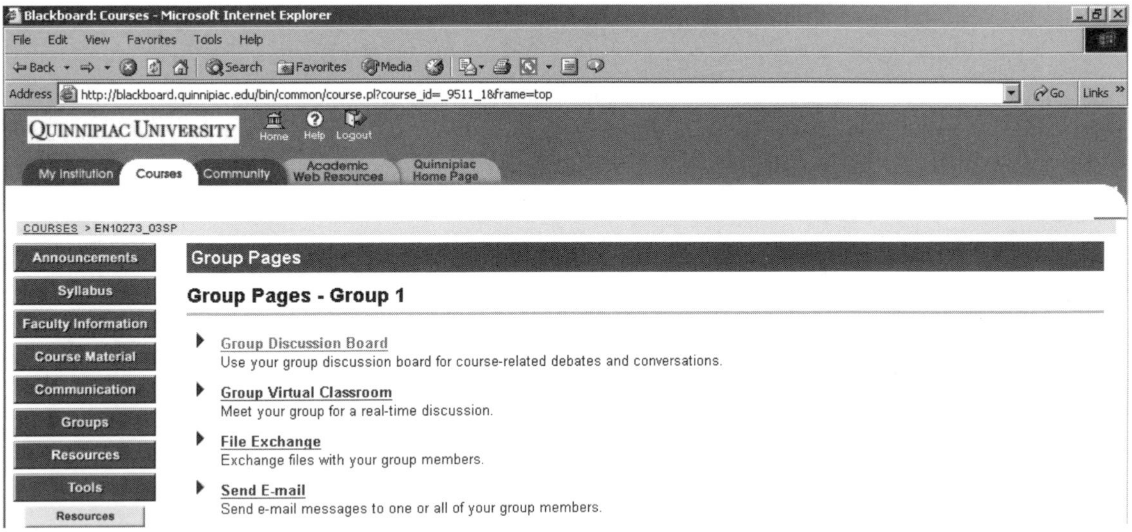

Fig. 7.12: The various tools available to independent groups in Blackboard. Property of Blackboard. Used with the permission of Blackboard. Microsoft Internet Explorer™ screenshot reprinted by permission from the trademark holder, Microsoft Corporation.

the student take a good look at the subject of the presentation from a perspective other than his own. Students often are reluctant to adopt a new perspective on work over which they have recently toiled, as many writing teachers have seen. By helping the student view the material from a different perspective you are helping the student better develop thinking skills.

A relatively simple assignment for beginning this process is to ask students to explain what they look for when they perform a Web-based search. What characteristics must a site have to make it useful to them? How do they evaluate its content? How do they remember the differences between the various sources they are reviewing? This simple assignment can be a presentation to the class, or it can be a semi-formalized response to you as part of the student's linked assignments associated with this project. As a presentation, however, it compels the student to articulate the decisions he made in a way that would not normally be a part of the project. Emphasis on the cognitive process changes perspective. The idea is to provide an opportunity for the student to reflect on his or her experiences from a different perspective.

Another assignment you might consider is to ask each student to present the thesis under consideration, followed by the top five resources he or she has collected. This is also a good way to share resources, model good research skills, and monitor students' progress while asking that they adopt a different perspective on the material and on their choices.

POTENTIAL PITFALLS

Organization of these Email messages can be an issue for both faculty and student. You may consider asking students to include a unique word or phrase in the subject line of the message so that you can create a filter to direct those specific Emails to a specific folder. Refer to Scenario 4 in Chapter 1 for information on this function.

Stay on track. Assignments that make use of different media can result in digression. Make sure that you have not asked your students to present so much evaluation that they lose sight of the project.

Shorter is better. Keep the length and the depth relatively short and shallow. It's better to build several shorter activities into the semester than to attempt one huge assignment.

SCENARIO 4: Reviewing Progress

Providing direction and support is another important aspect of assigning research to our students. Instructors also need to know whether students are progressing well or faltering. Dealing with research challenges early in the process can preclude that eleventh-hour query or plea for more time.

TRADITIONAL SOLUTIONS

Reviewing student work always takes time. In an effort to capitalize on a group audience, you may include review in class, asking students to share their experiences or sources. While this activity may generate some good discussion and model some good tactics, it also consumes class time.

Individual meetings offer another way to review students' research. These individual meetings, though more productive, increase the time you spend with students. Often they include the same discussion held during the previous individual meeting—that is, the student is not moving forward in the process.

Another means of reviewing research is to ask for copies of theses, outlines, or working bibliographies. These types of submissions may mitigate the various meetings with students, but you still need to review the material. In addition, this submission process can place more emphasis on the product than on the process.

It is best to provide feedback to students when they need it. Offering suggestions when students are most likely to see the potential for application can have significant effect on the students' work and help us understand their challenges that much better. Some technological alternatives exist to help you accomplish this.

TECHNOLOGICAL ALTERNATIVES

Email

Email remains a very easy, very fast way to provide better access to your students. Many of the details on providing access have been discussed in several chapters, specifically in Chapter 1. Traditionally you would ask a student to make an appointment during office hours to discuss research. This solution limits the student's options as well as your own. Email offers more timely, more efficient communication.

Using Email, students can send you whatever you decide is appropriate for review—drafts, URLs, questions. You have a variety of options, depending on your objective. You can simply review the material to get an idea of how the student is progressing, noting how much work has been done, what kind of sources have been used, and the focus of the topic. You may choose to save the submissions, keeping a record for future conferences or comparison with the final project. Saving submissions can be helpful when you assign a process assignment in which subsequent parts of the project are due at different times. For example, you may require that students send you their topic. Prior to the submission date, create a class folder on your computer, naming it for the assigned project. Then, in that folder, create a file for each student to which you can save submitted work. When the topics are sent via Email, copy the text and save it to the student's file. The same process works at the next stage of the project, when the student can send a list of questions that he or she has developed, perhaps, or a list of the five best sources. In this fashion you can create a timeline of the student's development in regard to this project.

Email also allows you to provide quick feedback and direction to your students. You can respond to their questions well before the next class meeting or the next office hour. You can offer resources by attaching files or copying URLs to the message. Students will benefit from faster response time, and you will benefit by knowing where they are in their project.

Threaded Discussion

As a means of communicating with students about research, threaded discussion may offer a few more advantages than Email, since the whole class can view it. Other students may well benefit from questions posted by a member of the class and your response to that question. Threaded discussions provide a record of the discussion, and you and your students can refer to previous questions and answers, using the thread as a resource page. Users also may attach documents and URLs to their threads. It may be that sharing information of this type supports one of your learning objectives.

Chat

Using a Chat function may serve as a way to expand your office hours and to make them more accessible to your students. Increasingly, many search engines offer a synchronous Chat function. (Setting up and using a third-party Chat for your class is discussed in detail in Scenario 1 of Chapter 3.) Among other things, Chat allows you to offer more office hours to more students by scheduling a time when you will be online and responding to questions.

Course management systems also provide a Chat feature, and you may prefer to use it for several reasons. Students enrolled in your class will already have access to this feature, so you won't have to load their names onto the list as you would in one of the free Chat applications. Also, the Chat sessions in most course management systems are automatically archived, so faculty and students can review previous sessions for pertinent information.

POTENTIAL PITFALLS

Remember that access is a two-way street and may add to your workload. Just as you have faster access to your students, they have faster access to you. Answering Email from home at night may offer faster contact with students, but it may also be a new task for you, something you have not scheduled before. It may take some time to acclimate to this new demand on your time, and you should monitor your workload accordingly.

Chat functions are synchronous; they allow real-time communication. Therefore, the messages will be posted in the order in which they are received, which can be confusing. In one Chat session you could be having as many different conversations as you have participants. Managing this will require some practice before you feel comfortable.

SCENARIO 5: Helping Students Avoid Plagiarism

TRADITIONAL SOLUTIONS

Traditional strategies for helping students understand and avoid plagiarism include education and thoughtful design of assignments. With the blurring of intellectual property caused by rampant audio and video file sharing, many students honestly seem to believe that anything they find on the Web is theirs. Spending time in class, particularly at times and places associated with assignments that might be obvious targets of plagiarism, is critical. Distribution of copies of institutional policy regarding plagiarism (along with consequences), and examples of differences between plagiarism, paraphrasing, citation, with the syllabus or at appropriate times in the semester is also a good idea. Make sure your students understand the definition and seriousness of plagiarism in the context of relevant assignments whenever possible.

It is also possible to design assignments in a way that minimizes the value and likelihood of plagiarism. Choosing topics that are unusual, personal, specific to the institution, and so forth make it less likely that students will find useful information from which to plagiarize. Requiring that students submit successive drafts of their work allows you can see the work evolving instead of appearing out of nowhere.

The technology alternatives suggested below build on these solutions in ways that can increase the quality of research while decreasing the likelihood of plagiarism.

TECHNOLOGY ALTERNATIVES

Require a Series of Linked Assignments with Online Accountability

Often students are more focused on product than on process. Rather than simply assigning a research paper, break the assignment into parts. Ask that students turn in a tentative thesis first, followed by an annotated working bibliography a few weeks later. Then, after some time has passed, ask that they turn in an outline that indicates the direction their research is taking. You may consider asking for a copy of their first draft to compare with the final copy.

All of this information can be sent via Email and collected into appropriate folders for review. Similarly, as you review the material, you will be in a good position to respond with questions or suggestions to direct their work.

You can also ask that your students send you, at several times over the project period, a short narrative or an outline indicating how they intend to support their topic or thesis so that you have a digital archive of their progress.

Another possibility is having students' initial research focus on a smaller aspect of the topic that you intend to introduce later in the semester. In fact, you could also reverse the process and have them research a larger concept at a more general level and then apply it more specifically to a topic later on.

Require a Bibliography Rather Than a Works Cited List

As students peruse their research they begin to generate ideas and make connections. Ask students to present a listing of the works they used to make sense of the topic. Often faculty ask for a list of the sources from which their students quoted material directly as opposed to a list of sources that their students used.

Of course, defining the word "used" to suit your needs may take some experimentation. Do you mean all the sources students review? Do you mean just those they read? What about the information a student finds in an abstract while searching databases? Could that material have directed the student a certain way?

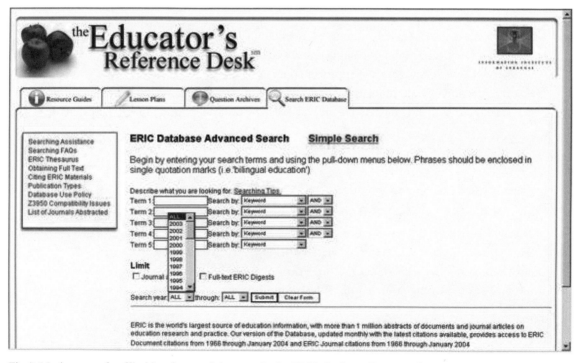

Fig. 7.13: An example of limiting the search by years in the ERIC database. Source: Educator's Reference Desk, Information Institute of Syracuse, Syracuse University.

Use of Current Research

Ask that your students use current research in their work. This will help keep them focused on the newer material. It may also preclude the use of purchased papers, which have often been in circulation for a while.

Many of the search pages in the databases allow you to restrict the dates of the material searched. This can make research a bit less cumbersome, and selecting specific dates limits the search to the appropriate material. An example of this function can be seen in figure 7.13.

Another way to promote a unique response to your assignment is to develop requirements that foster a unique response. Require that sources from a variety of venues be used for the assignment. Ask that your students make use of Web sites, databases, print resources, graphics resources, interviews, or other material when they do their research. Requiring different types of resources forces students to develop the skills to access and evaluate each type. The more you ask them to apply their skills to different sources, the better their skills will be honed and the better they will translate to other applications.

POTENTIAL PITFALLS

Don't ask for too much. You may not want to review the weekly responses of all your students.

Use whatever you ask for. Students will quickly perceive if this extra work serves a particular purpose or if it is window dressing.

You might consider simply requiring a list of the sites a student has used. It would be fairly easy for the student to highlight and copy the URLs to a working bibliography. In fact, the student is probably already recording the information somewhere. Simply formalize the process. Ask that your students send you an updated working bibliography for your files at the close of each week.

Focusing on the newest material may mean students will miss important—if dated—concepts. Your familiarity with the material should help here.

CHAPTER 8 Using Assessment and Feedback to Improve Learning

SCENARIO I: Identifying Points of Student Confusion

You assigned some reading for the next class meeting. You want to make sure everyone read the material, but you also anticipate confusion on some concepts from the reading and would like to identify which concepts are most "muddy" so that you can focus class discussion on these issues. A similar scenario, which can be addressed with the same tools, arises when you have just finished discussing a foundational issue in class and want to know that everyone understands it before you move on to material that builds on it.

SCENARIO 2: Teaching Students to Self- and Peer-Assess

You want students to learn to self-assess and give feedback, and you want to provide more, and more timely, feedback to students than your schedule allows.

SCENARIO 3: Improving Student Presentations

Your students have just made class presentations and you want to provide concrete and useful feedback that will help them improve their future presentations.

SCENARIO 4: Assessing and Managing Team Performance

You have students working in groups. You fear that one or two students in each group are carrying the weight and want to be able to assess that and manage it.

SCENARIO 5: Collecting Student Feedback on Course Activities

You want regular feedback throughout the term on the effectiveness of your teaching style, learning activities, the course's time requirements, and so forth.

Introduction

Assessment has become a dominant force in education over the past twenty years, as

- Various published studies have indicated the need for reform in education,
- The Total Quality Management ideas of Edwards Deming have spread,
- A growing body of research has focused on the value and strategies of assessment in education, and
- Most accrediting bodies and state legislatures have begun requiring increasingly rigorous assessment.

A good overview of the history, research, and strategies of assessment is provided in Huba and Freed.[1]

In this chapter we deal with several assessment-related scenarios in which faculty increasingly find themselves, and with strategies for using simple and reliable technologies to better manage those scenarios.

SCENARIO 1: Identifying Points of Student Confusion

TRADITIONAL SOLUTIONS

A commonly used strategy for finding out whether students did assigned readings and understood key points from readings and class discussion is to give brief quizzes at the start of class. The problems with in-class quizzes are that they use class time and that they don't provide immediate information that can be used to adjust activities in the current class session—and even if you take the time to quickly look at the quiz results to learn where students are confused, you may not have the materials on hand or activities prepared to make the desired adjustments.

Another way of finding out the students' points of confusion in readings and class activities is to ask them. You might begin class by asking whether there were any questions from the reading or from the previous class sessions, but we all know that few students will volunteer to look unprepared. Better still, you might ask students to write down their points of confusion, either at the start of class or before they come to class. Such surveys can be anonymous and very helpful in fostering a class discussion that is well targeted to your students' needs. As with the in-class quizzes, however, start-of-class surveys take class time. In addition to the time it takes you to read the comments you may be forced to give students a few minutes to write if you want full participation. Again, you may not have the materials on hand or activities prepared to make the adjustments suggested by the surveys.

TECHNOLOGY ALTERNATIVES

The technology alternatives for this scenario simply involve new ways of doing the same things, but those new ways bring both time savings and increased effectiveness.

Online Quiz—a quiz or test that can be taken on a computer through a network or the Web; when online quizzes are made up of objective questions, the results can almost always be generated automatically, often along with summary statistics

Online Grade Book—a feature of most course management systems that allows instructors to record and post grades, both for their own reference and so that individual students can see their own grades; online grade books almost always have the ability to apply instructor-assigned weightings to grades on course components so that overall course grades can be automatically calculated

All **Course Management Systems** offer the ability to quickly and easily create **Online Quizzes**. Using an input screen like that in figure 8.1 you will be able to create at least the following types of questions: true/false, multiple choice, multiple answer (more than one of the choices may be right), and matching.

Once such a quiz is created in the course management system, objective questions will automatically be graded, grades will automatically be reported to your **Online Grade Book,** and feedback given to the students. (You can choose whether you want students to get just their grades or various levels of detailed feedback on every question.)

It is also possible to create essay and short-answer questions using these tools, but grading them is less straightforward and unnecessarily complicated for the needs of this scenario. In general, the objective questions are well suited to this scenario, and the immediate feedback you get from them is important; remember that these are not major assessments but preliminary or check-up assessments

Add/Modify Question(s)

❶ Multiple Choice Question

Question Text:
You can type any question you want to here, or cut and paste it from somewhere else:

❷ Answers

Select the number of possible answers, fill in the fields with possible answers, and check the answers that will create a correct response.

Number of Answers: 4

Correct Answer	Answer Values
○	You can change the number of answers (Remove)
○	but (Remove)
○	need to be sure that you (Remove)
◉	designate one of them as correct at left (Remove)

Fig. 8.1: Template for creating an online quiz question in a course management system. Property of Blackboard. Used with the permission of Blackboard.

Name:	Pre-Class Mini-Survey: Chapter 8

Instructions:	Please complete this survey at least 2 hours before Tuesday's class to help me focus class discussion on concepts that need the most clarification and will be most valuable.

Question 1	**Multiple Answer**
Question:	Overall, the concepts in this chapter (please select all that apply)
	☐ Will be important to me in future school work
	☐ Will be important to me in my life and career
	☐ Were easy to understand and apply
	☐ Were too confusing for me to understand and apply

Question 2	**Fill in the Blank**
Question:	What was the most useful thing you learned from the reading?

Question 3	**Fill in the Blank**
Question:	What was the topic you found most confusing in the reading?

Question 4	**Fill in the Blank**
Question:	What topic in the reading would you most like to know more about?

Fig. 8.2: An online preclass survey can help assess student needs and interests. Property of Blackboard. Used with the permission of Blackboard.

aimed at helping you make sure students have done the reading and at identifying points of confusion with basic concepts.

Course management systems also let you easily create **Online Surveys** that give you immediate, anonymous feedback while automatically letting you know which students have participated in the surveys. Using the same screens used to create online quizzes, you can create short surveys like that in figure 8.2 (this is also the format in which quizzes are presented), asking students to identify points of confusion in reading or class activities.

Results from such a survey can help you identify which concepts need to be clarified in future class sessions—or with online supplements or suggested additional readings. Although students are not graded on their responses to your survey questions, they do automatically get check marks in your Online Grade Book once they have participated in the survey (as shown in figure 8.3), allowing you to keep track of which students are contributing.

You can view the survey results at any time, so setting the deadline for participation a few hours before class will give you time to view the results and make adjustments to planned class activities as necessary and desired.

> **Online Survey**—a survey that can be taken on a computer through a network or the Web; when online surveys are made up of objective questions, the results can almost always be generated automatically, often along with summary statistics.

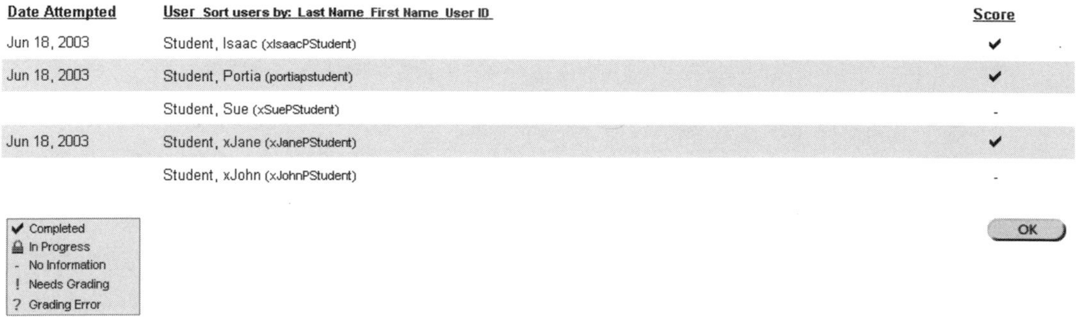

Date Attempted	User Sort users by: Last Name First Name User ID	Score
Jun 18, 2003	Student, Isaac (xIsaacPStudent)	✔
Jun 18, 2003	Student, Portia (portiapstudent)	✔
	Student, Sue (xSuePStudent)	-
Jun 18, 2003	Student, xJane (xJanePStudent)	✔
	Student, xJohn (xJohnPStudent)	-

✔ Completed
🔒 In Progress
- No Information
! Needs Grading
? Grading Error

OK

Fig. 8.3: Course management systems offer automatic accounting for student participation in surveys. Property of Blackboard. Used with the permission of Blackboard.

Overall, such online quizzes and surveys offer solutions to this scenario that

- Take no class time,
- Take five to fifteen minutes (per quiz or survey) to create,
- Take no time to grade/evaluate/record, and
- Provide feedback as to student knowledge/confusion before class begins, giving you time to react and adjust class activities.

POTENTIAL PITFALLS

One concern about using online quizzes is the potential for cheating: who took the quiz and under what circumstances? Since these are only minor assessments, this concern can be handled in part by assigning only a small weight to the grades achieved on these quizzes—but too low a weighting will result in students not taking the quizzes seriously.

But there is another solution to this concern. Online quizzes can be given passwords, without which students cannot take them. An assessment center—either as part of a learning center (which has a variety of incentives for supporting this) or, as demand increases, as a dedicated lab space—with graduate students or staff as proctors, can be used to require students to take quizzes only under supervision. The software allows you to set a maximum time allowed for the quiz, and the quiz can be set up so that students taking it cannot do anything (Email, search the Web, etc.) but take the quiz once they start it. This solution allows instructors to know who took the quiz, that the time allowed for the quiz was not exceeded, and that resources available during the quiz were those allowed— all without additional time commitment from the instructor.

SCENARIO 2: Teaching Students to Self- and Peer-Assess

There is significant evidence that being able to accurately self-assess—for students to be able to recognize whether they've produced good work, be it a science lab, a math proof, or a term paper—is a critical factor in determining an individual's success. To the extent students do learn and use these self-assessment skills, this is a win-win strategy—students will reach higher levels of competence and get better grades, and instructors will spend less time grading—well-done papers and projects are generally easier and more enjoyable to grade than those that still need significant revision.

> **Rubric**—a detailed list, often presented in a table, of features that will be used in evaluating an assignment, along with descriptive material indicating how each feature will be assessed

TRADITIONAL SOLUTIONS

Traditional strategies for teaching students to assess their work or that of their peers include in-class group assessment activities, modeling of instructor assessment, and the use of **Rubrics**.

Many instructors of writing-intensive courses spend class time having the class critique the written work of its members. The hope is that individual class members will then apply the critiquing skills learned in class to their own work. Underlying these activities is the belief that being able to recognize whether and in what ways something is well or poorly written is a critical skill in editing, and therefore in writing well.

A useful recent addition to this self-assessment training—and to assessment overall—is the rubric. A rubric like the one in table 8.1 gives students everything they need to evaluate and grade an assignment, including

- Attributes of the work, on the basis of which it will be evaluated,
- Components of each attribute to provide specificity,
- A weighting for each attribute to indicate its relative importance and to be used in calculating the overall grade, and
- Levels of quality for recording the extent to which each attribute is present and complete.

Using rubrics clarifies and even standardizes the evaluation process. Having the rubric available while working on a project allows students to better target and refine their efforts. All of this also means that students armed with well-written rubrics and trained in their use may be prepared to evaluate and assign grades to projects similar to the evaluations and grades the instructor would have assigned.

TECHNOLOGY ALTERNATIVES

Technology offers a variety of ways to enhance, extend, and supplement the traditional solutions to this scenario, allowing you and your students to get more value out of the traditional solutions you are using.

Table 8.1. Rubric for evaluating lab reports

Name: _____ Overall Grade: _____

Attribute—points out of total grade of 100 points (Components)	Level of Quality (points for each attribute are awarded in proportion to components present)			
	All components present	Most components present	Some components present	No components present
Overall Presentation—10 points (Content in logical order, pages clean, printing and graphics neat)				
Prelab Brief—15 Points (Concise, but all details required to complete case are included)				
Equations—15 Points (All equations necessary to complete case are included)				
Spreadsheet Correctness—15 Points (All calculations and references are correct)				
Organization—15 Points (Logic and layout are clear; use is intuitive)				
Postlab Accuracy of results—15 Points (All results reported are accurate)				
Discussion—15 Points (Each result is compared and contrasted to other results and related to theoretical concepts as relevant)				

Student instructions: Attach one of these to the top of each lab report and use it to evaluate yourself before you hand the report in. You will be given 2 bonus points on the lab if your attribute rating (Level of Quality) agrees with mine in each case and if your Overall Grade is within 3 points of that I give you.

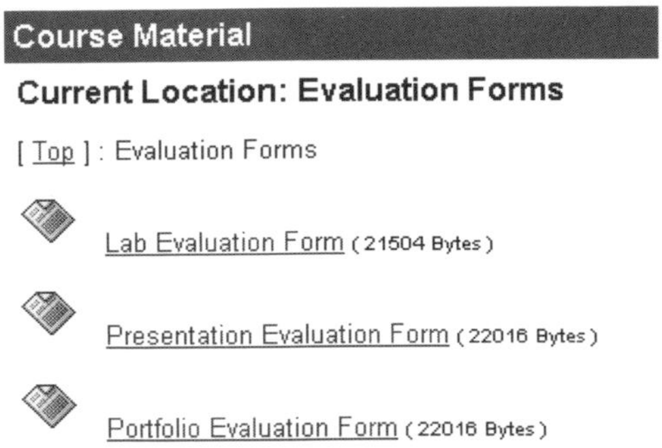

Course Material

Current Location: Evaluation Forms

[Top] : Evaluation Forms

Lab Evaluation Form (21504 Bytes)

Presentation Evaluation Form (22016 Bytes)

Portfolio Evaluation Form (22016 Bytes)

Fig. 8.4: Rubrics and other evaluation forms can easily be posted in the course management system, allowing students to access them at any time. Property of Blackboard. Used with the permission of Blackboard

First, every course management system allows instructors to easily post pages and files to the Web (see Chapter 3). Posting rubrics to the course Web pages gives students universal access to them (a sample page providing such access is shown in figure 8.4), meaning you never need to make copies and students can never lose them.

A second technology enhancement to the assessment/feedback process involves the ability to add comments or annotations to documents being read in a word processor (such as Word, WordPerfect, etc.). As shown in figure 8.5, a section of the document to which a comment is attached (the misspelled word "supplement" in the example) is bracketed, and the comment is inserted in a balloon at right. A document can have hundreds of such comments from various editors, and there is virtually no limit on their size.

This is a useful tool for instructors giving feedback, as it provides as much space for comments as necessary (which margins on paper may not) and, to the extent that your typing is faster and more legible than your writing, it may take you less time to provide more useful feedback. But this feature can also be used by students doing peer assessment—and is especially useful in conjunction with a third technology tool.

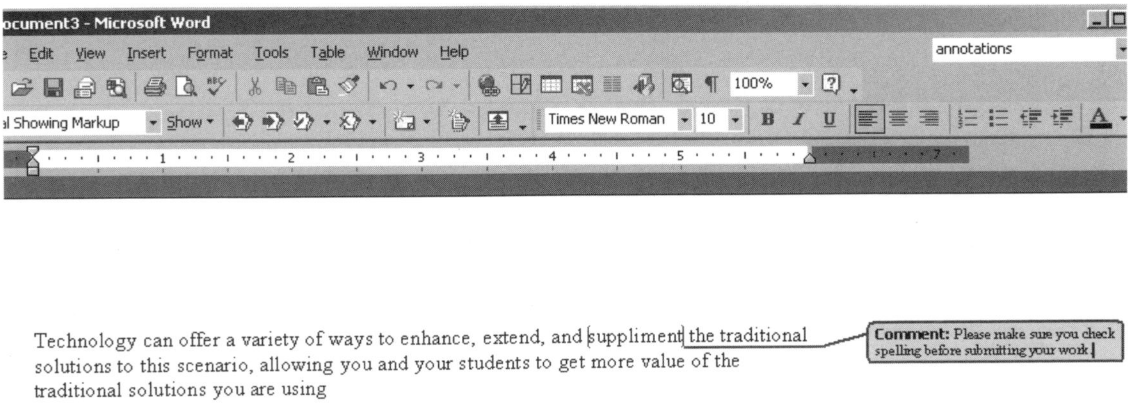

Document3 - Microsoft Word

Edit View Insert Format Tools Table Window Help   annotations

al Showing Markup   Show   Times New Roman   10   B I U

Technology can offer a variety of ways to enhance, extend, and supplement the traditional solutions to this scenario, allowing you and your students to get more value of the traditional solutions you are using

Comment: Please make sure you check spelling before submitting your work.

Fig. 8.5: Using the Comments feature in Word to provide feedback on documents. Microsoft Word™ screenshot reprinted by permission from the trademark holder, Microsoft Corporation.

▼ **Yankees are Great! (with apologies to Red Sox fans)**

Please contribute to this collection of original essays on various aspects of the Yankees by posting an anonymous message with your essay attached as a word processing document.

Once that is done, please read someone else's essay and edit it by providing annotations in the document to help them revise and improve the essay. Please post the document with your annotations as a reply to the original essay. Please post your reply anonymously. You are responsible to "edit" at least two essays posted by other people.

Fig. 8.6: Directions to a threaded discussion (in a course management system) used to coordinate peer evaluation of writing. Property of Blackboard. Used with the permission of Blackboard.

> That third tool is the **Threaded Discussion** (see Chapter 1, Scenario 3 and Chapter 3, Scenario 1 for more detail on setting up and using threaded discussions). Threaded discussions like that described in figure 8.6 can provide a nonthreatening forum for students to practice evaluating and editing the work of others.
>
> By clicking on the hyperlinked discussion title ("Yankees are Great! . . . ") students would be taken to the discussion itself, shown in figure 8.7. Here students have anonymously (they can include their names if they wish, and you can require them to do so if you wish) posted four essays ("An Ode to the Starters," "Swinging for the Right Field Fence," "Double Play!," and "The Old and the New") in the threaded discussion titled "Yankees are Great!" The paper clip at the right of each of these postings indicates that a file is attached to it—the word-processing file containing the essay. When a student clicks on the hyperlinked title for the posting ("An Ode to the Starters," for example), the text of the posting itself will open up, containing a message (perhaps something simple like "My essay is in the attached file," though the tool will handle a very long message) and, in this case, the attached file containing the essay. Posting the essays as attachments (instead of posting them directly in the text of the message) is necessary in this case only because the students are asked to add comments to each other's essays as comments or annotations (as shown in figure 8.5)—which they can do only when using word-processing software (Word, WordPerfect, etc.). In figure 8.7, two replies have been made to the first essay (each showing up as "Re: An Ode to the Starters"), one reply has been posted to the second essay, and no replies have been made to the third or fourth essays. Again, the paper clip at the right of each reply indicates that a file is attached—this time it's a word-processing file containing the original essay with the replier's comments now added.

⊟ An Ode to the Starters 🖉	Anonymous	Fri Jan 4 2002 3:54 pm	
Re: An Ode to the Starters 🖉	**Anonymous**	**Fri Jan 4 2002 3:57 pm**	New
Re: An Ode to the Starters 🖉	**Anonymous**	**Fri Jan 4 2002 4:19 pm**	New
⊟ Swinging for the Right Field Fence 🖉	Anonymous	Fri Jan 4 2002 3:55 pm	
Re: Swinging for the Right Fie... 🖉	**Anonymous**	**Fri Jan 4 2002 3:58 pm**	New
Double Play! 🖉	**Anonymous**	**Fri Jan 4 2002 3:56 pm**	New
The Old and the New 🖉	**Anonymous**	**Fri Jan 4 2002 3:57 pm**	New

Fig. 8.7: A threaded discussion used for peer evaluation of writing. Property of Blackboard. Used with the permission of Blackboard.

To the extent that students become knowledgeable evaluators of each other's work, those being evaluated will receive valuable and timely feedback on projects in progress. (There is evidence that students work on such projects around the clock, meaning that feedback from classmates is often received just minutes after the original posting.) Inclusion of rubrics in this process can help guide the feedback of editors, helping them become better editors and increasing the quality and value of the feedback provided.

POTENTIAL PITFALLS

The main concern in implementing these technology alternatives in support of Scenario 2 is making sure that faculty and students receive sufficient training in the use of threaded discussions and any word-processing features being used. Both of these are reasonably intuitive, and a small amount of training should allow students and faculty alike to reach proficiency in each, but it would be a mistake to assume that such training is unnecessary.

Another potential concern depends on your students and on the decision of whether to allow them to post messages anonymously. Doing so allows them to post their writing and editing in a public forum without fear of embarrassment if their work is below par. The potential problem is that, without having their names associated, immature students might take the opportunity to **Flame** each other's work. In most cases, an acknowledgement of this concern with an appeal that all postings be civil and helpful is enough to keep responders from being abusive. In the worst case, most course management systems allow the technology person running the system to uncover the poster of an inflammatory message, but this can be time consuming, and you don't want to have to resort to it often.

SCENARIO 3: Improving Student Presentations

The typical motivations for having students make class presentations of course material include

- Helping them grow comfortable speaking in front of a large group,
- Helping them develop communication skills more broadly, and
- Drawing them into the learning process by giving them responsibilities in it.

Well-targeted evaluation and feedback can help ensure that these goals are met—and that the presentations are good learning experiences for the class as a whole and not a waste of class time for all but the presenters.

TRADITIONAL SOLUTIONS

A useful tool for providing this well-targeted evaluation and feedback is a rubric like that in table 8.2. Having such a rubric while preparing and practicing for a presentation allows students to clearly

> **Flame**—to send an online message (an Email, an Instant Message, or a post to a threaded discussion, etc.) that is inflammatory, often personally

Table 8.2. Rubric for evaluating class presentations

Presenters: _____   Time used: _____   Grade: _____

Attribute (components)	Points out of the total 100	Level of Quality			
		A model for others	Well done in most regards	Satisfactory but not compelling	Unsatisfactory
Organization					
Clear introduction (speakers, outline)	5				
Good transitions (logical, smooth between topics)	5				
Logical conclusion (follows from presentation)	5				
Content					
Mission	10				
Goals	10				
Objectives	10				
Profitability	10				
Share price	10				
Professionalism					
Dress	5				
Eye contact	5				
Clear slides (font, colors, layout, amount of text are appropriate)	5				
Use of charts and graphs	5				
Interest generated					
Enthusiasm of speaker	5				
Audience involvement	5				
Audio visual elements	5				

understand and prepare for what you are looking for. Manipulation of the attributes and their weightings lets you massage and convey the priorities and coach students to better presentations. Receiving feedback in this format allows students to clearly understand where improvement is needed and to perceive more fairness in the grades they receive. An extension of this is to have classmates evaluate student presentations using the rubric, giving classmates the chance to learn by evaluating, and presenters the chance to receive feedback from peers.

TECHNOLOGY ALTERNATIVES

A simple way in which technology can help you reach this goal is by making your evaluation rubrics available online at all times. Posting your rubrics and evaluation forms to the pages in your course management system is quicker and easier than running off paper copies, and it ensures that your students will always know where to find them. The former saves you time and frustration; the latter increases the likelihood that students will refer to your rubrics while working on your projects, thereby increasing the effectiveness of the tool.

Having a videocamera on a tripod available in class during the presentations provides another relatively simple yet powerful technology enhancement. Such equipment is widely available through institutional audiovisual departments, meaning that this enhancement should not require faculty to do anything more than request the equipment. Each presenting student is required to bring in a blank videotape for recording the presentation. The presenting student then views the recording and evaluates his or her own performance before receiving the instructor's evaluation. Students going through this process are usually quick to pick up on many of the same things you might—especially if they are given a rubric to guide their self-evaluation. This process helps students practice self-assessment while adding credibility to the evaluation process—students see and hear themselves missing key content areas, fidgeting, mumbling, reading from cards, and so forth. Implementing this assessment strategy requires the faculty member to do nothing more than put in an equipment setup request to the A/V department.

POTENTIAL PITFALLS

There are really very few things to look out for with these technology alternatives. The A/V department should be able to get you running with the videocamera, and most students can figure out how to use them anyway. Students generally have widespread access to video players, and A/V probably has them available as backup.

The main concern with respect to posting rubrics (or any information) on the course management system is making sure that students are able to access those documents. That will not be an issue if the course management system is widely used at the institution, but it is always smart to ensure that students are able to access posted documents early in the semester to head off this concern.

SCENARIO 4: Assessing and Managing Team Performance

The use of student teams in projects and learning activities has increased with the growing literature on the value of **Collaborative Learning**. As discussed at the beginning of Chapter 3, there is now significant evidence that students reach deeper levels of understanding when working in groups instead of working alone. Group projects can also offer efficiencies to the instructor—students are learning from each other, and the grading load falls because only one project per group is submitted.

As was indicated in Chapter 3, one of the main problems with assigning group projects is that groups can be dominated by one or two members, and the work and learning may not be shared by all members of the group. Scenario 5 of Chapter 3 suggests ways in which threaded discussions can be used to manage and provide accountability for the contributions of group members.

SCENARIO 5: Collecting Student Feedback on Course Activities

Candid and frequent student feedback is more vital than ever for two reasons:

- It is critical in helping faculty assess the effectiveness of innovative learning activities increasingly being considered and used, and
- Students' learning styles and expectations are changing dramatically with their exposure to technology and a wide range of innovative learning activities, and faculty need ways to assess which of their traditional learning activities are still working and which are not.

TRADITIONAL SOLUTIONS

End-of-semester student evaluations are commonplace and required in most institutions, but they do not provide feedback while it could still be used to improve the current course. As such, students may not take the evaluations as seriously, knowing that they will not benefit directly from any suggestions they make. Further, these evaluations generally are standardized across the institution, meaning that the questions are probably not well targeted at the specific learning activities you are using in your class.

Having students take periodic surveys of your own provides one solution to these problems: you can create your own surveys focusing on your learning activities or course topics and administer them throughout the semester, ensuring that you will have timely, targeted feedback to help you improve your course as it develops. The main problem with this solution is that, depending on how often you decide to survey your students, you may end up using a

Collaborative Learning—a strategy for learning in which students work on projects or assignments in teams or groups

lot of class time over the semester to get this feedback. Whether or not you use class time to allow your students to complete surveys, you may have trouble balancing students' confidence in their anonymity (which will affect their candor) with enough accounting for participation to promote widespread participation (and keep the "squeaky wheels" from running the class).

TECHNOLOGY ALTERNATIVES

Online surveys administered through your course management system offer an efficient solution to this problem. A simple survey composed of multiple choice, multiple answer, true-false, or fill-in-the-blank questions can be composed and posted within a few minutes. You create each question in the survey by

1. Typing (or cutting and pasting in) the text of the question, and
2. Typing in the possible answers (except for essay or fill-in-the-blank questions, for which you provide no possible answers)

as shown in figure 8.8.

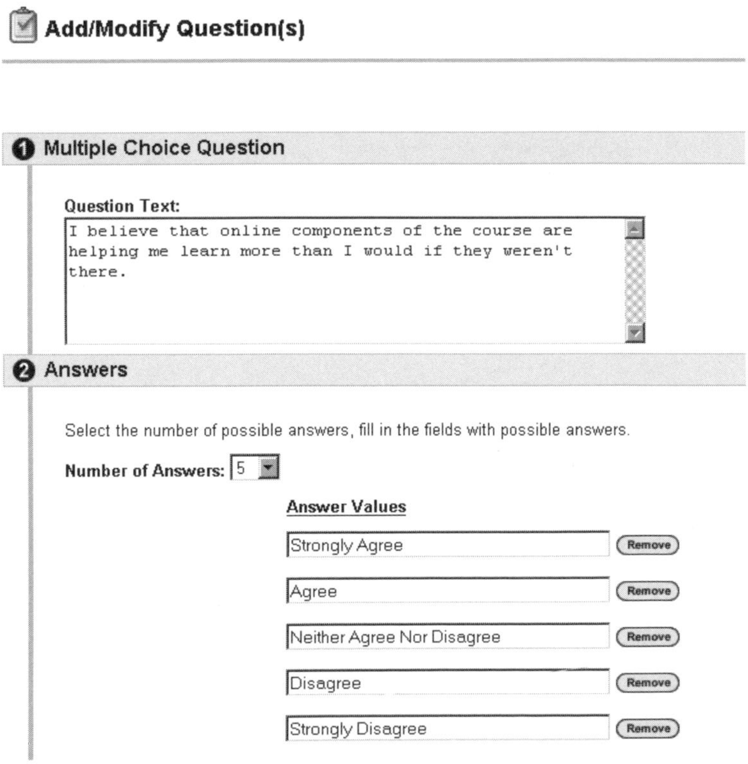

Add/Modify Question(s)

1 Multiple Choice Question

Question Text:

I believe that online components of the course are helping me learn more than I would if they weren't there.

2 Answers

Select the number of possible answers, fill in the fields with possible answers.

Number of Answers: 5

Answer Values

Strongly Agree   Remove

Agree   Remove

Neither Agree Nor Disagree   Remove

Disagree   Remove

Strongly Disagree   Remove

Fig. 8.8: Creating an online survey question in a course management system.
Property of Blackboard. Used with the permission of Blackboard.

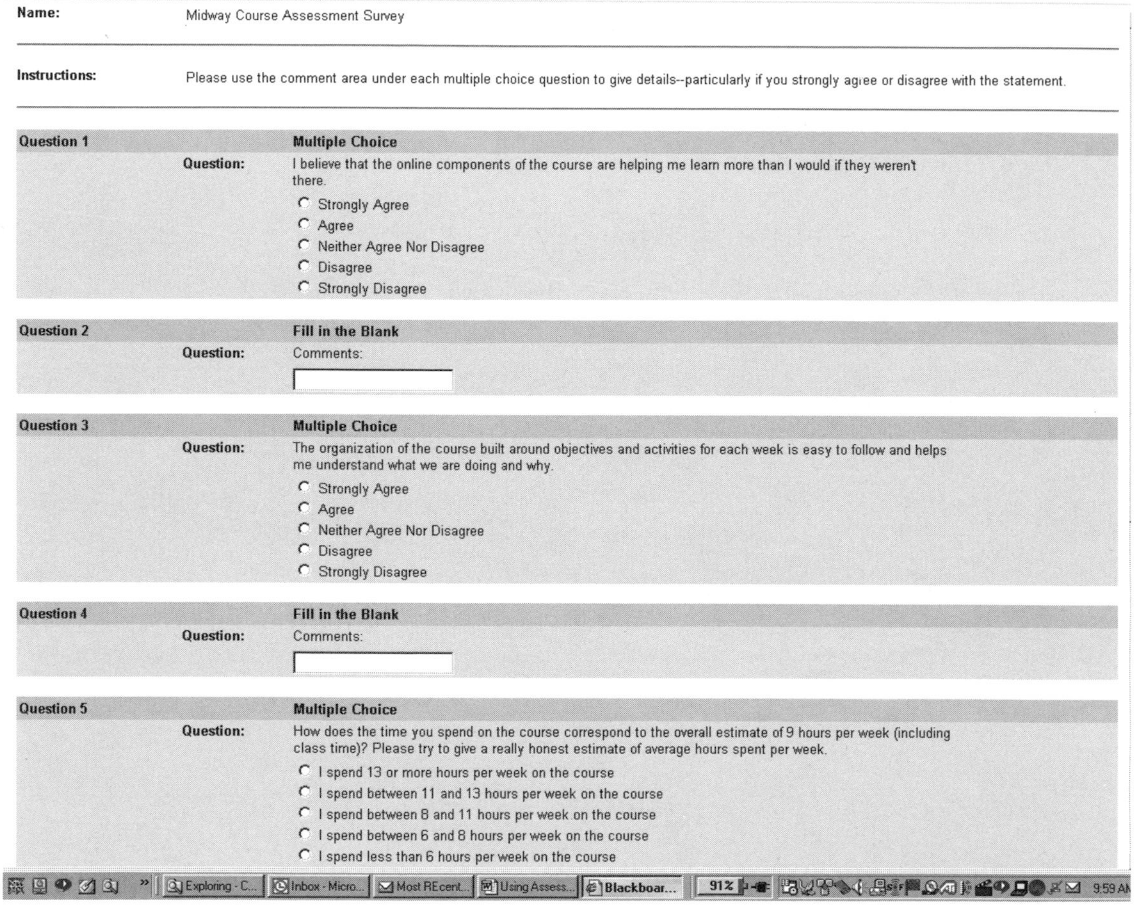

Name:	Midway Course Assessment Survey
Instructions:	Please use the comment area under each multiple choice question to give details--particularly if you strongly agree or disagree with the statement.

Question 1   **Multiple Choice**

Question: I believe that the online components of the course are helping me learn more than I would if they weren't there.

- ○ Strongly Agree
- ○ Agree
- ○ Neither Agree Nor Disagree
- ○ Disagree
- ○ Strongly Disagree

Question 2   **Fill in the Blank**

Question: Comments:

Question 3   **Multiple Choice**

Question: The organization of the course built around objectives and activities for each week is easy to follow and helps me understand what we are doing and why.

- ○ Strongly Agree
- ○ Agree
- ○ Neither Agree Nor Disagree
- ○ Disagree
- ○ Strongly Disagree

Question 4   **Fill in the Blank**

Question: Comments:

Question 5   **Multiple Choice**

Question: How does the time you spend on the course correspond to the overall estimate of 9 hours per week (including class time)? Please try to give a really honest estimate of average hours spent per week.

- ○ I spend 13 or more hours per week on the course
- ○ I spend between 11 and 13 hours per week on the course
- ○ I spend between 8 and 11 hours per week on the course
- ○ I spend between 6 and 8 hours per week on the course
- ○ I spend less than 6 hours per week on the course

Fig. 8.9: The student view of a survey in a course management system. Property of Blackboard. Used with the permission of Blackboard.

When you have created and posted your survey your students will see a survey like that in figure 8.9.

Once they've taken the survey, the cumulative results on all objective questions will automatically be calculated and viewable in a form such as that shown in figure 8.10, and any fill-in-the-blank answers are viewable in a form such as that shown in figure 8.11.

Though students' responses are anonymous, the course management system grade book will automatically record which students have participated, as shown in figure 8.12, meaning you will know whether or not everyone has provided input.

Online surveys, therefore, offer a solution to this scenario that

- Can take no class time to administer if students are asked to complete them outside of class,

Question 1: Multiple Choice	
I believe that the online components of the course are helping me learn more than I would if they weren't there.	% Responses
Strongly Agree	43%
Agree	43%
Neither Agree Nor Disagree	14%
Disagree	0%
Strongly Disagree	0%

Question 2: Fill In the Blank

Comments: [View Responses]

Click the **View Responses** button above to see a listing of all of the responses

Question 3: Multiple Choice	
The organization of the course built around objectives and activities for each week is easy to follow and helps me understand what we are doing and why.	% Responses
Strongly Agree	43%
Agree	57%
Neither Agree Nor Disagree	0%
Disagree	0%
Strongly Disagree	0%

Question 4: Fill In the Blank

Comments: [View Responses]

Click the **View Responses** button above to see a listing of all of the responses

Question 5: Multiple Choice	
How does the time you spent on the course correspond to the overall estimate of 9 hours per week (including class time)? Please try to give a really honest estimate of average hours spent per week.	% Responses
I spend 13 or more hours per week on the course	0%
I spend between 11 and 13 hours per week on the course	14%
I spend between 8 and 11 hours per week on the course	71%
I spend between 6 and 8 hours per week on the course	14%
I spend less than 6 hours per week on the course	0%

Fig. 8.10: The faculty view of quantitative results of a survey done in a course management system. Property of Blackboard. Used with the permission of Blackboard.

Question: Fill In the Blank

Comments:

1. being able to talk with other students on the subject is a real plus

2. I agree in the fact that I will learn more by going out myself and trying to figure things out. But the problem that I'm running into is time. I feel that I'm spen

3. No Response
4. You help us with what we need help with. Time isn't being wasted on lectures that we could learn just as well if we read the book

5. The interactive nature of class is an asset to my learning. I feel that our class is made up of a team of students and not individual students competing against ea

Fig. 8.11: The faculty view of qualitative results of a survey done in a course management system. Property of Blackboard. Used with the permission of Blackboard.

Date Attempted	User Sort users by: Last Name First Name User ID	Score
Jun 18, 2003	Student, Isaac (xIsaacPStudent)	✔
Jun 18, 2003	Student, Portia (portiapstudent)	✔
Jun 18, 2003	Student, Sue (xSuePStudent)	✔
Jun 18, 2003	Student, xJane (xJanePStudent)	✔
Jun 18, 2003	Student, xJohn (xJohnPStudent)	✔

[OK]

✔ Completed
🔒 In Progress
- No Information
! Needs Grading
? Grading Error

Fig. 8.12: Course management systems offer automatic accounting for student participation in surveys yet preserve anonymity relative to responses. Property of Blackboard. Used with the permission of Blackboard.

- Take between five and fifteen minutes (per survey) to create,
- Automatically calculate and provide access to cumulative results,
- Ensure student anonymity (increasing the probability that they will be candid), while
- Automatically account for participation, helping you make sure you are receiving feedback and making adjustments for the majority, and not a few, and
- Generally allow you to gather the timely, candid feedback you need to improve your course.

POTENTIAL PITFALLS

The most important potential pitfall when using online surveys is that you or your students will not know how to access or use this component of your course management system. Training sessions or one-on-one support are probably available to get you going, but it is critical that your students also feel comfortable finding and taking your online surveys (and any other online materials you post). Without this comfort you will probably not receive a high response rate on your survey and may even see some frustration show up in the responses you do receive. Institutionwide training, if available, is the best solution because it ensures that all students are comfortable with the course management system before they walk into any class. If this is not available you may be able to get someone from Information Services to give your class a brief session on the technology. In any case, it is critical to make sure that all students are ready before you begin using this tool.

CHAPTER 9

Gathering Course Learning Materials

SCENARIO 1: Identifying and Organizing Supplemental Resources

You have given your students a challenging assignment that will require deep investigation. Not seeking to cast them adrift, you want to point them toward supporting material, but you must identify that material before you can share it.

SCENARIO 2: Student Access to Specific Resources

Over the course of the semester you want your students to have access to specific information that supports or details a specific learning objective.

SCENARIO 3: Practice Tests and Quizzes

Your students have asked for a practice test with which to prepare for the coming exam.

SCENARIO 4: Supporting Learner-Centered Learning

You want to place more emphasis on students' creative engagement (constructivism/learner-centered activities) with your course material.

While the terminology varies—active learning, learner-centered learning, problem-based inquiry—research has shown that student-centered approaches to teaching have considerable merit (Bonk and Cunningham, 1998; Brown, Collins, and Duguid, 1989). One of the challenges to incorporating a more individualized environment for students has been logistical—how do you provide authenticity and multiple perspectives imbued with personal responsibility over learning? Increasingly, technology can play an important role in this process (Wilson, 1996; Cunningham, Duffy, and Knuth, 1993; Knuth and Cunningham, 1993). The technology available to you through many applications you already use can be helpful.

SCENARIO 1: Identifying and Organizing Supplemental Resources

Before you can offer material and direction to your students, you have to find it and evaluate it. In the past, this has meant spending time scanning books, magazines, newspapers, and journals, looking for something useful that didn't require a member of the Cirque de Soleil to copy it. You would traipse off to the library and scan the card catalogue, or you would do an electronic search using one of the library's electric catalogues. If you found a good citation, you would search the stacks for the hard copy so you could line up at the copier and make one and a half copies per student, enough for those who lost the original handout. More often than not you would find a good citation that would have to be ordered though interlibrary loan. Ah, the good old days.

Faculty continue to take the time to develop and organize supplemental information for their students' use. Whether it accompanies a particularly challenging assignment or is intended for the course at large, material outside the required texts can inform certain learning objectives.

TRADITIONAL SOLUTIONS

Developing support material for students has always had logistical hurdles simply because faculty had to go to the sources. Even as you made use of a particularly fruitful bibliography you still needed to make a trip to the library. Delving into card catalogues, you create a list of citations. Looking further, you squint at microfiche, feeding coins into a temperamental copier as you struggle to hold the image in focus. After searching the stacks for the right full-text article, you take your place in the line for the copier. Of course, over time, you will have collected the copies, videos, and texts that are pertinent to the material you are teaching. You may also place some of this material on reserve at the library. Each of these tasks is being made easier and faster with easy-to-use and accessible technology.

TECHNOLOGY ALTERNATIVES

Research Electronic Sources

With the advent of the Web and with networked computer systems, the onerous task of research and organization is becoming much easier. Electronic sources—Web pages on the Internet, organized databases maintained by your library, and file sharing—can be excellent sources of supplemental information. Rather than going to the library you can go online from your office, or even from home. In fact, many universities are installing wireless software on their campuses. This technology would allow you to take your laptop outside and research under a tree or on the quad.

Many of the guidelines you provide to your students apply when you are searching the Web. One finds all manner of information there, making source review critical. Spending some time reviewing evaluation criteria is worthwhile (see Scenario 1 in Chapter 7). Also, spending some time reviewing the operation of your favorite search engine will be helpful. Some engines offer more efficient ways to search than do others, as well as more effective ways to display the results. For example, the search engine AltaVista has a "collapse" feature, which allows you to regulate the number of results from the same site, as shown in figure 9.1.

Another profitable investment of time is to experiment with crafting a search using specific terms, often referred to as **Operators**. These operators indicate relationships between the key words of the search. Most search engines will have a resource page that discusses how the engine responds to specific operators. An example of this resource is seen in figure 7.3.

Many aspects of searching need to be sorted out by experimentation. For example, using different operators in your search can have different results. Google uses the following example. The word "bass" has more than one meaning. If you are interested in the word as it applies to fishing, Google would have you search for "bass -music" (meaning "bass" minus "music"), as shown in figure 9.2. AltaVista would have you search for "bass and not music" to accomplish the same search.

Databases will also offer different ways to perform a search. Databases are usually organized around the same logic as commercial search engines and will use the same operators. They may offer other operators as well, depending on their organization. An example of more operators is seen in the search page of the database JSTOR in figure 9.3. The downward-pointing arrows next to some of the boxes indicate pull-down menus listing the operators offered.

Again, experimenting with different databases will pay dividends over time.

A greatly underused resource is your reference librarian. An hour spent with one of these professionals will help you make connections more quickly. By understanding the relationships among

> **Operators**—logical words such as AND, OR, and NOT used in Boolean logic to determine how key words being used in a search will be processed

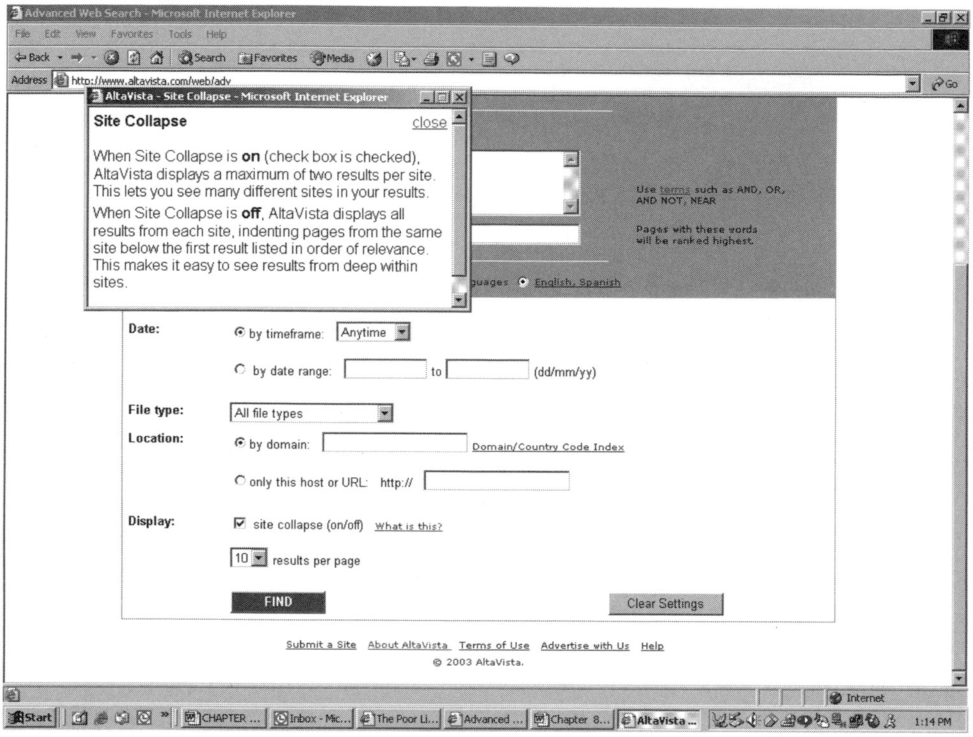

Fig. 9.1: The collapse feature in AltaVista. Reproduced with the kind permission of AltaVista Internet Solutions, LTD. Microsoft Internet Explorer™ screenshot reprinted by permission from the trademark holder, Microsoft Corporation.

the databases and their relevance to your assignment or your course objectives, these professionals can direct you to pertinent resources that you can incorporate into your assignment or your class. Reference librarians are also usually well versed in the institutional software, so they may see ways to use technology that have not yet occurred to you.

These aspects of technology can also support spontaneous research as well. Having just completed a class in which you identified the need for more information, you can return to your desk and perform a quick search for the topic. If you find something that

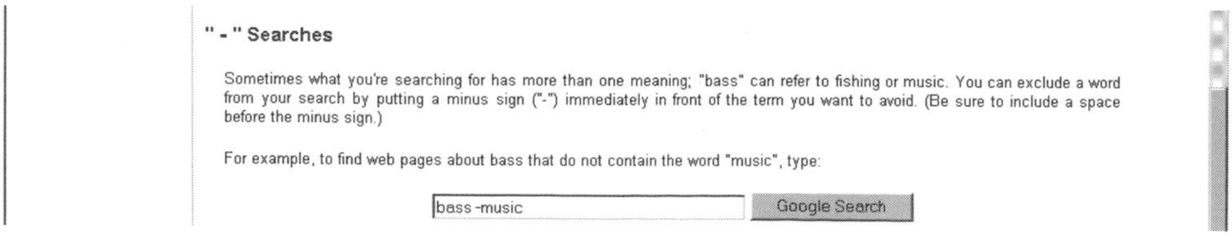

Fig. 9.2: An example of search terms in Google. Source: Google, Inc.

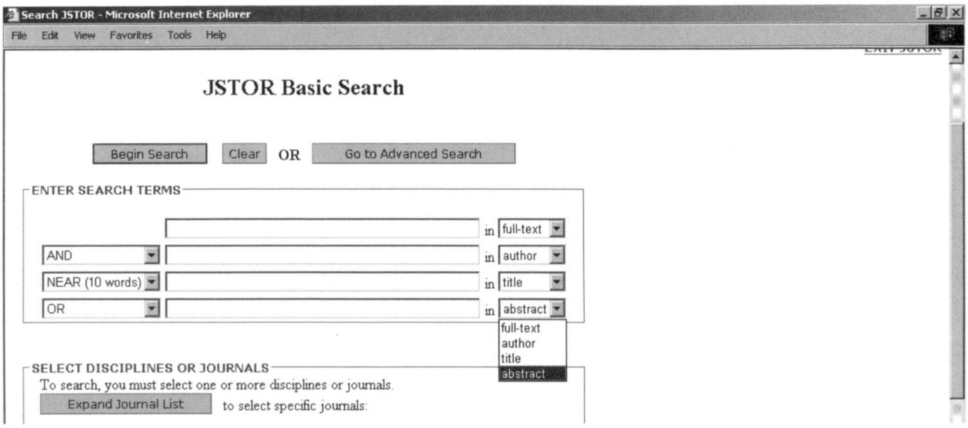

Fig. 9.3: An example showing the operator choices in the JSTOR database. © JSTOR. Reprinted courtesy of JSTOR. Microsoft Internet Explorer™ screenshot reprinted by permission of the trademark holder, Microsoft Corporation.

helps, you can copy the **URL** to an Email and distribute it to your class. You could also post the URL to a resources page in your course management system.

Email

The ease with which you copy a URL and paste it into an Email is apparent. However, at this stage of collecting your research, you may not want to send six different Emails to your class distribution list, each containing the URL of a recommended reading. In fact, you will have to leave the Web browser giving you access to the Internet, open your Email application, craft the message, paste the URL, and send the Email. What about your copy? Did you remember to include yourself on the class distribution list? Will you have to open your folder of sent items to access a copy of this URL tomorrow? Depending on your objective and the expected use of the material you have found, you may consider some options.

If you are gathering material for an assignment, Emailing the URLs is a fast way to get the information to the students. However, if this is an assignment you might do again, or if this is information that really should be in your syllabus, you might want a better record of your research. Consider pasting the URLs you collect into a Word document instead of an Email. As you research, keep the open document (which you have already named and saved) minimized. As you find material, copy the URL and then maximize the Word document so that you can paste in the URL. It may be that jotting down a few notes or perhaps even annotating the entry will help you later. After finishing, make sure to save the document again before returning to the Web browser. Now you have a file of URLs to which you can return and develop into a more usable tool than a single URL in an Email

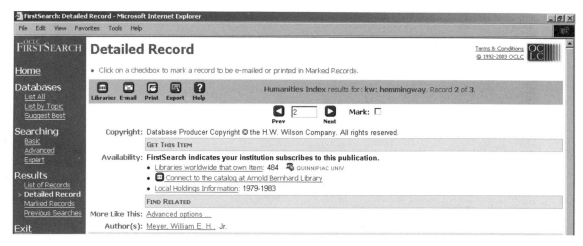

Fig. 9.4: A view of the Email option in FirstSearch. Microsoft Internet Explorer™ screenshot reprinted by permission of the trademark holder, Microsoft Corporation.

would be. You will still be able to enjoy the ease and timeliness of Email by attaching this document to the message you send. In addition, the document is saved in your files for your review and for additional distribution.

Many Web sites and databases recognize the virtues of Email and incorporate its use into their sites. Somewhere on the page you may find a link that asks whether you would like to Email this page, document, or image. Figure 9.4 shows an example of this option in the FirstSearch database. Note the second icon in the gray toolbar.

If you are using the Email function provided by these electronic resources, consider developing a set of rules that will filter incoming Email, directing each message to the file you choose. This can help you manage the research you do and the sources you choose to incorporate into your class. Many Email applications offer this function. In Microsoft Outlook, you can access the Rules **Wizard** to set up this type of filtering. Figure 9.5 shows how to access the Rules Wizard in the Tools menu of Outlook.

Follow the prompts indicated in the pop-up boxes to set up your filters. To create a new rule, click on the New button. This will bring you to a series of options from which you can pick what will serve you best (figure 9.6). Outlook also provides the Office Assistant feature for additional help.

Some of the free Email applications also offer filtering. Figure 9.7 shows the set-up page in Hotmail, which is accessed from the Options button.

Depending on the database, you may be offered other functions as well. JSTOR, for example, offers you the ability to download the resource directly to your computer. Having your own electronic copy may serve your objectives better than a copied URL. Figure 9.8 shows a resource page from JSTOR. In the links just below the toolbar you will see

Wizard—a feature of many software packages that allows the user to control how it will run; a rules wizard in an Email system, for instance, allows the user to easily set up the rules that will be applied to sort and manage incoming Email

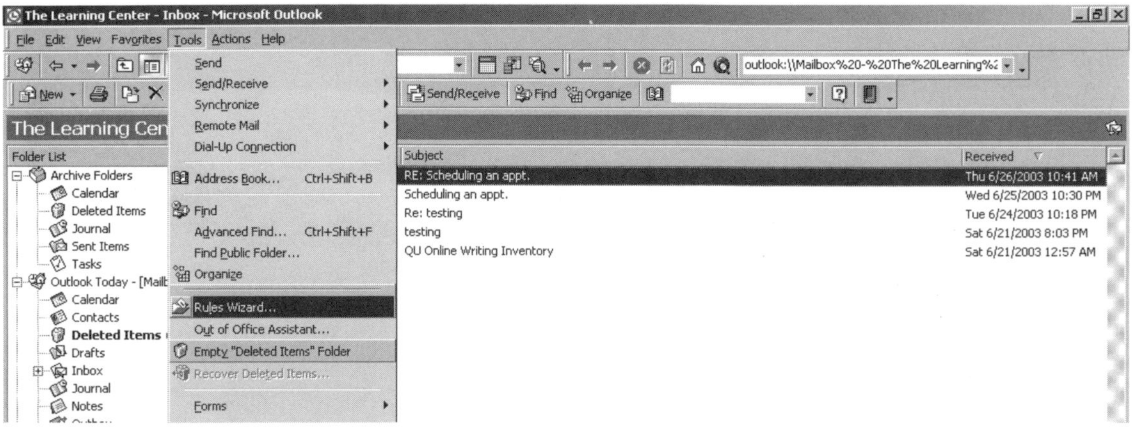

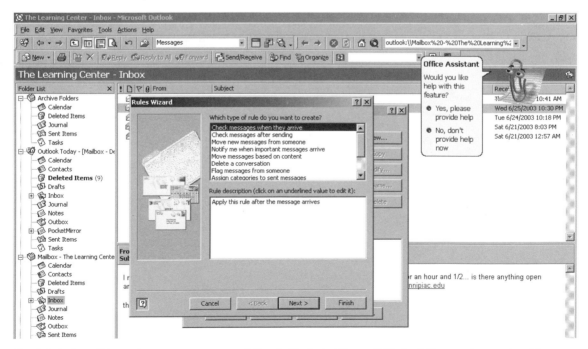

Fig. 9.5: Finding the Rules Wizard function in Microsoft Outlook. Microsoft Outlook™ screenshot reprinted by permission of the trademark holder, Microsoft Corporation.

several options, among them the ability to print the document and the ability to download it to your computer.

POTENTIAL PITFALLS

One downside to the ease of electronic searching is that it's easy to get off track and lose significant time surfing. Stay on task by referring to your objective.

Fig. 9.6: A view of the options to set up your mail filter in Outlook. Microsoft Outlook™ screenshot reprinted by permission of the trademark holder, Microsoft Corporation.

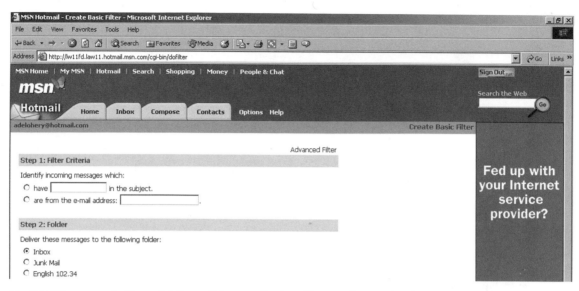

Fig. 9.7: Filter set-up in Hotmail. Microsoft Internet Explorer™ screenshot reprinted by permission from the trademark holder, Microsoft Corporation.

The speed with which you can do Web-based research can take some managing. Remember to record the citations you find useful. A quick way to do this is by copying the URLs to a resources document you have created for this purpose.

When you are using a database, the URL produced by the search may be too long to conveniently copy. You may consider experimenting with other means of recording the information need to get back to this source, such as noting the title and author, along with the database name.

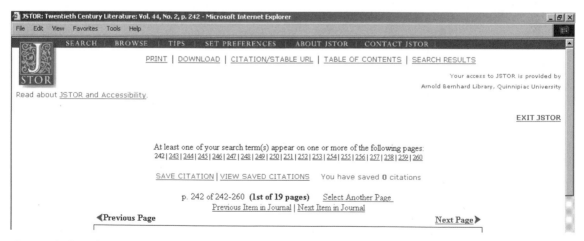

Fig. 9.8: A view of the options available in JSTOR. Underlined text indicates links. © JSTOR. Reprinted courtesy of JSTOR. Microsoft Internet Explorer™ screenshot reprinted by permission from the trademark holder, Microsoft Corporation.

Downloading documents from a database to your own computer has several advantages over simply recording a URL or a hyperlink. Downloading allows you to organize and access the information more easily. You will be able to offer students easier access to the content than if you give them a URL. If you are searching Web pages that do not offer a download option, check to see if the Email option is offered. You can also highlight and copy what you like to an appropriate file and then save it in your computer. Again, make sure you understand copyright issues before distributing copies of downloaded material (see Appendix).

Remember that most filters identify a specific word or phrase in a specific place. Make sure that your students address their messages to you in the appropriate manner. For example, if you have set up your rules to filter all Email messages with the word "essay" into a specific folder, make sure that your students know to label accordingly.

SCENARIO 2: Student Access to Specific Resources

As you research and teach a specific class, you find material that helps provide insight or that challenges expectations. Some of this you may incorporate into a reading list, but much of it lies beyond the realm of "required text." Consequently, you consider it supplemental material and hope your students will use it, appreciating your effort to offer new material from different perspectives. Two challenges usually accompany student use of this material: pertinence and access.

TRADITIONAL SOLUTIONS

Student access to faculty-generated supplementary material is made possible through faculty effort. If you bring this information to your students, it is usually in the form of handouts, copies of bibliographies, articles, or graphics. If you expect your students to go to the material, you place it on reserve at the library or in your department office. Technology offers more efficient ways to connect the student with the material.

TECHNOLOGY ALTERNATIVES

Email

After collecting your supplementary material, you can certainly use Email to distribute it. Its ease of use and its timeliness make it a good tool for giving students access to supplemental material and reminding them how that material can be useful.

At the beginning of the semester you probably have a good idea of the supplemental material you want your students to access. You may decide to give them access to everything at once, or you may decide to send them pertinent pieces as they are needed. Whatever your intent, you should take advantage of the distribution list you created for this class. As you have researched, you've recorded the URLs, perhaps printed out a citation page, copied a journal article, or done some other act of organization. Consider collecting the citations into one document and sending that document to your students. A way to further expedite students' access to this material is to insert hyperlinks in the citations page. In the same way you insert hyperlinks into your syllabus you can insert hyperlinks into a resource page or an assignment page, which you can send it to your students via Email. Students can then click on the link and retrieve the information quickly, as long as they have Internet access.

Hyperlinks in Your Syllabus

Placing the supplementary material in one easily accessible place lessens the number of requests for more copies. Placing the material near the assignment in the course schedule reinforces your expectations of student use and aids easy access. You can also consider grouping the supplementary materials closer to the required text portion of your syllabus, but incorporating them into the course schedule of your syllabus may offer students more clarity. An example can be seen in figure 9.9.

You can copy the links directly to the syllabus from the URL on the browser. The code behind the text (which makes the hyperlink work) will transfer with the text. You can also consider inserting hyperlinks into the text itself.

Course Management System

Posting your material to a course management system removes many of the concerns of student access through Email. The course page is static—you control its content and organization, and the process by which students access the information never varies. Most institutions using course management systems arrange access so that students can get to their information from off-campus locations as well as on-campus ones. Blackboard, one purveyor of this software, offers a specific page, named Course Material, on which you can place supplementary material, as seen in figure 9.10. A course management system

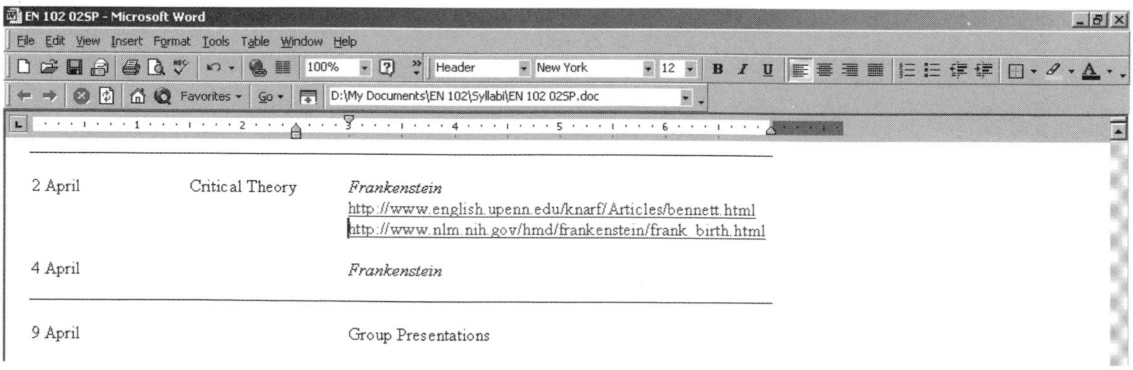

Fig. 9.9: Hyperlinking supplementary material in your syllabus. Microsoft Word™ screenshot reprinted by permission from the trademark holder, Microsoft Corporation.

can combine many technological benefits, including Email, distribution lists, and access to material.

> **Internet Service Provider (ISP)**—a company or other organization that provides users access to the Internet, probably the best known being AOL

A Third-Party Web Page

If your institution does not offer a course management system, you might consider developing your own Web page. Most **Internet Service Providers** offer some space on their servers for client use. Many even point you toward easily accessible technology that will help you create your own Web page. In fact, Microsoft Word allows you to save a Word document in Web format, which you can then copy and paste to your Web site.

A personal home page can also provide more flexibility to those already using a course management system. Many institutions use a standard template—design and functions—for their course management system. Faculty wishing to try other designs or tools may consider designing a Web page and making use of ISP space.

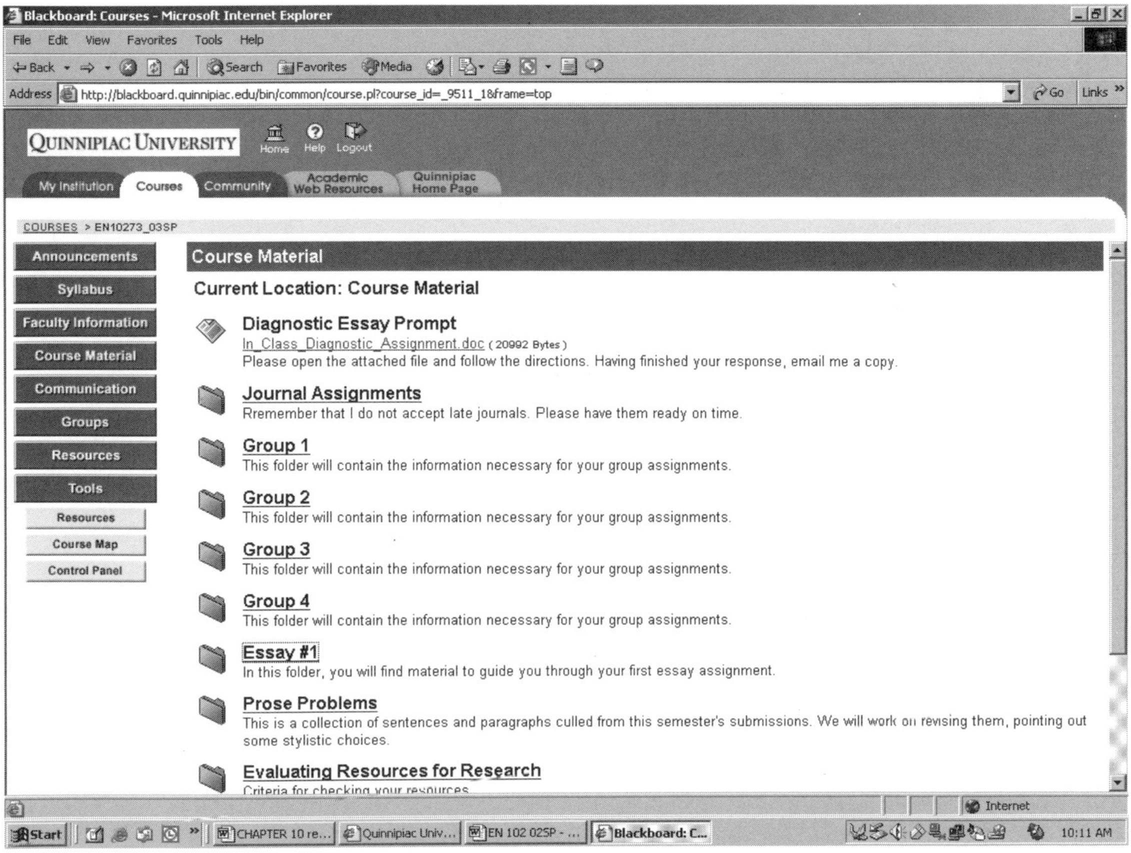

Fig. 9.10: The Course Material page in Blackboard. Property of Blackboard. Used with the permission of Blackboard. Microsoft Internet Explorer™ screenshot reprinted by permission from the trademark holder, Microsoft Corporation.

POTENTIAL PITFALLS

Management of Email messages is critical. When you send an Email to students, you make the assumption they will save the material it contains. They, like you, may place Email messages regarding this class in a specific folder. They, like you, may open the attached document and save it to their own computer so as to easily access it later. This assumed part of the process is a potential weak link. Students may misplace material or may not save the material in a way that makes it easily accessible. You might consider discussing how they can save these resources to make the best use of the material you send.

Make sure you check any hyperlinks you offer your students to make sure they are current. Links are revised for a variety of reasons. Sites often are reorganized or upgraded. If you posted the link earlier in the semester, it's a good idea to make sure it is ready for student use.

SCENARIO 3: Practice Tests and Quizzes

Offering opportunities to pretest a student's grasp of material is often helpful. When dealing with foundational information, certain aspects of technology lend themselves to efficient use of time and to schedule flexibility for the student. Evaluating these pretest opportunities can, however, take time. Whether you collect and review the assignments yourself or have students self-correct in class, you are still adding time to your schedule. Certain technology can not only lessen the time involved but can also organize the tests and their results in more usable formats.

TRADITIONAL SOLUTIONS

The tools you provide to help prepare students for upcoming assessments usually take time to develop and review. You create study sheets of the most important concepts, or perhaps practice questions. Some faculty may give over the day before an assessment to questions and drill. Practice tests and quizzes can consume significant time, depending on the methods you employ. And if you review the students' answers, you certainly increase your time investment. Quite often you expect students to shoulder the bulk of this load, reviewing the material themselves.

TECHNOLOGY ALTERNATIVES

Quiz Function in Your Course Management System

Course management systems offer various assessment tools for your use. Most allow you to place content directly into their templates to create assessment opportunities. Blackboard offers many options under the Assessment Manager button in its Control Panel. This Assessment Manager page offers the options to add a quiz or a survey to your course page, as seen in figure 9.11.

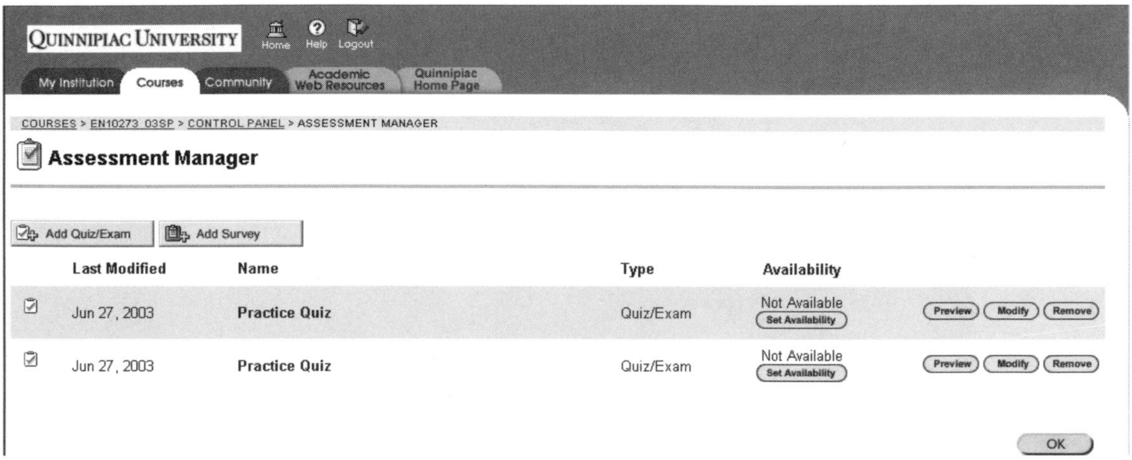

Fig. 9.11: Assessment Manager page in Blackboard. Property of Blackboard. Used with the permission of Blackboard.

Selecting the Add Quiz/Exam button will begin the process of creating your own assessment tool. You can also choose to use the Survey function (see Scenario 5 of Chapter 8). Blackboard also offers several question formats. Figure 9.12 shows the choices available.

There are some options for organizing these testing opportunities. You can, for example, create a Quiz/Test folder in one of your course pages. In Blackboard you might consider creating the folder in the Course Material page and direct your student to that page for access. The page shown in figure 9.13 is an example of a page in which all of the quizzes are collected in one folder in the Course Material page.

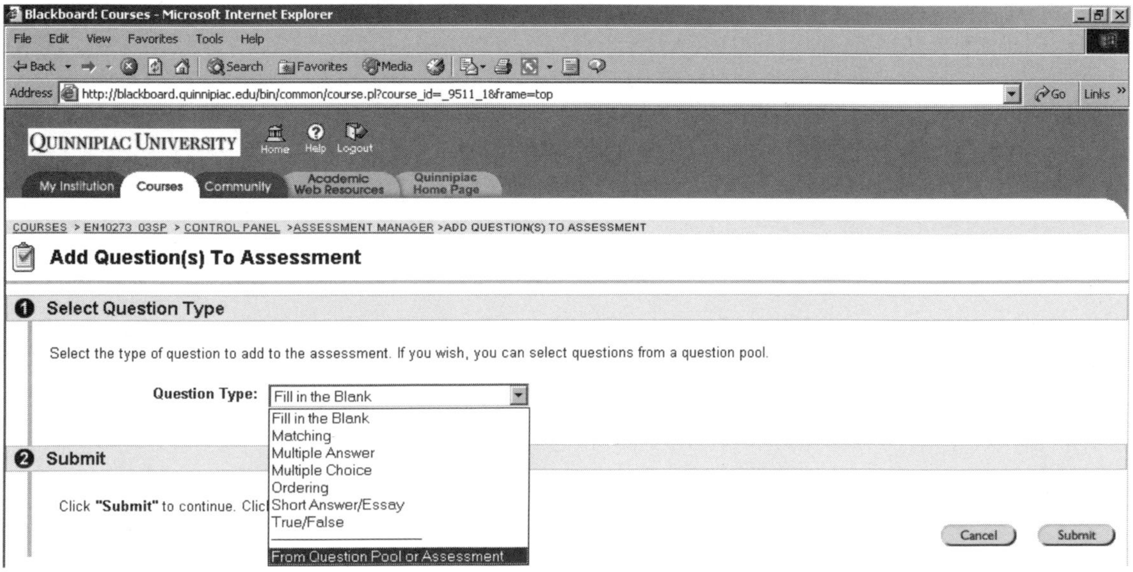

Fig. 9.12: Question format choices in Blackboard. Property of Blackboard. Used with the permission of Blackboard. Microsoft Internet Explorer™ screenshot reprinted by permission from the trademark holder, Microsoft Corporation.

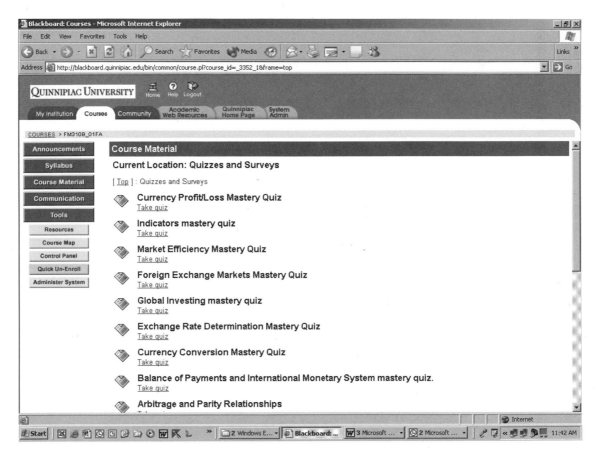

Fig. 9.13: All quizzes collected in one folder in Course Material. Property of Blackboard. Used with the permission of Blackboard. Microsoft Internet Explorer™ screenshot reprinted by permission from the trademark holder, Microsoft Corporation.

While this organization does provide one place in which all of the quizzes are stored, it also removes the link from its context within the course. You might consider another way to organize access to these links. As discussed in Scenario 2 of Chapter 5, providing the links to support activities in context can help students see the relevance of contextual material. It can also help them construct their own sense of knowledge by providing them just enough scaffolding to indicate your expectation of how the material should be used. (See figure 5.5 and table 5.1.)

Tests Provided by Publishers

Many textbook publishers offer support material that takes advantage of technology. Web sites that support individual texts and CDs that accompany the texts are two of the most common types of support.

The Web sites supporting these texts can vary greatly in content and organization. You should consider taking the time to review the material offered. What they call a study sheet may be simply a version of the table of contents or a list of the learning objectives from the beginning of a specific chapter. Despite this similarity, the change in format may have a positive effect on your students. In addition, these resources can be arranged easily by the student to suit his or her learning style.

Another feature of these support sites is practice quizzes and tests. Most of these features are organized with the chapter material, so a student works with contextual information and must make a conscious effort to move to another chapter. Students can access these tests by clicking on the link and following the instructions that appear. After selecting his or her answers, the student can click on a submission button that will score the practice test and return some degree of information. The type of information returned varies from publisher to publisher and even from text to text. Some sites can send an Email to the instructor with the test results. The results page varies, but students are almost always given more information than a score.

At present, not every text is supported by a Web page. If the publisher does provide this kind of support, the sales representative should be able to direct you to it. In addition, the front matter of most texts usually discusses support available to faculty and students, often providing the URL to the page in a prominent place. Review the text you are using to see if Web support exists.

Email or Discussion Thread Collaboration

Engaging your students in collaboration can reduce your workload as it increases their level of thinking. You might consider taking advantage of Email or **Threaded Discussion** to facilitate this collaboration. You can assign students to study groups in which they must discuss the best answers to a series of questions or problems you post. This collaboration can result in powerful learning, since each student is participating in the gathering and evaluation of the information.

Another idea may be to assign a specific problem or concept to each student. This student would then field the questions of his or her peers, using Email or using a threaded discussion. A student who can lead a discussion on a concept will be more prepared for the test.

POTENTIAL PITFALLS

While self-directed, the self-assessment options offered by publishers are best used to reinforce foundational information or information acquisition. Application of the information tends to be more subjective, requiring more sophisticated thinking than is required in the mainly objective questions offered by most publishers' Web sites.

While Email is a helpful medium for communicating, it does not lend itself to the level of organization and archiving one finds with threaded discussions. Asking students to use a thread creates a record for those not actively participating to view. The thread also organizes and archives the discussion for use as a study tool.

SCENARIO 4: Supporting Learner-Centered Learning

Current research about teaching and learning has been yielding interesting information. More and more instructors are dabbling with student-centered learning. One of the challenges instructors face, however, is providing a variety of perspectives from which the student can choose information that best suits his or her use. Arranging the various elements required to provide a suitable environment can be daunting. Arranging them in a way that fosters active learning—student-directed inquiry and response—can be harder still.

TRADITIONAL SOLUTIONS

Students coming to postsecondary education usually arrive from a fairly well-structured environment. This structure tends to reinforce passive learning rather than active learning. Consequently, creating an environment that supports student-centered learning takes time and effort. It seems that the more you expect students to direct their own learning, the more time you need to spend modeling the appropriate behavior and giving over class time. You hand out carefully crafted assignments, accompanied by extensive lists of resources. You put students in groups for collaboration and send them to the library. And, of course, you spend time following up their progress. Overseeing student-centered learning requires considerable time and energy. Certain technological alternatives can make the process more efficient.

TECHNOLOGY ALTERNATIVES

Work with Your Reference Librarian

We all need to be reminded to take advantage of the resources that exist at our institution. Reference librarians often have suggestions to help support learner-centered learning. In fact, they often have the means to carry out those suggestions. After some discussion about your assignment or your course objectives, they can help you identify appropriate resources for support. Chatting with someone who knows the system may save you time, precluding a long search of sources. In some cases, reference librarians may help beyond the search. The scope of the assignment may inform the scope of collaboration. The page seen in figure 9.14 is an example of the potential ability of reference librarians to support an assignment. The page offers a series of links, arranged by topic, for students and fac-

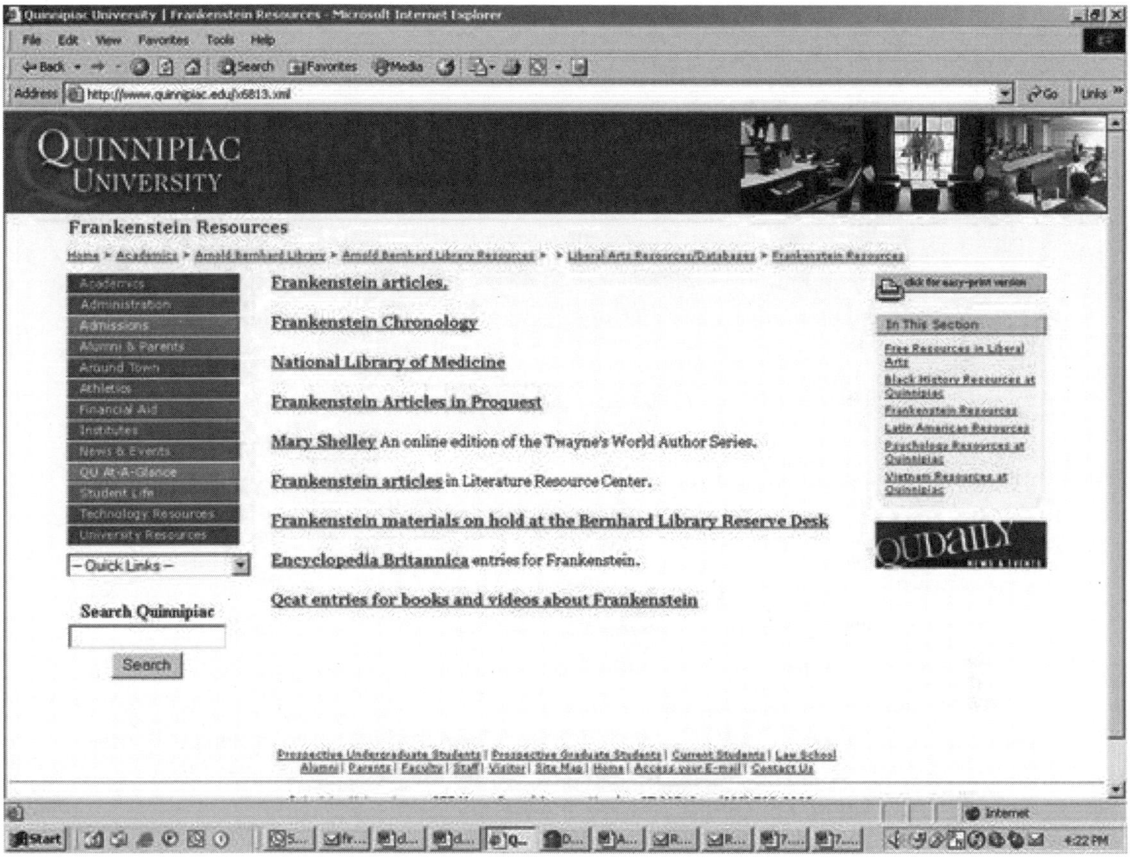

Fig. 9.14: A library Web page posting a collection of links in support of an assignment. Source: www.quinnipiac.edu/x6813.xml. Courtesy of Quinnipiac University. Property of Blackboard. Used with the permission of Blackboard. Microsoft Internet Explorer™ screenshot reprinted by permission from the trademark holder, Microsoft Corporation.

ulty alike. Such a resource page offers tremendous support to those instructors positioning their students for self-direction among appropriate sources.

Instructors will also benefit from reviewing this material. You need to know what it can do, as well as its limitations. Currency with the process, if not the product, lends credence to student-centered learning.

Course Cartridges for Your Course Management System

Publishers have begun working with purveyors of course management systems to develop **Course Cartridges** containing content that can be loaded directly to your course page. This material often contains a wealth of information that can support the text you are using in the classroom. Since you will be working through the publisher from whom you bought the text, the material in the course cartridge will support your required text as well.

Using a course cartridge can offer students information from various perspectives, one of the needed characteristics of student-centered learning. In addition, however, it also offers material that has been reviewed by the publisher and will support the text you are using. Consequently, it strikes a nice balance. It offers students an opportunity to create a new, unique, and meaningful response to their assignment. It also provides enough direction so that students are choosing among relevant sources as they respond.

Course Management Systems

Course management systems incorporate two very helpful features of technology, asynchronous discussion and the ability to attach documents. When used well, these aspects of technology can create an environment more inclined to support student-centered learning. Instructors can develop such an environment through these features by promoting access to information and access to peers and instructor.

Student access to information, often an individual activity, is facilitated through the instructor's ability to post information to the course materials pages, as well as all users' ability to attach files to threaded discussions. Students searching among the attachments and folders can review the information at their own pace and in their own sense of order. Students can also contribute to the dialogue by posting relevant URLs of Web resources they may have gathered.

Student access to peers and instructor is also accomplished through a feature provided by course management systems. Faster, more convenient communication between student and instructor and among students can facilitate student-centered learning. Threads promote dialogue through a series of electronic communications organized in clear relation to one another. A user can begin a thread, posting a problem to solve or a thesis to argue. Subsequent respondents can fashion a reply, which is then posted to the thread for review by the other users. Just as information can be organized and maintained, so too can discussions be organized to facilitate learning.

Course management systems can be a good tool by which to organize information and facilitate communication, giving students more control over their own learning.

POTENTIAL PITFALLS

While you want students to direct as much of their inquiry as possible, you also need to make them comfortable in doing so. Early discussion and modeling of this type of resource and its potential is necessary for student engagement.

Material in these cartridges has been researched and organized by someone whose sense of organization is quite likely different from your own. It may also be that you would prefer to direct your student toward some information and away from other information, given the varying depth and breadth of the information provided.

As with any use of technology, make sure that your students know how to use the features discussed above. Provide opportunities for them to practice them features before incorporating them into an assignment.

Appendix

THE DIGITAL MILLENNIUM COPYRIGHT ACT OF 1998

Enacted during the Clinton administration, this act is an attempt to address copyright issues in an increasingly digital world. Advances in computer access and computer literacy have simplified the copying and transmitting of content. In response to concerns about copyright infringement, President Clinton's Information Infrastructure Task Force developed a report titled *Intellectual Property and the National Information Infrastructure*. This report led to further discussion and to the ultimate passage of the Digital Millennium Copyright Act of 1998 (DMCA).

The act addresses, among other things, management of rights held by copyright owners and the possible circumvention of technologies that guarded these rights. Consequently, the accepted meaning of "fair use," the phrase that attempts to indicate appropriate levels of reproduction and distribution of copyrighted material, continues to be tested.

Information about the Digital Millennium Copyright Act of 1998 and the Report on *Intellectual Property and the National Information Infrastructure* is posted on the Internet. (You will need Adobe Acrobat to view these files.) You may also consider searching the Internet with appropriate keywords for more discussion of the DMCA.

> A summary by the U.S. Copyright Office: *http://www.loc.gov/copyright/ legislation/dmca.pdf*
>
> The Conference Report from the House of Representatives: *http:// www.lcweb.loc.gov/copyright/legislation/hr2281.pdf*
>
> Intellectual Property and the National Information Infrastructure: *http:// www.uspto.gov/web/offices/com/doc/ipnii*

FAIR USE

Within the bulk of law that governs copyright issues is a section that allows faculty to copy and distribute material that is not their own.

Section 7 of Title 17 of the U.S. Code addresses fair use as a limitation on owners' exclusive rights to copyrighted material. Fair use allows use of someone else's material without his or her permission and without payment.

Section 7 indicates that reproducing material for "criticism, comment, news reporting, teaching (including multiple copies for classroom use), scholarship or research is not an infringement of copyright." Perhaps more helpful for faculty, however, are the four factors that this section sets forth for evaluating our use of other people's material.

1. the purpose and character of the use, including whether such use is of a commercial nature or is for nonprofit educational purposes;
2. the nature of the copyrighted work;
3. the amount and substantiality of the portion used in relation to the copyrighted work as a whole; and
4. the effect of the use upon the potential market for or value of the copyrighted work.

Each of these factors should be weighed as you evaluate your use of someone else's work. Discussion with your reference librarian or your instructional technology staff can also help you feel more confident.

More information on fair use is posted on the Internet. You might consider searching there for more discussion regarding the application of fair use.

Section 107: *http://www.copyright.gov/title17/92chap1.html#107*
Title 17 of the United State Code: *http://www.copyright.gov/title17/ 92chap1.html*

WEB-BASED PLAGIARISM DETECTION SERVICES

Responding to the concerns of many faculty, various Web-based plagiarism detection services continue to develop. Faculty can send a copy of the file they wish to review via Email. These services will search their own databases, the Web, or a combination of both sources, looking for similarities. They then provide a report for the person submitting the file.

Several sites offer free trials, limited by time or by number of submissions. Response times vary by service. In addition to plagiarism detection, many sites are increasing the services they offer to include archiving, peer review, and online grading.

As in other aspects of technology, change occurs fast and often with these services. Over the course of our writing this book, we have found that several services no longer have active URLs, and some have been subsumed by larger companies. As you decide you want to explore these services, simply Google "Plagiarism Detection" and begin your review. Look for cost, response time, comparison resources, and report accessibility.

EVE 2

EVE 2 is a service that searches the Internet. Instructors have the ability to submit files in several formats. EVE returns a copy of the essay in Rich Text format with suspected occurrences of plagiarism underlined in red and the correlating Web sites listed at the bottom. Many of EVE's features are discussed in the FAQ page. While it used to offer a shareware version for a fifteen-day trial, it now asks that you purchase a license. Its site claims that Eve 2 has performed in excess of 86 million searches since February 7, 2000 (*http://www.canexus.com/eve/index.shtml*).

MYDROPBOX

MyDropBox is another online plagiarism sevice. In its Web pages it claims to be set up to search three sources: the Internet, password-protected paper mills, and your institution's own databases. Its "originality report" offers an "overall matching index" to indicate the general level of suspect text. The report uses colored text to indicate various findings within the body of the submitted text. It also offers a direct comparison of the submitted text with the found text, along with the URL of the found text. Also of note, it claims to be able to act as a teaching tool, offering the ability to be set up as a service through which students can check their own papers and be instructed where they need to include citation (*http://www.mydropbox.com*).

PLAGISERVE

Plagiserve offers to compare your submissions with its database of essays and papers, as well as search the Web for similar text. It also claims to search paper mills. There is a discussion board feature, allowing anyone to post questions or comments. Plagiserve will return an originality report that underlines suspect text in the body of the submission that is then compared directly with text found in the search. The found text is hyperlinked to the source. This service is free, but some of the postings in the various threaded discussions indicate that this may change (*http://www.plagiserve.com*).

TURNITIN

Turnitin claims to be the oldest plagiarism detection service on the Internet, growing from a 1996 Web service called Plagiarism.org. It searches the Internet, various password-protected databases, and its own growing database of papers submitted for review. It returns an originality report that offers an "overall similarity index," a colorful scale that indicates the percentage of similar material found on the Internet. The suspect text in the submission is underlined and color-coded to match the URL of the suspected source, also provided in the report. Turnitin has developed many other services as well, including a portfolio service, a grade book function, and the ability to support peer review (*http://www.turnitin.com*).

Glossary

Many online glossaries of technology terms are available on the Web. These can be found by using your favorite search engine, but some useful online glossaries can be found at:

- Computer User (http://www.computeruser.com/resources/dictionary/dictionary.htm)
- TechWeb (http://www.techweb.com/encyclopedia/)

Ancillary Resources—additional materials available, often for free, from publishers upon adoption of a textbook. These may include PowerPoint presentations, digital video clips, online tests, and a wide range of Web resources

Annotation—a feature (sometimes called Comments) available on most word processors that allows the reader of a document to insert suggestions or comments as a bubble or margin note that does not disrupt the flow of the original document

Announcements—a feature of all course management systems (usually the first thing a student sees when entering the Web pages for a course) that allows faculty to easily post information they want their students to see

Archive—a feature of many components of a course management system that allows the instructor and sometimes the student to record and save a digital copy of an online event such as a Chat session

Asynchronous Chat—a Chat session that takes place over hours, days, or even weeks instead of over a few minutes, and in which all participants may not be online and participating at the same time (as would be true in a Synchronous Chat) but will check in and out, reading contributions that others have added since the last visit, and replying and contributing at each visit

Attach Files—the ability to add a file containing a document, spreadsheet, presentation, video, etc., to an Email, a threaded discussion, or other message

Authenticated—recognized by a computer or network with restricted access; usually accomplished by providing a user name and password, which the restricted access system compares to records it already holds regarding acceptable user name/password combinations

Banner—an image on a Web page (usually a rectangle) used to advertise a product or service, often giving the reader a link to Web pages supporting the sale of that product or service

Boolean—a logical method applied to online searches for information in which the search connects key words with operators such as AND if both key words must be present in the search results, OR if either word being present is sufficient, NOT if a key word should not be present in the search results, etc.

Browse—to view a list of files and/or folders of files, or to view the contents of a file or group of files

Browser—a program that lets the user view a list of files and folders and/or their contents, most commonly Web pages

Campus Computing Project—an ongoing study of the impact of technology on higher education in America, based on annual surveys going back to 1990

Cc'd—when a person besides the primary recipient of an Email message is also sent the message, that secondary person is said to be "copied" on the Email correspondence (based on the idea of the carbon copy)

CD Texts—some textbook publishers offer some of their books—complete with all text, illustrations, tables, etc.—in a digital form on compact disc. In this form textbooks are usually cheaper and include such features as video, audio, and simulators

Change Tracking—a feature of word processors in which the reader can edit a document in a way that highlights or otherwise marks all additions or deletions made by that reader

Chat—software that gives two or more users the ability to communicate with each other at the same time, usually by typing messages that all participants in the Chat can see

Chat Room—a location on the Internet or on a network that users can visit to Chat; Chat rooms on the Internet are often dedicated to a specific topic

Clicking—depressing a mouse button, usually when the cursor is over a specific on-screen object; unless otherwise indicated, clicking means left-clicking

Clipboard—part of a computer's memory dedicated to holding data (text, images, files, etc.) that have been copied or cut from one application (e.g., text from a word-processing document) so that they can be pasted into another

Collaborative Learning—a strategy for learning in which students work on projects or assignments in teams or groups

Comment—a word-processing feature (also called Annotation) that allows the reader of a document to insert suggestions or comments as a bubble or margin note that does not disrupt the flow of the original document

Content Management Systems—software that allows users to create libraries of digital files and hyperlinks; these items are accessible via an organized folder structure and/or searches for key words associated with each file or hyperlink. Content management systems usually allow the person submitting a file or hyperlink to decide the universe of users who will be able to gain access to the submitted item

Copy and Paste—the ability to highlight data (text, an image, a file, etc.), save a copy of it to the digital clipboard, and then paste that data somewhere else; this ability is available in most applications

Course Cartridge—a set of Web pages and online course materials (assessments, videos, presentations, threaded discussions, etc.) that have been created to accompany a textbook and can be loaded directly into a course management system and used without editing (though editing is possible); course cartridges are often among the free ancillary materials available to an instructor upon adoption of a textbook

Course Management System—a system of software that allows faculty to easily create and manage a range of online classroom tools, including announcements, file posting, threaded discussions, and online assessments; Blackboard and WebCT are two well-known examples

Course Web Pages—a set of Web pages and online classroom tools created for a specific course

Cursor—the shape or symbol controlled by the mouse and used to point to items appearing on the screen

Dead Link—a hyperlink for which the associated Web page does not exist or is not available; the user will get an error message instead of being taken to the intended Web page

Disguised Identity—when a user represents himself as someone else or uses a fictitious name when working on a computer, network, or the Internet

Distribution List—a premade list of Email addresses, usually available to users of an Email system, for sending Email to groups of people; in an academic environment, there are probably distribution lists for "All Faculty," "All Students," "All Staff," and subgroups within these groups

Double-Click—to left-click twice in rapid succession to do something like open a file or start a software program

Drop Box—a feature of a course management system that allows students to post messages or files to a space accessible only to the instructor; once an item is posted, the posting student cannot edit or remove the item. A digital drop box is usually used as a space in which students can submit assignments online, and all student assignments are collected there by the instructor

Drop-Down Box—a list of subheadings, features, instructions, capabilities, etc., that appears just below the onscreen item to which it refers; sometimes the user has to click on the item to make the drop-down box appear, and sometimes the box appears when you move the cursor over the item

Email—broadly speaking, the transmission of messages and associated data over a network or the Internet; this broad definition would include submissions to Chat and threaded discussions, but Email is most commonly treated as a distinct system for sending, receiving, and collecting messages to and from the user's account (mailbox) to the account or accounts of other users

Experiential Strategy—a strategy for learning built on the idea that students learn best by experience, or that experience is a critical component of learning

Find—a feature of word-processing and other applications in which the user types in a string of letters and/or numbers (a word, phrase, number, etc.) that can be found in each occurrence within the file (e.g., a document) to which the search is applied

Flame—to send an online message (an Email, an Instant Message, or a post to a threaded discussion, etc.) that is inflammatory, often personally

Formative Assessment—an assessment given in the midst of a course, the results of which are used by the students and/or the instructor to adjust activities and behavior in what remains of the course

Frames—blocks or sections of a Web page that have been created and loaded separately to be combined into the complete Web page; frames may be thought of as mini-Web pages, as each frame will have its own Web address or URL

Higher-Order Learning Activities—referring to a taxonomy of learning such as that presented by B. S. Bloom (1956), in which learning is classified into levels or orders, usually with knowledge of basic facts and definitions at the first level, and the abilities to apply, critique, and synthesize ideas at higher levels

Highlighted—when an onscreen item has been visibly chosen (changed in color), usually so that some operation such as copying can be applied; items are highlighted by clicking on them, or, in the case of more than one item, by clicking on one of the items and then dragging the cursor over all of the items to be highlighted

Hyperlink—programming associated with an onscreen item (a word, phrase, image, etc.) that creates a link between that item and another, target, resource, usually something on the Internet; the user accesses the resource targeted by clicking on the hyperlink; often the cursor will change into a hand or other shape when moved over an item with a hyperlink

Hypertext—a word or phase in a document, presentation, spreadsheet, etc., that is linked (via hyperlink) to additional information, often something on the Internet. hypertext is almost always underlined and in a different color from the rest of the text. When you click on a hypertext word or phrase, you are automatically taken to the additional information on that term or phrase. You can return to the original passage (where you found the hypertext) by clicking the Back button on the browser screen

Icon—a small onscreen picture, usually hyperlinked or otherwise associated with a Web page, start-up of a software application, or other resource in such a way that clicking or double-clicking on it gives the user access to that associated resource

Instant Messenger—software that allows two or more users to exchange messages immediately; as in a phone conversation, all participants in an Instant Messenger session must be online at the time of the exchange

Internet Service Provider (ISP)—a company or other organization that provides users access to the Internet, probably the best known being AOL

Learner-Centered Learning—a perspective and strategy for learning in which learning (as opposed to teaching) is emphasized

Left-Clicking—depressing the left mouse button, usually when the cursor is over a specific onscreen object; unless otherwise indicated, clicking means left-clicking

Listserv—software for managing Email lists in which users can subscribe (to become part of a list and receive Email sent to the list) and unsubscribe (to remove themselves from the list); listservs are often used by organizations to send messages and information to members

Misdirected Link—hyperlink to the wrong target material or pages

Navigate—to use hyperlinks to move from page to page in a network or on the Web

Online Assessment—a quiz, test, or survey that can be taken on a computer through a network or the Web; when online assessments are made up of objective questions, the results can almost always be generated automatically, often along with summary statistics

Online Grade Book—a feature of most course management systems that allows instructors to record and post grades, both for their own reference and so that individual students can see their own grades; online grade books almost always have the ability to apply instructor-assigned weightings to grades on course components so that overall course grades can be automatically calculated

Online Quiz—a quiz or test that can be taken on a computer through a network or the Web; when online quizzes are made up of objective questions, the results can almost always be generated automatically, often along with summary statistics

Online Survey—a survey that can be taken on a computer through a network or the Web; when online surveys are made up of objective questions, the results can almost always be generated automatically, often along with summary statistics

Operators—logical words such as AND, OR, NOT used in Boolean logic to determine how key words being used in a search will be processed

Pop-Up Box—a box that appears, and can be manipulated, as layered above the other objects on the screen; sometimes a pop-up box appears as part of a process the user is executing, providing additional detail or choices. Increasingly, pop-up boxes appear with advertisements while the user views pages on the Web

Portfolio Assessment—a strategy that relies on evaluation of student projects (in a student portfolio) for assessment of the student or of a program, instead of, or in addition to, the use of tests

Post—to submit data (text, an image, a file, etc.) to a computer on a network or the Web for display to others

Right-Clicking—depressing the right mouse button, usually when the cursor is over a specific onscreen object; right-clicking is done only when the user wants to display features or options (which appear in a drop-down box) related to an onscreen object

Rubric—a detailed list, often presented in a table, of features that will be used in evaluating an assignment, along with descriptive material indicating how each feature will be assessed

Screensaver—a software program that prevents a monitor's screen from being ruined, which might happen if the same display remains on a monitor for hours at a time; after a specified period of time (determined by the owner of the computer), the screensaver replaces whatever is displayed on the monitor with the images from the screensaver (bouncing balls, swimming fish, etc.), only to return the monitor to its original display when a user moves the mouse or strikes the keyboard

Screenshot—an image of what is on a computer screen; a screenshot can be captured on the clipboard (to be pasted elsewhere) by pressing the Prnt Scrn (Print Screen) key on the top row of most computer keyboards

Scrolling—used whenever the item (page, document, or image) being viewed is too large to fit on the screen; scrolling up and down or right and left lets the user see other parts of the item

Simulator—a software package that allows the user to experience some aspect or aspects of a real-world object, environment, situation, etc.

Strategic Planning Model—a plan for creating, implementing, assessing, and revising the strategy of an organization; components usually include a mission statement, measurable objectives that support that mission (that, if accomplished, will mean the mission has been accomplished), and action plans (actions needed to accomplish the objectives)

Student-Centered Learning—a perspective and strategy for learning in which the activities of the student (as opposed to those of the instructor) are emphasized

Summative Assessment—assessment done at the end of a project or course, usually for the purpose of assigning a grade

Synchronous tool—a tool that requires all participants to be online and participating at the same time (as opposed to checking in and out and contributing over hours, days, or weeks, as with an asynchronous tool); a phone would be a synchronous tool, while a letter would be asynchronous

Target—the Web page or resource to which a hyperlink takes the reader

Template—a page in a software program with prompts for information or data (including files holding documents, presentations, video, etc.), and a space accompanying each prompt in which the information or data may be typed or pasted

Thread—a posting identifying a primary component or aspect of a subject being discussed in a threaded discussion, along with all replies and subsequent postings related to that original posting

Threaded Discussion—an ongoing collection of electronic submissions or postings on a particular subject, arranged by "threads" of the subject, with each posting being submitted as the creation of a new thread or a reply to ideas expressed in an existing thread; also an application that provides this capability

24/7—service or availability is around the clock (24 hours) and every day of the week (7 days per week)

URL (Uniform Resource Locator)—the unique string of characters assigned to, and used to access, material posted on a network or the Web (in the case of material posted to the Web, the URL is the Web address)

Video Clip—a small segment of video footage that, if in digital format (storable in a file on a computer instead of just on a videotape), can be inserted into Web pages or otherwise accessed through a network or over the Web

Video Projector—a light-emitting device that can project the output from a VHS player, DVD player, or computer (showing what is on the screen of the computer) onto a large movie screen so that everyone in the room can see it

Virtual Library—a collection of digital materials (documents, images, videos, audio files, etc.) that is usually accessible to a community of workers or learners

Web Address—the unique string of characters (usually beginning with www.) assigned to a Web page and used to access it from the Web

Web Posting—a Web page or file that has been posted to a Web site

Web Site—a location (made up of a Web page or set of Web pages) on the World Wide Web (abbreviated as WWW or Web) that is uniquely identified by, and found by accessing, the Web address(es) or URL(s) assigned to it

Wizard—a feature of many software packages that allows the user to control how it will run; a rules wizard in an Email system, for instance, allows the user to easily set up the rules that will be applied to sort and manage incoming Email

Word Processor—a software package (such as Word or WordPerfect) that allows users to easily create, edit, format, and otherwise manipulate a document

Notes

CHAPTER THREE

1. John Dewey, *Democracy and Education: An Introduction to the Philosophy of Education* (New York: Macmillan, 1916). Jean Piaget, *The Moral Judgement of the Child* (New York: Harcourt, 1932).

2. R. E. Slavin, *Cooperative Learning: Student Teams* (New Haven, Conn.: NEA Professional Library, 1987), and "Synthesis of Research in Cooperative Learning," *Educational Leadership* 48, pp. 71–82, 1991. J. Evans, *Bias in Human Reasoning: Causes and Consequences* (London: Erlbaum, 1989). K. Topping, "Cooperative Learning and Peer Tutoring: An Overview," *Psychologist* 5, pp. 151–157, 1992. J. D. Nichols and R. B. Miller, "Cooperative Learning and Student Motivation," *Contemporary Educational Psychology* 19, pp. 167–178, 1994. S. E. Newstead and J. S. T. Evans, eds., *Perspectives on Thinking and Reasoning: Essays in Honor of Peter Wilson* (Hillsdale, N.J.: Erlbaum, 1995). N. J. Vye, S. R. Goldman, C. Hmelo, J. F. Voss, S. Williams, and the Cognition and Teaching Group at Vanderbilt, "Complex Mathematical Problem Solving by Individuals and Dyads," *Cognition and Instruction* 15, 1998. C. Tang, "Effects of Collaborative Learning on the Quality of Assignments," in B. Dart and G. Boulton-Lewis, eds., *Teaching and Learning in Higher Education* (Melbourne: Acer, 1998).

CHAPTER FOUR

1. Morris Keeton and Pamela Tate, eds., *Learning by Experience—What, Why, How* (San Francisco: Jossey-Bass, 1978), p. 2.

2. John Dewey, *Experience and Education* (New York: Collier and Kappa Delta Pi, 1938), p. 20.

3. John D. Bransford, Ann L. Brown, Rodney R. Cocking, M. Suzanne Donovan, and James W. Pellegrino, eds., *How People Learn: Brain, Mind, Experience, and School* (Washington, D.C.: National Academy Press, 2000), p. 126.

CHAPTER EIGHT

1. Mary E. Huba and Jan E. Freed, *Learner-Centered Assessment on College Campuses: Shifting the Focus from Teaching to Learning* (Needham Heights, Mass.: Allyn and Bacon, 2000).

Index